Sex After Life

 # Critical Climate Change

Series Editors: Tom Cohen and Claire Colebrook

The era of climate change involves the mutation of systems beyond 20th century anthropomorphic models and has stood, until recently, outside representation or address. Understood in a broad and critical sense, climate change concerns material agencies that impact on biomass and energy, erased borders and microbial invention, geological and nanographic time, and extinction events. The possibility of extinction has always been a latent figure in textual production and archives; but the current sense of depletion, decay, mutation and exhaustion calls for new modes of address, new styles of publishing and authoring, and new formats and speeds of distribution. As the pressures and re-alignments of this re-arrangement occur, so must the critical languages and conceptual templates, political premises and definitions of 'life.' There is a particular need to publish in timely fashion experimental monographs that redefine the boundaries of disciplinary fields, rhetorical invasions, the interface of conceptual and scientific languages, and geomorphic and geopolitical interventions. Critical Climate Change is oriented, in this general manner, toward the epistemo-political mutations that correspond to the temporalities of terrestrial mutation.

Sex After Life

Essays on Extinction, Vol. 2

Claire Colebrook

O
OPEN HUMANITIES PRESS

with Michigan Publishing – University of Michigan Library, Ann Arbor
2014

First edition published by OPEN HUMANITIES PRESS 2014
Freely available online at http://dx.doi.org/10.3998/ohp.12329363.0001.001

Copyright © 2014 Claire Colebrook

This is an open access book, licensed under Creative Commons By Attribution Share Alike license. Under this license, authors allow anyone to download, reuse, reprint, modify, distribute, and/or copy their work so long as the authors and source are cited and resulting derivative works are licensed under the same or similar license. No permission is required from the authors or the publisher. Statutory fair use and other rights are in no way affected by the above.

Read more about the license at creativecommons.org/licenses/by-sa/3.0

Cover Art, figures, and other media included with this book may be under different copyright restrictions. Please see the *Permissions* section at the back of this book for more information.

PRINT ISBN 978-1-78542-012-2
PDF ISBN 978-1-60785-300-8

OPEN HUMANITIES PRESS is an international, scholar-led open access publishing collective whose mission is to make leading works of contemporary critical thought freely available worldwide. Books published under the OPEN HUMANITIES PRESS imprint at Michigan Publishing are produced through a unique partnership between OHP's editorial board and the University of Michigan Library, which provides a library-based managing and production support infrastructure to facilitate scholars to publish leading research in book form.

MICHIGAN PUBLISHING
www.publishing.umich.edu

OPEN HUMANITIES PRESS
www.openhumanitiespress.org

Contents

1. Feminist Extinction — 7
2. Norm Wars — 23
3. Post-Phenomenology's Evil Cartesian Demon — 49
4. Queer Aesthetics — 75
5. Queer Vitalism — 100
6. Difference, Time and Organic Extinction — 126
7. Ethics of Extinction — 137
8. Just Say No to Becoming Woman (and Post-Feminism) — 149
9. How Queer Can You Go? — 179
10. Postmodernism Is a Humanism: Deleuze and Equivocity — 203
11. On the Very Possibility of Queer Theory — 236

Works Cited — 253
Permissions — 265

Chapter 1

Feminist Extinction

The Bloated Monster

As the human race hurtles toward extinction, primarily as a result annihilating its own milieu, we feminists might respond by saying, 'I told you so.' Feminism is, like any 'ism,' perhaps too diverse to be given any grounding identity, yet it has most certainly been marked by critiques of man. Even in its earliest, liberal, and inclusive phases, feminism's claim to include women within the category of 'man' or humanity did so not so much for its own sake as for the sake of life in general. It was not a question of women selfishly making a claim for themselves so much as a call for a better life for all in a new world of sex equality. Feminism has never been a special interests claim but has always appealed to some broader justice in which all humans would be included. As long as man excluded and enslaved what was other than himself—as long as he treated women as mere chattels—his own humanity would be diminished. As Mary Wollstonecraft pointed out in 1792, the relation of master to slave not only enslaves the weaker party, but also precludes the full development of 'man' as a rational being: 'Birth, riches, and every extrinsic advantage that exalt a man above his fellows, without any mental exertion, sink him in reality below them. In proportion to his weakness, he is played upon by designing men, till the bloated monster has lost all traces of humanity' (Wollstonecraft 2008, 53).

Wollstonecraft's argument is a typical early instance of an insistence on feminism as a better logic for all life. Even before the emergence of explicitly ecological modes of feminism, there had been a long-standing criticism of the limits or self-enclosure of man. But this long-standing resistance to man is intrinsic to the history of humanist self-critique.

Feminism is best seen as an ultra-humanism in that it has, from its inception, been based on the idea that man can only come to himself and be properly human through the recognition of women. The very concept of feminist emancipation harbors an implicit ecology. From liberal to radical and post-structuralist feminisms, women have always fought for themselves in the name of justice and equilibrium (and not as a warring special-interest group). It should come as no surprise, then, that feminism would eventually claim an affinity to otherness in general (Schwab 1996, 34; Hitchcock 1993), and see itself as extending naturally into environmental and class concerns:

> More and more men are embracing eco-feminism because they see the depth of the analysis and realize that in shedding the privileges of a male-dominated culture they do more than create equal rights for all, that this great effort may actually save the earth and the life it supports. (Plant 1997, 129)

There is—according to most forms of eco-feminism—something like an affinity and passion for life as such that has been deflected by a male or masculinist tendency towards mastery and domination of all otherness; this care or concern for life in general might be redeemed by a return to a saved earth. The relation between environmentalism and ethics is co-determining: without a concern for our milieu or the earth we could not possibly build a world of social justice, but without a harmonious and sexually ethical social order we could not possibly respond properly to our ecological milieu. It is not only in the specific branch of an 'ethics of care' or eco-feminism that the critique of masculinism becomes intertwined with a concern for the nonhuman. Eco-feminism is no minor offshoot of feminist thought but structures its genealogy: liberal feminism begins by saying that one cannot exclude a group of bodies from the rights of the humanity in general. Insofar as one is human (and therefore finite) there can be no precedence or pre-political mastery over any other being: sexual equality follows on from a liberal refusal of transcendence. But that refusal of transcendence not only precludes human-human mastery but indicates an overcoming of mastery as such. In the absence of any transcendent or absolute moral order we are all placed in a position of humility (Langton 1988). If an appeal to humanity in general overturns any possibility of a pre-given political hierarchy, because all humans are born equally rational, then that same humanizing gesture will lead to a questioning of the human. By what right can humanity be declared to be definitively rational, definitively self-conscious or definitively social-political? Who defines these privileged predicates?

Second-wave feminism questions the very nature of 'the human,' and certainly does not embrace liberalism's 'self-evident' values of instrumental reason and universalism. Perhaps the notion of the self freed from all prejudice is an elevation of a certain type of self, and perhaps another ethics of local attachments, embodied passions and specificity would be just as worthy of being deemed to be human. By the time eco-feminism emerges, the concern for the environment explicitly takes feminism from a mode of human-human combat (women fighting for their rights, for the sake of all humanity) to a war on the man of reason; for it is man whose drive to mastery for the sake of his own self-maintenance has resulted in an unwitting suicide. Enter posthumanism: 'we' no longer contest what should count as the properly human, for the very definition of the 'properly human' constitutes a chauvinistic exceptionalism of the species and enables an ongoing hegemony in which the label of 'human' smuggles in historical, cultural, sexual, racial and class norms. Posthumanism, of course, takes many forms—ranging from granting non-humans highly human qualities such as rights and cognition, to a questioning or rejection of the very qualities that had defined humanity (such as reason, language and technological progress). In all cases, though, there is a rejection of any simple notion of 'man' as a proper form or ground. Far from the posthuman 'turn' being a vanquishing of feminism, one might say that the posthuman is required by feminism's critical trajectory. The very concept of the feminine splits humanity in two, precluding any simple human norm: either humanity must be redefined or broadened to include women, *or* the very question that enabled women to challenge the rights of man, will lead to a full-scale destruction of any assumed right whatsoever.

Feminism's recent turn to life (in environmentalism and 'new materialisms') should not appear as an addition or supplement but as the unfolding of the women's movement's proper potentiality. Indeed, this is just how eco-feminism has presented itself. It makes no sense to strive to transform our relation to the environment without transforming our own mode of being. Feminist criticisms of man would not be add-ons to environmentalism but would be crucial to any reconfiguration of ecological thinking. Insofar as man has always been defined as a rational animal who calculates, manipulates, and represents a world that is his proper domain—and if we assume that 'a dominating position alienates human beings from the environment on which their survival depends'—a thought of life without or beyond man becomes imperative: 'When human beings ignore natural processes, their antagonistic attitude towards nature leads not only to the destruction of the environment but also to self-destruction' (Braidotti, Charkiewicz, Hausler and Wieringa 1994, 149).

It is with this recognition of self-destruction that feminism gains general purchase. Feminism's criticism of man will not only transform humanity and its milieu but will open up a new thought of life. It is not only the case that a reformed relation to the environment requires a reconfiguration of man; it is also the case that the project of transforming man—allowing him to become something other than the subject of instrumental reason—requires going beyond the bounds of the organism to consider life in general.

But here we arrive at two questions: is care for the environment really an exit from the mode of anthropocentric blindness that has accelerated the destruction of the biosphere? And, would not a thought of life *beyond* the human environment—beyond *our* world, *our* environment, the place or home for which *we* care—be a more adequate response to man's suicidal world tour?[1] Put differently, what I am suggesting here is that the very concept of 'the environment' (seen as that which environs, is vulnerable to our destruction and therefore worthy of concern) shares all those features and affective tendencies that structured the self-enclosed Cartesian subject that feminism has always had in its sites. The very notion of an environment that encircles our range of living practice, and the very notion of 'woman' as tied to place and oriented to care, always figure the world as *our* world. To say, as eco-feminists do, that we are essentially world-oriented and placed in a relation of care and concern to a world that is always place rather than meaningless space is to repeat the (masculine) reduction of the world to its sense *for us*. The problem, despite our protestations, is that we do *not* care. All the shrill protestations of proper care and connectedness maintain the anthropocentric alibi. Indeed, the criticism of the scientific disenchantment of the world, along with the lament that the world loses its meaning to become mere raw material as we fall further into a mode of patriarchal domination, maintains an insistence on the figure of the connected globe, or the environment as an auto-poetic, self-furthering and self-organizing totality: it is assumed that the proper relation to the milieu that sustains us would be an *extension* of virtues of respect, care, concern, and even communication to a nonhuman that is always presented in a normatively homely manner.[2] What remains out of play is a consideration of forces of life that are not discernible from within our milieu, and that do not perturb our coupling with nature.

Even when the word vitalism is not used explicitly, we might observe, today, a vitalist ethics in general that dominates our time. Just as traditional vitalism set itself against René Descartes' positing of an extended substance that was the basis for a mechanistic and calculable material world, so there is now a persistent, vehement, and near-universal denunciation of Cartesianism, summed up by Antonio Damasio as 'Descartes' error' (Damasio 1994). Against the idea of a mental substance that represents an inert material world, neuroscientists, cognitive scientists, cognitive archaeologists, researchers of artificial life, and philosophers have insisted on characterizing life not in static or centered terms but as a plural and dynamic creativity. The mind or the self emerges *from life* rather than being the privileged point from which life is known. One could characterize this late twentieth-century anti-cognitive turn to life as a vitalism precisely because, like its pre-modern counterpart, it places an emphasis on dynamism, relations, active becoming, and creativity. Cartesianism, today, is deemed to be horrific for all the same reasons that it was condemned (mainly by theologians) in its first articulation: the Cartesian subject is a disconnected, character-less, disembodied, disenchanted, and disaffected ghost in a machine. If life has meaning—if it is never mere matter but always this particular felt life for this particular living organism—then one must discard Descartes' error and arrive at a new Spinozism. For Damasio, this means that there is no self who perceives the world in a certain way and who is then affected emotionally by some external input. Rather, in the beginning is affect: an emotion that may or may not come to consciousness. The self is the 'feeling' of this event, which is also to say that the self does not end with the borders of the biological body.

In terms of environmentalism and questions of the human being's relation to the milieu that it has for so long disregarded, this might seem to be a salutary elimination of man as *homo faber*. It appears, perhaps, that from within their own trajectory, theories of 'mind' have arrived at the immersion of mind in life, at the recognition of the inextricable intertwining of the mind with its milieu—and perhaps even at the most profound of feminisms. Man as master of representation, cognition, calculation and disembodied distance has, without assistance, and in his own good time, recognized himself as an originally environmental being. Feminists have, in other words, been right all along, but man was capable of realizing the truths of feminist care and concern without the explicit intervention of feminism. Indeed, one of the definitive theorists of posthumanism, Cary Wolfe, negotiates his definition of posthumanism by shuttling back and forth between feminism's insistence on the power relations among various knowledge practices and systems theory's emphasis on embodied, situated and world-constituting knowledge, and then concludes that both disciplines have their limits in their containment within the human, the limit of which needs to be shattered by an exit from the human, possibly towards the animal: 'the question is not who will get to be human, but what kinds of couplings across the humanist divide are possible and indeed unavoidable when we begin to observe the end of man' (Wolfe 1995, 66).

But is redemption this easy? Although we know that events are occurring for which the old models of calculative reason are inadequate, it is uncertain just what or how much we could tackle from our supposedly new point of view of engaged, dynamic, extended, embodied, and emotive selfhood. Is this new vitalism or anim(al)ism really a felicitous shift in modes of thinking that will allow us to deal with the current critical state of our milieu, or is it a reaction formation? I would suggest the latter, especially if we consider not only the joyous affirmations of life—with the discovery of empathy (Rivkin 2009), affect (Gregg and Seigworth 2010), embodiment (Rowlands 2010), universal creativity (Russell

2007), and wondrous futures (Levy 1997)—but also *seemingly* dire warnings. James Lovelock's 'final' warning is, after all, a warning *for us*—otherwise it would not be final. It assumes our duration, the end of life for us (Lovelock 2009). To say that Gaia is vanishing is to equate our system of life with systematicity *tout court*. Could we not see the present as the end of *this* Gaia, if Gaia really is an apt figure? What is not considered—beyond questions of warning, surviving, saving, and death knells—is what kind of life the actual death of man might enable, whether 'we' ought to live on, and just what or who this saved 'we' approaching finality might be. If we are seeking to save ourselves then are we also saving the survival mechanisms that have brought the human species and its milieu to the brink of destruction? If we wish to destroy 'man' as the rapacious Cartesian, calculative subject of instrumental reason in order to save life, who is the ground of this futural and counter-human annihilation? For all the problems of destroying man in the name of something other than the human, and for all the resonance of this survivalist self-destruction with the very grips of humanism it is aiming to vanquish, so much of the posthuman rhetoric today appears to declare itself as already attuned to the life that 'man' so lamentable ignored (up until now).

It is just at the point at which the future's potentiality and openness appears to be radically *lacking* in life that what counts as thinking (ranging from high theory to popular science) has discovered a life that goes beyond the old, limited, finite, and all too concrete models of mind. This seeming revolution of over-turning man for the sake of the life that man has denied is—far from being man's other—the very hallmark of the end of man. Man has always existed as a being who ends himself: as soon as the human is given some natural or limited definition, man discovers that his real, creative, futural being lies in some not-yet realized becoming that will always save him from a past that he can denounce as both misguided and as at an end (Derrida 1969). Today, just as the human species faces possible and quite literal extinction, 'man' extinguishes himself: he declares that he is neither a brain in a body nor a mind in a machine, but always already ecological—sympathetically, emotionally, and systemically attuned to a broader milieu of life. Such claims range from popular neuroscience's claims for emotional and affective selves, to system theory's arguments for a self that extends beyond the bounds of the individual body and a whole series of appropriations of non-Western traditions of mindfulness in which the self can overcome its egoistic prison. Once again what is affirmed—against all the evidence for a malevolent relation or intrinsically suicidal system of humanity and its environs—is an original human connectedness, an irreducible system in which the world is never alien raw matter but always this particular world as it is disclosed for this particular organic life.

But has man really extinguished himself? Has there not always been an insistence that thinking and being are the same, that—in old Parmenidean terms—to think is to be in accord with a movement of life that affirms and sustains itself? That is to say, man has continually realized that the world that he has depicted is to some extent a projection of his own mastering reason, and he has then gone on to claim that—after the Enlightenment—the same mythic world of his own imagination has been extirpated in order that man might arrive at life *as it really is* (Adorno and Horkheimer 2002). If there has continually—since Aristotle—been a reaction against Platonism and intellectualism, has this not been because such idealisms set themselves and their values above life? For the systems theory of Humberto Maturana and Francisco Varela, which has been so influential across a range of domains, there is not a primary world that is taken up and represented by a separate subject, since there is just this coupling of organism and the world that the organism inhabits (Maturana and Varela 1992). It is against this anti-Platonism or naïve literalism that I would suggest that we consider the world not as our own milieu but in its own duration. Perhaps we should think again about the supposedly evil Cartesian separation between mind and world, not as separate substances but as a separation between one being (man) for whom there can be something like substance, and whatever else in all its contingency would remain? Should we not be considering ourselves and conscious life *not* as emergent properties, but as a monstrosity that we do *not* feel, live, or determine but rather witness partially and ex post facto? That is to say: the end of man is both desirable and necessary, yet also impossible. Any attempt to vanquish man as a blight on earth has always depended on the notion of a proper human who would find himself, again, being at one with the earth.

The Sex of Extinction

Here we must turn to the sex of extinction, or what I will refer to as (s)extinction: life, at least as it has been figured through the imaginary of man, always desires to exit itself, negating any determined or merely actual being. As man, today, faces his death in the literal sense, he summons forth his figural death; he demands and declares that man must become one with the life of which he is an expression. In this becoming-with-the-world has man become woman? In one sense the answer is yes, but this is not a *new* becoming-woman, nor is it a *new* vitalism. There has always been an affirmation of the life from which man emerges, a life that can be relived, reaffirmed, and plundered so that man may overcome his isolated subjective detachment in order to feel at one with his world. (This was, indeed, the shift from Platonism to Neo-Platonism, where the gap between ideals and the world as it is is covered over with a theory of emanation, in which all forms emerge from one fecund life.) Man has always been an environmental animal, has always viewed the world as his environs, has always been a mode of becoming-woman: he lives his proper being not in fully actualized and detached isolation, but through a more profound autonomy in which he recognizes and affirms himself through a world that is never alien, never mere matter, but always a sign of his proper and profound life. That is—and this is in the spirit of a quick, moral, and unthinking anti-Cartesianism—man is most properly himself when he relates to and lives himself through his own indispensable otherness.[3] If there has been a historical shift from instrumental Cartesianism—where the world is dead matter to be mastered—to environmentalism, then the latter move is a hyper-Cartesianism (since for the environmentalist the world is not *really* other, alien, or inhuman but always already at one with man's proper life).

A feminist critique of man—a man who has always been vitalist in his profound communion with life—would be the most tired of gestures. Man lives on by feminist critique, by continually surpassing and reviving his rationality through imbibing the blood of the dead, by returning to and retrieving the life beyond the bounds of his own life. Neither a traditional vitalism that regards matter as supplemented by spirit, nor a 'new' vitalism where matter is already dynamic will save us. What any vitalism will sustain is just this lure of *saving life* (as though one might find, in life, means for salvation). What we need to consider is the dead end of life: man lives on either by gathering all proper life within himself (seeing all life as mindful) or by positing a good life that will save him from himself.

It is perhaps in this double bind (where man maintains himself in the face of extinction by extinguishing himself) that a radical feminism could provide a genuine thought of life beyond the human. Here, there would be no woman who remains close to the earth, life, and cosmos: no woman who provides man with the other he has always required for his own redemption. Feminism, today, facing the extinction of the human, should turn neither to man nor to woman: both of these figures remain human, all too human, as does the concept of the environment that has always allowed man to live on through a vitalist ethic. One would also need to say the same about posthumanism, which is more often than not an ultra-humanism. In many ways, what passes for posthumanism consists in the assertion that man is not an isolated animal with any specific features that would mark him off from life, for he is always already at one with life, animality, and technology. Rather than thinking of woman, the finality and redemption of man, or living beyond man in an era of the unified posthuman (which takes heed of the final warning for us), what really needs to be confronted is the way in which the figure of 'life' has always justified man as an intrinsically posthuman animal. Man has always been other than himself, always more than his own mere being.

If vitalism has any general sense—and it has at least a performative force in current calls for a new vitalism—then it does so in opposition to what is perceived to be a long-standing condition of Western man. Man, according to anti-Cartesian and posthuman critiques, has conceived of himself as an autonomous, mastering, representing, elevated, and rational near-divinity who owes nothing to his world. The turn to the environment, to becoming one with a vitality that exceeds the bounds of his own being, would supposedly be a departure from a history of instrumental reason. But the turn to vitalism is another vampire gesture: man consumes himself, and then imagines that he is no longer the rapacious animal he once was. Man believes he has exited his self-enclosure to find the world and his better post-feminist self. The concept of the environment—as that surrounding and infusing life from which we have emerged, and which, so the argument goes, would be retrievable through a vitalist overcoming of our malevolent detachment—maintains the same structure of anthropomorphism. What needs to be thought today is that which cannot be thought, lived, retrieved, or revitalized as the saving grace of man or woman.

Not the Post-apocalyptic (Not the Posthuman), Not Now

To give a sense of what this might mean both critically and positively, we should perhaps ask what the future would be like beyond the figure of man (a figure that has always included both the posthuman and woman). What if we were to approach the future through sexual difference, where sexual desire would be distinct from any notion of survival or organic self-maintenance? Here, one would need to abandon notions of survival, and of the *post*human, precisely because these are recuperating gestures. If one considered sexual difference outside dualist gender binaries, one might confront proliferating differences. Difference is *sexual*, rather than gendered, when it is not the coupling of two kinds (or genres) for the sake of mutual self-maintenance and ongoing recognition. If a body connects with another body, not for the sake of its own survival or reproduction but through something like touch as such, then sexual difference would relate to what is other than itself without a view to shoring up its own being. To be open to what is not one's own—to what cannot be figured as environment, ecology (with all its motifs of *oikos* and interconnectedness) or the *post*human—would have two consequences.

First, one might ask about future modes of existence that are not based on survival (for any survival, as living on, would always be an extension of the present). Margaret Atwood's great counter-post-apocalyptic novel *The Year of the Flood* does just that. In this novel, Atwood seems to be opening with a (now) standard post-apocalyptic landscape in which human life in its civilized and urbane modes has been destroyed, leaving a world of fragile *living on*. Through the use of flashbacks, Atwood describes a world prior to this wasted landscape: a world of traffic in women, of the manipulation of life for corporate expediency and commercial novelty, of a subclass of humans who function as manipulable matter for a techno-scientific capitalist elite, and of a language of noise and brandnames. Here, Atwood opens one path for thought: our post-apocalyptic future has already arrived. The nightmare dystopia of some supposedly science-fiction inhuman future whereby we have sacrificed our humanity to rapacity and venality has already arrived, and that is because that is how *man* has always lived. It is no accident that Atwood's earlier fiction was remarkably prescient. Her depiction of a world in *The Handmaid's Tale* in which women are bio-politically managed is not so much a warning for the future as it is a diagnosis of what humanity has always been: a passionate commitment to life that will allow the vital order to act as a foundation for moral managerialism. Second, and more important for my purposes here, *The Year of the Flood* describes another cult of the future— the Gardeners—whose ecological discourse of sacred life and the purity of the origins of their own retrieved humanity is structurally akin to the imagined 'biopolitical' corporatism that also establishes the extension and maximization of life as its lore. What Atwood suggests, against the present idea that man might surpass himself and find a new ecological future, is that such redemptive imaginaries have always allowed man to master life in order to maintain himself. Life—or its moral imaginary— has always been biopolitical: green, eco-feminist, vitalist and posthuman 'turns' to animality and the ecology all vanquish man as he has been for the sake of a new redeemed future, and do so because of a commitment to an ethical self who can always cast off what he is in order to *become*.

But *The Year of the Flood* is not only critical and diagnostic. (This is where it differs from other twenty-first century critiques of life management, such as Kazuo Ishiguro's *Never Let Me Go* of 2005). In addition to the ironic depiction of a world war between green appeals to life as it is and biopolitical futures celebrating a life that has survived beyond all human limits, Atwood presents the hint of a future of *refusal* in which the women who are traded, exchanged, and managed for the sake of biological variation and reproduction reject the biological family and familial production to produce new modes of haphazard social bonding (beyond sexuality) and new forms of bio-art that decay upon impact. In a world where a war takes place between eco-fascism (or saving life at all costs) and bio-politics (the management of life for the sake of maximized reproduction), Atwood describes fragile female characters who make their way through this landscape, forming lateral alliances of friendship rather than filial communities of reproduction. One of the characters has a successful career in bio-art, where she uses wasted bodily materials to produce artworks that are fleeting and ephemeral: 'She liked to watch things move and grow and then disappear.'[4] Atwood challenges the fetishized motif of life, the human mode of monumental archives, and the idea that in turning to 'life,' art and man might find endurance.

What Atwood poses is a world beyond 'woman' as man's better other. *The Year of the Flood* continues two critical traditions in feminist writing—one Romantic (that refuses what Freud referred to as the oceanic feeling or pre-Oedipal plenitude), and one modernist (that refuses a feminine fecundity that would revitalize all the dead systems of reified language and technology). Like Mary Shelley in *Frankenstein*, a novel that aligned the romantic artists who imagine nature as a benevolent feminine other with the scientist's domination of nature as dead matter, *The Year of the Flood* presents a world in which ecological redemption (as eco-fascism) is the flipside of a bio-political management of life. The two warring factions in Atwood's novel both make a claim to be acting for a life that would destroy previous modes of human self-imprisonment: the Adamic cult of Gardeners appeal to the vital value of the earth as a way of controlling bodies, production, and reproduction, while the governing corporation (CorpSeCorp) aims at maximizing life through genetic manipulation and data management. Both these factions are enabled by the post-apocalyptic imaginary or, to borrow a phrase from Lovelock, the imaginary of 'final warning.' If our only value and horizon is that of life, then only one path is permitted: that which saves and survives.

Both Shelley's *Frankenstein* and Atwood's *Year of the Flood* display a quite common motif in feminist fiction writing to question the value of the maximization of life. In this respect one would have to associate at least one form of feminism, *not* with finding a 'woman' beyond man, but with a critique of all that has stood for 'woman' as man's other. Such literature instead conducts thought experiments of futures that open up reproduction beyond any notion of self-managing humanity. *The Year of the Flood* continues a feminist-novelistic-radical capacity to question the very value of survival (which is also to say the value of value, if value has always been given as that which furthers life). It would be incorrect to label this tradition as science fiction, for the worlds depicted are those of the present scientific imaginary: in both *Frankenstein* and *The Year of the*

Flood it is both science (as instrumental reason) and its supposed other (the ecological connectedness with life) that are presented as redemption narratives that fail to question just who this 'man' is whose survival we seek to maintain. One might say that the consequences one can draw from this feminist tradition are that man always plans his escape through imagined posthuman futures and others, and that what is required to think beyond man as survival machine is a sense of the contamination of the ecological imaginary. This brings us to the second consequence, and the second tradition, in which the very figures of art, creativity, and production—tied to fruitful life—are also interrogated.

This second critical tradition extended and radicalized by *The Year of the Flood* is the feminist modernist counter-aesthetic. In Virginia Woolf's *To the Lighthouse*—a novel that, like Atwood's, ends with an ambivalent figure of the approach to (or refusal of) light—the central maternal nurturing figure, Mrs. Ramsay, dies. After an interlude ('Time Passes') that presents a falling of darkness, the final section of the novel concludes with the young female artist, Lily Briscoe, having a vision that prompts her to act almost destructively toward the conventional canvas. Not only does her vision result in a single dark line painted down the center of the picture of Mrs. Ramsay that she has been struggling to compose throughout the novel; her creative act is coupled with a recognition of art's decay—as though Briscoe's refusal of art history and representation is also an embrace of transience. This is not man as *homo faber*, being infused with a life other than his own that he goes on to present, represent, and preserve, for Lily's approach to her canvas occurs quickly and almost as a distraction:

> Quickly, as if she were recalled by something over there, she turned to her canvas. There it was—her picture. Yes, with all its green and blues, its lines running up and across, its attempt at something [...]. With a sudden intensity, as if she saw it clear for a second, she drew a line there, in the centre. It was done; it was finished. Yes, she thought, laying down her brush in extreme fatigue, I have had my vision. (Woolf 2006, 170)

The Year of the Flood also presents an art event amid a world of destruction, where the artwork is similarly confronted with impersonal forces of transience and that takes place in a milieu of posthuman destruction, a destruction that has occurred *because* of the shrill and myopic desire for life. Just as *To the Lighthouse* is structured around the falling of an immense darkness (the 'great' war) that is the consequence rather than the overcoming of man's apocalyptic imaginary (where man will arrive fully at nothing other than his own mastery), so *The Year of the Flood* presents the future of man. This future is one in which life is maximized, in which survival harnesses technology and nature for the sake of a time of continuity and extended futures. The minor ray of disturbance is given in a practice of bio-art that, quite unlike the dominant bio-art of the present that maintains man's watchfulness over life, embraces disappearance:

> Amanda was in the Wisconsin desert, putting together one of the Bioart installations she's been doing now that she's into what she calls the art caper. It was cow bones this time. Wisconsin's covered with cow bones [...] and she was dragging the cow bones into a pattern so big it could only be seen from above: huge capital letters, spelling out a word. Later she'd cover it in pancake syrup and wait until the insect life was all over it, and then take videos of it from the air, to put into galleries. She liked to watch things move and grow and then disappear [...]. Her Wisconsin thing was part of a series called The Living Word—she said for a joke that it was inspired by the Gardeners because they'd repressed us so much about writing things down. She'd begun with one-letter words—*I* and *A* and *O*—and then done two-letter words like *It*, and then three letters, and four, and five. Now she was up to six. They'd been written in all different materials, including fish guts and toxic-spill-killed birds and toilets from building demolition sites filled with used cooking oil and set on fire. (Atwood 2009, 56-57)

Atwood depicts the artist, Amanda, not as one who will retrieve all that is proper, foundational, and eternal in life, but as a scammer, joker, or player who will take man's game of life, money, and survival—including the sanctity of the word—and play with nonexistence. Beyond 'man,' there is perhaps only 'woman' and 'life'; and this is why man has always sustained himself by (figures of) becoming woman. Rather than think apocalyptically in terms of our own finality (or our own beyond or our very own posthumanity) we might—finally—be given the opportunity to think of a world without ends.

Here lies the significance of Atwood's work. First, she presents the imagined nightmare of a future world of man's psychotic drive to master life as already evidenced in the present (rather than being some imagined or possible post-apocalyptic future). We are always and already so tied to life that it becomes the screen or tableau upon which we imagine nothing other than our own living. Second, like Shelley before her, she does not place a feminized nature outside man, for beyond 'man' one cannot figure *the good life* but only contingent, fragile, insecure, and ephemeral lives. Finally, one cannot appeal here to art or the aesthetic, for here, too, one encounters the fetishized figure of redemptive creation. In its place, Atwood, like Woolf and Shelley before her, imagines what life would be like if one could abandon the fantasy of one's own endurance.

Notes

1. I use the term *man* quite deliberately here: for it is this figure of man that has been adopted by both parties, both those who deploy notions of a generic humanity *and* those feminists who seek to find a space of 'woman' outside the man of reason. The concept of man also brings with it a certain concept of world: as Heidegger and others have pointed out, the earth becomes 'world' when it is *lived as our own*.

2. For a stringent critique of the myopias of environmental thinking, see Donna Haraway, *When Species Meet* (Minneapolis: University of Minnesota Press, 2008) 18.

3. It is for this reason that Luce Irigaray (1985) does not see Descartes as an 'error' in the history of thought but instead recognizes in the Cartesian cogito an ongoing appeal to a necessary otherness that will enable man to return to himself, and live himself as nothing more than the process of reflecting his own outside.

4. For an insightful criticism of bio-art's putative break with 'man' —a critique that would resonate with Atwood's attempt to figure a bio-art of dead waste— see Nicole Anderson, '(Auto)Immunity: The Deconstruction and Politics of 'Bio-Art' and Criticism,' *Parallax* 16:4 (2010): 101–116.

Chapter 2

Norm Wars

It might seem at first glance that Gilles Deleuze would be *the* anti-normative theorist par excellence and that we could turn to his work to draw from his rich lexicon of seemingly counter-normative concepts, including immanence (as the refusal of any imposed order), affect (or forces disruptive of calculated propriety) and the body without organs (that appears to signal, even if he did not used the word, some sense of a body's capacity to generate instability). The body without organs, more than immanence and affect, offers two modes of counter-normativity: the first lies with the use of the word *organs,* for it is organs or parts that seem to grant some functioning wholeness to bodies. The body without organs seems to reverse the organicist idea that beings become what they are (and take on function, order and organization) only in relations to a whole. The body *without organs* suggests that there can be something like a body—a whole—that does not have functioning parts; as long as fragments, parts or forces are not organized or functional then they cannot be said to be organs. By contrast, another performative mode of reading this term would suggest just the reverse; there are acts or performances—movements or functions—that compose or perform a body, but that body never takes on a final or definitive wholeness. Despite the complexity and polyvalence of the term 'body without organs' it can nevertheless provide a clear and distinct path beyond performative approaches to normativity. On a generally performative account, immanence is true and good because it frees us from any imposed or given norms; immanence is a radical liberal refusal of any authority that might dictate order in advance. Further, affect also disturbs standard, prescriptive, calculative or imposed orders of the self; affects occur without decision or mastery and the politics of affect takes us out of the domain of selves and interests and into a realm where politics would proceed by creating and performing: producing or working with affects rather than simply negotiating information. As already suggested, immanence and affect seem to have the vogue that they do today (if they still do) both because of Deleuze's work *and* because of a general shift towards performativity, or the idea that politics and identity occur through ongoing creation and not by appeal to principles. If performativity is true then it follows that selves become what they are in ongoing actions that relate to, are affected by, and affect, others. If performativity is true then it also follows that we have no foundation outside our self-creating performance of who we are. We would all, potentially, be 'bodies witout organs' capable of dismantling any identity to which we have been subjected, but never by decision or fiat so much as precarious and heteronomous engagements with others. It would seem then that immanence, affect and performativity would be the anti-normative concepts par excellence, freeing us from the negativity of critique.

I will argue that all these concepts of immanance, affect and performativity—have two sides: one is anti-normative, and therefore defined against (and within the same terrain as) normativity. The other side would neither be normative nor anti-normative but would be posed in terms of a different problem, a problem on a plane distinct from that of performativity. For it is performativity—in its shift from linguistic to political modes—that stresses that there are not identities, forms, systems, meanings or terms that are then repeated by language users; nor is language use or the taking on of identity the adoption of some external system. Rather, terms and systems are created and constituted through ongoing performance. It would follow then that individuals do not take up norms and identities and *then* find space for critique, for there is no norm or identity outside performance, and so all performance is at once repetition and disturbance, consolidation and critique. In this respect the very possibility of a norm—that it is given through repetition and performance—is also the impossibility of a norm, for no repetition *is* or coincides with the norm itself. One is always necessarily subjected, for there is no self or subject outside the norm, but one is also necessarily never fully or finally 'a subject' precisely because every performance of a norm is never the norm *as such*. Norms emerge from, but are disturbed by, the very performance they make possible. But it is for just this reason that performative modes of defining affect and immanence remain subjectivist. Affect becomes that destabilizing force of bodies in performance and relation, while immanence precludes any reference to a force or power that would exceed performing bodies. These reactive modes of defining anti-normativity are *subjectivist* in Heidegger's sense: they posit some ground from which all relations emerge (and, further, in rejecting *Descartes'* subject of mental substance they posit some other ultimate subject—such as life, affect, embodiment or immanence). Deleuze's concepts of immanence, affect and act or fiat (rather than performativity) are—I will argue—composed on another plane, from a different style of problem.[1] It might seem at first that performativity might be a countervitalist concept: without any foundation or appeal to life all we have are actions and relations among bodies, *from which* we then posit some foundation or subject that must have been. Certainly such a mode of thinking performativity might be possible but it would need first to free performance both from language acts and acting bodies, perhaps thinking of performative forces beyond all that we have come to think of as acting, and would also need to be freed from the problems of norm and identity. (As an example one might think of all the cosmic performances of geological powers that do not seem to have been active or identified until now and that have a being or force beyond systems of recognition.) As conceived, the concepts of immanence, affect and performative—those that seem to have waged war on normativity and especially insofar as they are opposed to normativity—constitute something like a new subjectivism of life. For if one appeals to the affects of bodies as destabilizing powers that would wage war on the rigidity of norms, or if one thinks of performativity as radical insofar as it takes on (and then destabilizes) norms then one repeats, reactively, a disjunction between the system of norms on the one hand and the force of disturbance on the other.

This has direct consequences for disciplines and disciplinarity. If it were the case that one might appeal to some generative ground—such as life—from which relations would emerge, then knowledge would be a single field, and may enjoy something like interdisciplinarity, which would encompass all the different but conversant and convergent ways in which life appears. Seeming disciplinary divergence—such as literary theorists' or art critics' tendencies to treat works of art as detached from life, or philosophy's approach to logic as having some Platonic reality, or the scientist's disenchantment and reification of life—could all be remedied by an acknowledgment of the genesis and emergence of all these faculties from one self-furthering life. Habermas, the great theorist of inescapable normativity, has insisted that we need some reflective practice—such as critical philosophy—that locates and negotiates the knowledge practices of various lifeworlds:

> The difference between lifeworld and communicative action is not taken back in any unity; it is even *deepened* to the extent that the reproduction of the lifeworld is no longer merely routed *through* the medium of action oriented toward reaching understanding, but is saddled *on* the interpretive performances of its agents. To the degree that yes/no decisions that sustain the communicative practice of everyday life do not derive from an ascribed normative consensus but emerge from the cooperative interpretive processes of the participants themselves, *concrete* forms of life and *universal* structures of the lifeworld become separated. Naturally, there are family resemblances among the plurality of totalities of life forms; they overlap and interlock, but they are not embraced in turn by some supertotality. Multiplicity and diffusion arise in the course of an abstraction process through which the *contents* of particular lifeworlds are set off ever more starkly from the universal structures of the lifeworld. (Habermas 1990, 343)

No discipline should be a world unto itself, rigidly imposing its field upon life. The task of the disciplines, and especially the humanities, today would lie in just this *ideal*, but not actuality of, convergence. All this would seem to follow from at least one notion of immanence: disciplines emerge from life and cannot stand above life (or other disciplines); nor could there be a specialist 'moral' or biological science that would provide some law *for* life, for these practices too emerge from, and are therefore immanent to, life.

By contrast, Deleuze and Guattari (1994) focus on the incommensurable and divergent nature of the faculties—lacking anything like a *sensus communis,* good sense, common sense, lifeworld or 'lived.' The concepts created by philosophy have a thought and consistency of their own, and are responses to problems that take hold of and do violence to thinking. If there is an immanence it is not immanence to a life of the 'lived'—not this life of ours that we negotiate from practices and can never step outside. Rather, the immanence is inhuman, which means that 'we' (we humans) cannot locate all that is within any life, for life is not given as such, as some ground from which difference emerges. The disciplines—then—far from being traceable back to praxis exist and insist in their immanence, irreducible to anything other than themselves. Works of art manage (at least in part) to tear something like 'affects' from affections: as though the lived affection were the expression of a pure power or quality. Scientific functions are definitely not those of the lived, but have success insofar as they formulate new 'observers' that would allow for a consistency and truth that is certainly not that of human experience. It is not the case, then, that we have competing systems—all emerging from life, each composing a reality of its own that we then need to adjudicate via reflective critique. Nor are we imprisoned in a human domain of performed or constituted normative orders from which the only exit would be destabilization from within. If we think beyond normativity and its others to a different way of thinking about the concept of immanence we would be presented with multiple powers, all of them opening up divergent potentials and assembled systems. Each such diverging line would be expressive of the infinite in its own way. The problem with normativity would neither be that norms in their rigidity do violence to the dynamic praxis of life, nor that without norms we would fall into the chaos of the undifferentiated. Certainly, then, there would be no distinction between the hard world of scientific facts, and then the norm-constitutive or meaning-productive humanities. Nor would there be some imprisoning and reactively nihilist sense that the sciences, too, are normative or value-producing, and that beyond normativity there only exists some reality or life that is known *ex post facto* as beyond the sense we make of it.

Life, as articulated by Deleuze, is not a generative ground. It is not life in general as some force or algorithm that generates a 'vital normativity,' such as the imperative for life to maintain and persevere in itself (Esposito 2008). Nor is life some negated or mourned real that is given only through the narrow forms that we impose upon it. Rather, by referring to 'a' life that is distinct from the actualized individual, life does not become some imperative of retrieval, redemption or repair. It does not have the sense of drawing our attention *back* to the ground of life from which individuals have emerged. On the contrary, 'life' is—like the three faculties of Deleuze and Guattari's *What is Philosophy?*—a detaching power.

This is because it is 'a' life: neither the life of an individual, nor life in general:

> We will say of pure immanence that it is A LIFE, and nothing else. It is not immanence to life, but the immanent that is in nothing is itself a life. A life is the immanence of immanence, absolute immanence; it is complete power, complete bliss[...] it is an absolute immediate consciousness whose very activity no longer refers to a being but is ceaselessly posed in a life. (Deleuze 1991, 27)

If normativity is a commitment to *one's* life, such that I could not be who I am if I were not committed to some ongoing, stable and disciplined self, then 'a' life shifts the terrain of the problem. One is neither a free, self-creating individual, always other than any reified or imposed norm (anti-normative subjectivism); *nor* is one a self who gives a law to oneself, recognizing oneself through the capacity to be *someone*. In contrast to *one's* life or dynamic life in general, Deleuze's 'a' life has two distinguishing features. First, Deleuze argues that this potential for thought—for thinking about immanence as 'a' life—is expressed in literature. That is, in order for this strange thought of 'a' life to emerge it needs to be distilled, articulated or constituted through some specific faculty. When Charles Dickens describes the loathsome character Riderhood—whose organized and identifiable individuality no one would seek to save—he manages to articulate a moment at which all the general and stable qualities, including the character's personal striving, fall away:

> Between his life and his death there is a moment that is only that of *a* life playing with death. The life of the individual gives way to an impersonal and yet singular life that releases a pure event freed from the accidents of internal and external life, that is, from the subjectivity and objectivity of what happens: a 'Homo tantum' with whom everyone empathizes and who

attains a sort of beatitude. It is a heacceity no longer of individuation but of singularization: a life of pure immanence, neutral, beyond good and evil, for it was only the subject that incarnated it in the midst of things that made it good or bad. (Deleuze 1991, 28-29)

One is given not an individual who wants to live, nor life in general but something like a 'spark'—one force in an eternity and infinity of forces that flickers here and now, and that may or may not endure. If there is an individual who endures as a relatively stable ongoing collection of predicates, all given form through relations to other individuals and predicates, then this is because there are individuating 'sparks,' flickers of 'a' life that might create a differentiated person located in a specific point of view. Life, given as 'a' life, would therefore be closer to a power of dispersal and positive destruction: 'a' life is that which is stabilized when individuals are brought into being, but which appears *as individuating* when the individual falls apart and is now the potentiality for individuation. Second, this way of thinking about immanence is radically destructive and antifoundational. Rather than posit something like life, humanity, labor, responsiveness, affect, being or the lived as that receding ground from which relations emerge, 'a' life is counter-actualizing or anti-relational. It does not express itself via some normative commitment that something *is* only insofar as it is recognized, maintained as itself, and constitutive of ongoing stability; nor is life that which is given as other than any fixed norm (as it would be in the Romanticist notion of the subject as above and beyond any of his expressed personae).

This can be explained more concretely by looking at one of the few occasions when Deleuze and Guattari address the relation between norms and desire. In *Anti-Oedipus* they examine the colonizing power of the figure of Oedipus. The power of their diatribe against psychoanalysis lay in their astute understanding of the truth of the Oedipus complex, that Oedipus was, indeed, the structure of the modern subject. We imagine that *either* we subject ourselves to the prohibiting normativity of *the* law, or fall back into a chaotic and nightmarish psychosis. Discussing the ways in which psychoanalysts approached an African tribe, Deleuze and Guattari criticize the assumption that psychoanalysis can and *should* begin *not* when disturbances and forces are distributed beyond individuals humans but when crises are located within a subject and a psyche. Why, they ask, should *individuation* be tied exclusively to an *individual* and a subject's relation to norms?

> Why think that supernatural powers and magical aggressions constitute a myth that is inferior to Oedipus? On the contrary, is it not true that they move desire in the direction of more intense and more adequate investments of the social field, in its organization as well as its disorganizations? [...]
>
> Could it not be said that Oedipus is also a traditional norm— our own to be exact? How can one say that Oedipus makes us speak in our own name, when one also goes on to say that its resolution teaches us 'the incurable inadequacy of being' and universal castration? And what is this 'demand' that is invoked to justify Oedipus? It goes without saying, the subject demands and redemands daddy-mommy: but which subject, and in what state? Is that the means 'to situate oneself personally in one own's society'? And which society? The neo-colonized society that is constructed for the subject, and that finally succeeds in what colonization was only able to outline: an effective reduction of the forces of the desire to Oedipus, to a father's name, in the grotesque triangle? (Deleuze and Guattari 1983, 170-71)

Deleuze and Guattari's argument against Oedipus as a structure pertains directly to normativity: the structural account of Oedipus insists that *either* one submit to the prohibiting law of normativity and renounce the fullness of desire, *or* one falls back into the dark night of the undifferentiated. One accepts normativity as the very condition for being a self; other than the normative recognized self there is only a silent and inarticulable negativity. In terms of theories of the political subject this can be charted in terms of two positions today: normativity is the enabling, ennobling and productive condition of granting one's life sense, worth and recognition (Korsgaard 1996, 237); *or*, the self that is constituted through normativity and recognition is the outcome of a process of subjection, beyond which lies a negated, mourned, inarticulable and precarious life that can only be posited after the event of its loss:

our identification with the active side of our nature is what binds us to the moral law. That the moral self is a self normatively conceived, what I call a practical identity, emerges nicely when Kant says that 'even the most malicious villain (provided he is otherwise accustomed to using his reason)'—that is, provided he is reflective—'imagines himself to be this better person when he transfers himself to the standpoint of a member of the intelligible world.' The 'better person' here functions as an object of aspiration and identification. The idea of identifying normatively with a certain conception of one's nature—the conception of oneself as active and rational—therefore plays a central role in Kant's view, just as identifying normatively with the conception of oneself as human does in mine. (Korsgaard 1996, 237-38)

Performativity is thus not a singular 'act' , for it is always a reiteration of a norm or set of norms, and to the extent that it acquires an act-like status in the present, it conceals or dissimulates the conventions of which it is a repetition. Moreover this act is not primarily theatrical; indeed, its apparent theatricality is produced to the extent that its historicity remains dissimulated (and, conversely, its theatricality gains a certain inevitability given the impossibility of a full disclosure of its historicity). (Butler 1993, xxi)

Either (as in Korsgaard) the self is tied to normativity insofar as it is active and reflects upon itself; or, (as in Butler) the performance of norms gives the appearance of one who has acted. Both agree that the self, one way or the other is normative. For Korsgaard the norm is, and ought to be, properly one's own (otherwise it would not be a norm). For Butler, the norm is precisely *not one's own*—therein lies its status as performative, as that which constitutes an 'act' through its dissimulation.

One way of defining the current theoretical landscape is to chart various positions according to a war on normativity. These could be parsed into three general orientations. First: only normativity can save us. Second: normativity needs to be defined against normalization. Third, and finally—the question of norms is a false or badly posed problem.

These three orientations allow for different attitudes towards the problem of disciplines. If normativity is the condition for the possibility of a future, then we require disciplines as positive and enabling practices. The humanities, with its generation of meaning and legitimation procedures, would be crucial for 'our' ongoing survival. If, however, disciplines have been intertwined genealogically with processes of normalization, then our normative future would require a radical upheaval of the humanities. This would demand something like a Foucaultian approach, where the very modes of knowing from which the humanities have emerged would need to be criticized in light of the distribution of powers that constituted something like 'life' that could function as a transcendental ground. Life would be the horizon that enabled the formation of human sciences, the division of labor that would yield the humanities, and a relation among disciplines that would subsequently generate a conversation concerning man as a norm-constituting animal. Against these two modes of approaching disciplines, both of which would support a defence of the humanities—to some extent—and would present interdisciplinarity as a prima facie good, I would like to propose a Deleuzian approach. Here, one neither appeals to normativity as the definitive human horizon, nor aims to disengage normativity from human normalization. Rather, by destroying both the positive and critical aspects of disciplines it would be possible to achieve modes of thinking that look to a posthumanities future.

Before launching into some of the academic and disciplinary accounts of normativity we can begin by considering the unstated war on normativity that dominates the present. In its naïve form this has been deployed by marketing strategists, consciousness-raising forms of identity politics, and certain unreflective readings of theory. From early forms of liberation feminism and other seemingly radical approaches to politics, the word 'stereotype' is a clear pejorative. Rather than be defined and determined by images or cliches, selves should be defined via one equal and self-organizing humanity; selves should be pure creativity and self-definition adopting a critical distance to anything other than their own real and authentic individuality. That is, one should either reject stereotypes by arguing that beneath color, sexual orientation, gender or religion we are all ultimately human, and capable of recognizing each other across manifest divides. Or, one could appeal to the unique and distinct nature of each individual. Both of these notions have been common marketing and moralizing ploys. In the late 1980s Benetton's United Colors of Benetton campaign featured posters of ethnic diversity—a range of bodies all wearing the varied colors of Benetton. The 'family of man' motif celebrates difference as apparent and enriching, but beneath which lies a friendly and affirmative sameness. This 'unity in diversity' notion (that was ironized by William Blake's 'I am black but O! my soul is white') has continually been expressed in popular song lyrics, including Michael Jackson's 'Black or White' of 1991: 'I'm not going to spend my life being a color.' Even more cloying was the earlier Ebony and Ivory (of 1982 by Stevie Wonder):

> *We all know that people are the same where ever you go*
> *there is good and bad in everyone*
> *we learn to live when we learn to give each other what we*
>   *need to survive*
> *together alive'*

The 'deep down we are all human' motif survives happily in cinema as well, ranging from Paul Haggis's *Crash* of 2004—in which the urban conflict and racial violence of interweaving narratives resolve in a final moment of cross-racial human recognition—to the more recent *Avatar* of 2009, in which the rapacious human species, living in end times, meets a different species only to find that these blue humanoids seem to embody all the virtues of community, reciprocity, altruism and patriarchal lineage that had (once) defined humanity. One might refer to this knee-jerk humanism as the normativity that dare not speak its name: there is no norm other than the norm that 'we' have no norms. Despite race, creed or (in the case of *Avatar*) species differences 'we' are all capable of recognition of each other, for there is no real otherness—no norm that does not, in the end, give way to humanity. Religion? Not significant, if we just converse and face each other. Race? Nothing more than a color—akin perhaps to the cohabiting keys on a piano keyboard ('Ebony and Ivory'...). Gender, sexuality? Don't mention it. (This ultra-humanism is—I would suggest—masked by what passes in theory today for many modes of posthumanism: we no longer believe in the exceptional distinction of privileged white 'man,' for *everything that lives* is an agent—subjected to the one norm of unity, community, communication, reciprocity and ecology: deep down we are all human.)

Perhaps more significant, though, is the more explicit counter-normative resistance to any image or figure that is in any way transcendent to the individual's very own being. The first notion—that deep down, despite manifest appearances we are all human—derives from a liberal commitment to human self-regulation: I am free to be anything I want, to pursue anything I want *because* I am a member of one human community that recognizes and tolerates all others of its kind. There is a minimal transcendence here: the only regulation is self-regulation, and this occurs by way of acknowledging that one is nothing more than human; any other norm (religious, sexual, ethnic, political...) is of one's choosing and cannot impede the broader recognition of humanity in general. The second and more stringently counter-normative position both extends and reacts against liberalism. Differences between earlier modes of liberalism were that traditional post-Kantian forms relied on a minimal and formal normativity: a just society would be one that would be chosen by all, regardless of one's social position. The good self would be one who was not defined through any specific norm, but who recognized that *some* normative structure—giving a law to oneself—is constitutive of reason and selfhood. Against this liberal commitment to minimal and formal normativity, one might define the present as shrilly anti-normative: not only should there be no norm imposed on the individual flexibility of my own being, I ought not to enslave myself to any overly stringent idea of who I ought to be. The self-help industry is largely built on an imperative of self-acceptance—of not judging oneself, of not imposing any figure or ideal upon the self. (Sometimes these imperatives have a 'feminist' slant—such that one ought to avoid internalizing media images of ideal women; or sometimes the pitch is apparently ecological or anti-capitalist, so that one is warned not to be a victim of gimmicks and hype. A recent campaign of a popular form of soft drink worked by urging consumers to be intelligent enough to realize they were buying a drink, not an image of coolness or masculinity.) New forms of branding rely less on the appeal to a unified humanity, and more on a rebellious individualism; this can range from Nike's 'id' (or individually designed range) to limited edition versions of street-wear. Advertising now draws heavily from counter-culture, so that environmentalism, anti-corporatism, non-conformism and feminism can be branded. The beauty brand 'Dove' used the notion of 'real' women to market its products; Starbucks has been one of many companies selling itself through 'fair' trade; other brands such as The Body Shop or Pret a Manger, despite their vast sales empires trade on setting themselves against 'chain' branding, beauty hype and fast food. Nothing sells like counter-culture; nothing constitutes the uniqueness of an individual more than a rebellion against normativity.

In terms of theory it is possible to observe an anti-normativity in at least three tendencies. First: 'immanence' in one of its popular versions sets itself against any image, norm, law or state that does not derive from the self-constituting act. In Hardt and Negri's formulation of it, immanence would be distinguished from liberalism's seemingly similar 'freedom from imposed tutelage,' for there is no individual or presumed rationality that would guide the formation of the polity. Instead, humanity constitutes itself; whatever counts as human is achieved through an ongoing and collective becoming. Liberalism's ultimate value of *liberty* has always impeded collective self-formation, because liberty was liberty of the individual. (We can see this in the way Rawls's definition of freedom imposed a responsibility on the individual to choose in such a way that her decision could be universalizable for all.) Against this, Hardt and Negri's collective discourse abandons any already given subject or grounding agent, arguing for a self-forming humanity, with the multiple nature of the political precluding any settled norm (236). The human is neither a norm of reason, nor an underlying ground. Contemporary capitalism has already, they argue, abandoned norm-regulated forms of behavior in favor of corporate efficiency (178), and so democracy cannot take the earlier forms of city-state models but requires global creativity. This creativity cannot be calculated by any measure other than itself, not capital, and not the free individual:

> 'living labor' [is] the form-giving fire of our creative capacities. Living labor is the fundamental human faculty: the ability to engage the world actively and create social life. Living labor can be corralled by capital and pared down to the labor

> power that is bought and sold and that produces commodities and capital, but living labor always exceeds that. Our innovative and creative capacities are always greater than our productive labor—productive, that is, of capital. At this point we can recognize that this biopolitical production is on the one hand *immeasurable,* because it cannot be quantified in fixed units of time, and, on the other hand, always excessive with respect to the value that capital can extract from it because capital can never capture all of life. (Hardt and Negri 2004, 146)

Outside of 'high' theory, recent economic crises and corporate corruption—or the war between Wall Street and Main Street—have prompted left-wing calls for individual participation and collective constitution of the polity alongside right-wing 'small government' imperatives. What distinguishes these recent maneuvers from standard liberalism is a rejection of any norm or model of reason or regulation that is not that of a continually self-creating and self-inventing becoming. This is also how movements of 'new' labor or the third way managed to cast off notions of being constrained by leftist ideology: rather than having a revolutionary program or privileged norm of the primacy of the working class, the model of government was primarily managerial and procedural. It is not surprising, then, that Hardt and Negri's multitude had to expend quite a bit of labor of its own on distinguishing itself from 'third way' movements: the new collectivity of humanity should not be grounded on appeals to global security or war alliance, but should be generated from a creative, rather than managed, multitude (Hardt and Negri 2004, 233, 398).

Second, we might consider the concept of affect. Defined against mind-centered, Cartesian, cognitive and computational models of consciousness, affect has (in its less critical articulations) enabled a privileging of life that is regressively organicist. Rather than the body being seen as a part of the world or as a known object, the body and its responsiveness is now the horizon from which knowledge emerges. In the beginning is the affect or feeling *from which* systems, relations and terms have their genesis. In its relatively popular scientific mode this affective turn—away from rigid entities and systems to dynamic relationality—is perhaps most clearly expressed by Antonio Damasio, whose work, even more than that of Hardt and Negri, crosses from university culture to a broader reading public. The titles of Damasio's books read like a series of theses: *Descartes' Error* describes the problem of beginning from the position of the cognitive self, and in that regard expresses a widespread anti-Cartesianism that has much resonance with counter-normativity. For what at least *one* mode of anti-Cartesianism expresses is a hyper-subjectivism. The properly relational, emotive, responsive, affective and living self has been reified into some normative 'ghost' in a body that has become a machine. Damasio's *The Feeling of What Happens* argues for the primacy of emotion, which far from being a state of mind or mental phenomenon is given or felt after its bodily and definitely non-cognitive occurrence. ('Bodily' is not quite the right word here, for there is no body as object; there is a domain of emotive responsive and autopoetic interactive self-regulation, which is then felt—and it is from that feeling that a self is formed.) *Looking for Spinoza* enables Damasio to strengthen the philosophical ground of his anti-Cartesianism, but his Spinoza is a curious beast. Yes, Spinoza was a philosopher of the affections who defined mind *not* in opposition to the body, but as an aspect or perceptive feeling of what occurs affectively. But Spinoza was also a philosopher of reason, whose positing of a third kind of knowledge, or a capacity to consider substance—or what is—beyond the point of view of our own affections, opened up a theology (even if pantheistic) that would be distinctly out of tune with any insistence on the primacy of the lived body. Damasio's most recent work focuses on what he refers to as 'biological value,' which—as described—accounts for the genesis of the self not so much from extrinsic, historical or transcendent systems but from minute selections:

> in addition to the logic imposed by the unfolding of events in the reality external to the brain—a logical arrangement that the naturally selected circuitry of our brains foreshadows from the very early stages of development—the images in our minds are given more or less saliency in the mental stream according to their value for the individual. And where does that value come from? It comes from the original set of dispositions that orients our life regulation, as well as from the valuations that all images we have gradually acquired in our experience have been accorded, based on the original set of value dispositions during our past history. In other words, minds

are not just about images entering their procession naturally. They are about the cinemalike editing choices that our pervasive system of biological value has promoted. (Damasio 71)

I would suggest that Damasio's use of 'logic' here—for all its appeal to individual bodily immediacy, reveals what Derrida diagnosed as 'logocentrism': some ground determines systems and relations in advance. Here, that ground is 'life.'

Finally, the concept of performativity—especially as one tracks its migration from linguistics to ethico-political accounts of the self—demonstrates the contraction of action away from any consideration that would be beyond processes of subjectivity and subjection (as it might once have been in its linguistic mode). The force of the concept of the performative lay in a capacity of language as action—as *doing things with words*—that would free philosophy from having to deal with odd immaterial or mental entities such as 'meanings.' The performative, as a concept, was always two-sided: it opened the possibility of forces, actions, and acts that are not those of humans beings or lived bodies, but it also— by focusing on act—tended to reground systems on some will or 'doing.' Language works, in speech act theory, not because our exchange of tokens allows some transfer of some pure sense that would exist outside our usage: a term works because of conventions of interaction, exchange, use and processes of relative stability. When the concept of the performative was translated into the problem of identity it had (again) two sides: on the one hand, in Butler's formulation of the term, it produced an affirmative concept of matter, whereby there is no such thing as life or matter that lies outside language, for language—like anything that could be said to *be*—exists only in its differential distribution: 'What I would propose in place of these conceptions of construction is a return to the notion of matter, not as site or surface, but as *a process of materialization that stabilizes over time to produce the effect of boundary, fixity, and surface we call matter*' (Butler 1993, 9). One might, following this, consider matter to be performative: in this case, Butler's work would open up a new materialism that would pose questions quite distinct from those of subjective normativity. This did, indeed, occur but Butler's own work went on to pose questions (of recognition, subjection and what counts as grievable) that tended to return processes of performativity to an agent who (admittedly) is not a 'doer' so much as one who is given as a subject through the exclusion of something extra-discursive:

> Indeed, to 'refer' naively or directly to such an extra-discursive object will always require the prior delimitation of the extra-discursive. And insofar as the extra-discursive is delimited, it is formed by the very discourse from which it seeks to free itself. This delimitation, which is often enacted as an untheorized presupposition in any act of description, marks a boundary that includes and excludes, that decides, as it were, what will and will not be the stuff of the object to which we then refer. This marking off will have some normative force and, indeed, some violence, for it can construct only through erasing: it can bound a thing only through enforcing a certain criterion, a principle of selectivity. (Butler 1993, 11)

Only normativity can save us

Strangely, despite all the incoming evidence regarding a widespread human destructiveness—both to man's own species and his milieu—there has been a number of appeals, celebrations and defenses of the definitively human capacity for normativity. The argument takes two general forms—one that appeals to a tradition of human normativity, grounded in a faculty of philosophy (such that human beings cannot avoid a constitutive relation to ongoing lawfulness), and another that addresses a present sense of groundlessness and loss of meaning, and that can only be ameliorated through practices of normativity. The first position is best expressed by a humanized neo-Kantianism. There is no appeal to what lies beyond nature, as might have been suggested by some readings of Kant's account of the noumenal or supersensible (but necessarily presupposed) subject. (This is the subject or *non*-ground that Heidegger [1967] approached when he questioned the 'source' of Kant's various faculties.) Rather, there is something quotidian or post-metaphysical about the necessity of normativity:

> Outside of human nature, there is no normative point of view from which morality can be challenged. But morality can

> meet the internal challenge that is made from the point of view of self-interest, and it also approves of itself. It is human nature to be governed by morality, and from every point of view, including its own, morality earns its right to govern us. We therefore have no reason to reject our nature, and can allow it to be a law to us. Human nature, moral government included, is therefore normative, and has authority for us. (Korsgaard 2004, 66)

It would be a performative contradiction for me at one and the same time to use the word 'I,' and to affirm some value, and then on another occasion affirm the opposite. Without some minimal ongoing normativity 'I' would have no being; this is not because the subject has some nature or essence that entails or dictates law, but because *in the absence of nature and essence* 'I' am nothing other than a lawfulness that I grant to myself. One might say that the governing, or normative, 'idea of humanity' is that of the pure form of the self-regulating subject: because there is no human nature that I can know, or that can provide a ground for my actions, I must give a law to myself. 'I' am nothing other than this act of self-regulation. Inflected somewhat differently, this inescapable normativity of humanity can take a negative, but no less subjective form.

We return to Judith Butler: selves are constituted through normativity and recognition. However, one should not simply celebrate this lawgiving event of constitution. First, the stabilization of the self through a repeatable norm, sacrifices or mourns that which is occluded or not taken up as worthy of recognition (even though this lost ground is known only *as lost*, only in being other than, or negated by the normative). Second, one needs to politicize rather than individualize normativity: just *what* modes of self one will recognize as normative, both for oneself and others, are restricted—not least by what Butler referred to as the 'heterosexual matrix' or what has been marked more generally as heteronormativity.

> Here a certain normative crisis ensues. On the one hand it is important to mark how the field of intelligible and speakable sexuality is circumscribed, so that we can see how options outside of marriage are becoming foreclosed as the unthinkable, and how the terms of thinkability are enforced

by the narrow debates over who and what will be included in the norm. On the other hand, there is always the possibility of savoring the status of unthinkability, if it is a status, as the most critical, the most radical, the most valuable. As the sexually unpresentable, such sexual possibilities can figure the sublime within the contemporary field of sexuality, a site of pure resistance, a site unco-opted by normativity. But how does one think politics from such a site of unrepresentability? (Butler 2004, 106-07)

Without some mode of normativity there would be no selfhood or subjectivity. But in both the neo-Kantian affirmation of self-legislation and Butler's more critical idea that the performative structures that enable selves are not decided by selves, what would be required is some form of discipline as critique. One could not simply have a world of fact-based natural sciences, nor a social science assumption that one might be able to chart and analyze various systems of norms (cultures, languages, textual systems, societies, polities). What would be required is a critical notion of the humanities: if 'we' are always subjected to some norm of humanity, whether that be enabling or restricting, then some reflective procedure needs to be constantly vigilant of normative figurations of the (unavoidably) human.

Normativity versus Normalization

One might say, in response to the idea that humans are norm-producing and norm-constitutive animals, that this is a highly *normalizing* assumption. Here, a certain reading of Foucault would be in order. Consider one notion of norm, grounded on a certain motif of man (one that Foucault aligns with a specific reading of Kant, and a specific trajectory of the human sciences—a trajectory from which he would distinguish what he refers to as literature). This notion of norm emerged with *man*; for man is the being who must on the one hand (by nature) give a law unto himself, but whose positive content is left blank: 'Before the end of the eighteenth century, *man* did not exist—any more than the potency of life, the fecundity of labour, or the historical density of language' (Foucault 336). On or around 1700 there emerged a new episteme of life, and from then on no *morality* was possible, only ethics. *Morality* would have been just the assertion, perhaps grounded on a notion of God, nature or even humans in relation to some moral nature, that certain values are worthy. Ethics, however, is possible only with the idea of *man*. Here, I do not assert a value because I say that this is how the world *is*. Rather, it is because man is that being who realizes that as a cultural (linguistic, historical, desiring) animal he has no nature other than the nature he gives to himself; that he must not simply assert a value, but come up with some formal value-generating procedure:

> It seems obvious enough that, from the moment when man first constituted himself as a positive figure in the field of knowledge, the old privilege of reflexive knowledge, of thought thinking itself, could not but disappear; but that it became possible, by this very fact, for an objective form of thought to investigate man in his entirety—at the risk of discovering what could never be reached by his reflection or even by his consciousness: dim mechanisms, faceless determinations, a whole landscape of shadow that has been termed, directly or indirectly, the unconscious. [...]. Man has not been able to describe himself as a configuration in the *episteme* without thought at the same time discovering, both in itself and outside itself, at its borders yet also in its very warp and woof, an element of darkness, an apparently inert destiny in which it is embedded, an unthought which it contains entirely, yet in which it is also caught.
>
> [...] Superficially, one might say that knowledge of man, unlike the sciences of nature, is always linked, even in its vaguest form, to ethics or politics; more fundamentally, modern thought is advancing towards that region where man's Other must become the Same as himself. (Foucault 2002, 355; 358)

For Foucault, this has concrete consequences for the disciplines. Human sciences are only possible if man is at once a being with a certain *cultural nature*; these 'sciences' study man as an effect of hidden forces of which he can be only dimly aware. There now becomes a possibility both of bio-politics—managing man according to his life requirements (the health of populations)—but also a conception of the humanities. For now there is ethics: if man cannot know himself as he is in himself, then he can at least read his own cultural production as an expression of this unthought. (Foucault's own suggested direction was quite different: to tear language away from man would open up a domain of forces beyond normalizing life. Deleuze extended this path to life: how might we imagine mutations of life not based on the living—such as the geneses enabled by silicon? [Deleuze 2006, 74].)

Today, with the 'humanities' turning to historicism, cognitive archaeology, neuroscience, and other interdisciplinary sources, it is presupposed that concrete forces can provide the ground for interpretive reading. What is assumed is both a notion of man as a being with certain imperatives of life (requiring him to speak and labor) and also as a being who *properly* gives himself his own lawful being. This might be Kantian liberalism—act in such a way that your act could be assented to by all. Or it might, more insidiously, be what Foucault referred to as 'biopolitics'; whatever 'we' do has no value or morality, but is nothing more than the effective management and regulation of a population. Added to this world of managerial facts would then be the reflective or normative discussions of the humanities. What has happened is that something like 'life'—a concept that explains the emergence and self-maintenance of all living beings—destroys any immediate or unreflective morality; instead, one sees all moralities as expressions of a human life that is given in various languages, cultures, epochs or systems.

Foucault's project was at once historical in demonstrating that this seemingly anti-foundational maneuver was normalizing: if 'man' is that animal who has no nature other than the law he gives to himself then we at once assert the universal primacy of the liberal, reasoning, self-furthering subject of reason and calculation *and* (more alarmingly) posit something like 'life' that is the manageable ground of this subject. It 'follows' that polities ought to act in such a way that they maximize this subject's capacity to give himself his own norms: education as the creation of critical, reasoning subjects; health care reforms that enable the fruition of life; intervention in areas that would impede rational activity (protecting individuals from drugs, gambling, debt, pornography, poor diets—anything that would corrupt their supreme capacity of choice). Foucault did not, as some have suggested, want to retreat from a managerial and biopolitical modernity to some golden past where (either) one simply acted with mastery and fiat to create oneself as a work of art. He *did* chart a genealogy of the self, demonstrating that what we (today) deem to be the inescapable horizon of normativity—the liberal subject who gives a law to himself in a world of self-regulation—ought to be seen as transcendent rather than transcendental. That is, it is something that we encounter as opaque and contingent, not the ultimate horizon of 'our' being. Further—and this is where we can mark a distinction between Foucault's genealogy and Deleuze and Guattari's geology or stratigraphy—one needs to mark a disciplinary distinction. The human sciences are possible because of the assumption of normativity *as normal*: we study cultures, languages, epochs, counter-cultures, genders, sexualities, ethnicities or societies because we assume that man is an animal who constructs himself through enabling normative systems, systems that ought to be the object of our (managerial) critique and reflection. Today, as the humanities (*especially* literature) has become an amalgam of historical positivism, sociology of knowledge and (worst of all) evolutionary criticism, it would be possible to distinguish a different mode of the humanities (if one wanted to call it that). Foucault argued that man emerged from the complex of life, labour and language: man speaks and works because he is the living being whose nature compels him to work and speak in common. If we uncoupled language from its grounding in man as the being who gives himself self-furthering laws we would have *literature*. Language—considered not as sign of our self-creating being—but as something that has its own being (its own density or shining) would give us a positive criticism. How do texts form relatively autonomous field of problems, and with what other problems do they intersect? How do they mutate, and what do they enable?

Not 'Beyond Normativity'

Deleuze is not one of those thinkers who defines himself *against* a terrain. Even, with Guattari, *Anti-Oedipus* (for all its 'anti') has a positive condition. It is only possible to have the repressive normative strictures of Oedipus—*either you submit to the family or you are psychotic!*—because of a broader synthesis. The terms that make up a normative domain, such as the subject who submits to regulation, or the body that becomes sexed, or the thinker who works with a logic, are possible because of what we might refer to (but this time differently) as immanence, affect and fiat. In his book on Foucault, Deleuze makes two remarks that suggest a subtle but important difference from Foucault. First, Deleuze suggests that there is a Kantian limit in Foucault's work: one knows power in its differential effects, as a distributive force, but one never crosses the line to power itself. (And this is why, by contrast, Deleuze and Guattari will choose to write about desire, as something their method seeks to intuit *itself* as productive synthesis, not as produced.) Second, Deleuze suggests that it is possible to decouple (or deterritorialize) 'life' (and not just language) from the normalizing motif of man. I have already suggested that immanence, considered in the multiple singular—immanence always as 'a' life—a disturbing force or 'spark,' creates a new challenge for the discipline of thinking. If life is given in these sparks, from which individuals emerge but which might also have produced different syntheses of individuation, then 'a' discipline would be the posing of a problem from a differential field. Such a field would not be one view among others on the same general terrain, but would encounter other fields, composed differently by different problems—different actualizations or individuations of 'a' life. One uses the singular 'a' life to mark its distinction, but desists from granting this 'life' a body or individuality. This brings us to affect, which would not be emotion, feeling and certainly not responsiveness (and *certainly not*) a vital normativity. Let us consider inertia or weariness or stupid malevolence as 'an' affect. This potentiality would insist and persist, always there, and capable both of seizing hold of us, and of being detached or deterritorialized.

I am in a debate with my parliamentary colleague, and we are both engaging in a discourse about managing the nation's debts (both its financial and political debts to the present, and its possibly imagined geological debts to its future); there is a potentiality for positive destruction: we might talk, gesture and move in such a way that the thought of 'a' future seizes hold of us, or we might speak and act in such a way that we become gripped by the inertia of all the old figures. Who knows what syntheses might allow one affect rather than another to take hold? One might want to think of such questions in geological terms, by looking at the strata that compose such a scene. (I imagine, writing now, that talks between Obama and Boehner regarding the supposed US debt crisis were gripped by all sorts of free-floating affects—naïve hope, regressive racism, financial fear, political expediency, nostalgia for a real America, panic, psychotic incapacity to imagine dire consequences, the lure of smooth rhetoric, the strictures of procedural and managerial discourse, the visual affects of gentlemanly comportment, visceral anger …..I am not saying that Obama or Boehner felt these affects, nor that the Tea-party or 'left' expressed these feelings. Rather, just as an artist can capture an affect—such as the litigious torpor that is the affect of *Bleak House*—one might say that no one in the USA in July 2011 was panicking, and yet the *affect* of panic haunted the scene: *that there may be panic*. This would differ markedly from looking at the scene in terms of competing norms—leftist welfare liberalism versus competitive small government conservatism—because the scene would not be motivated by deliberation or cognition alone. It would also differ from rabidly anti-normative reactivisms: either the individualism that resented systemic government enclosure in party-political timelines *or* appeals to one creative, immanent, global and self-creating humanity. Immanence would not be immanent *to* a domain that would be structured by (or belied by) normativity. Rather, immanence would place us—or the questions we pose—among a field and plane of problems. It would not be a question of deliberating norms, as though there were a field of life to which we must give a law; nor would it be a question of negotiating some negated but lost outside beyond normativity. We would be exposed to all manner of powers: institutions, affects, habits, desires, pure predicates, potentialities, order-words, spatial distributions, a general interweaving of multiple and discordant strata. But it would not be 'us' as self-legislating beings who approached this terrain—as if we were within this life to which we were immanent. Immanence is not *our* immanence that allows us to eliminate the outside. Finally, we might think of the difference between act as performative and act as fiat: 'problems are inseparable from a power of decision, a fiat which, when we are infused by it, makes us semi-divine beings' (Deleuze 2004, 247). Here, also, I would like to return to the quotation from Deleuze's essay on immanence: 'for it was only the subject that incarnated it in the midst of things that made it good or bad' (Deleuze 1991, 28-29). Consider the difference between the performative, where there is no difference between doer and deed, and where the self is an ex post facto effect of an act, an act that occurs and is possible because of a normative matrix, even as it disturbs that very normativity through a differing repetition.

In this case what is dominant is what Deleuze and Guattari refer to as exclusive disjunction: only in submitting to the laws of action do 'I' become a being or subject at all, and yet at the same time I mourn that presupposed but lost real that can only be thought of as other than the normative matrix. Either I submit to recognition or fall into the dark night of indifference; I am either male or female; either I become a subject by demanding inclusion in the State or I refuse recognition and flirt with psychosis. And this is because without performance—without the act that marks out a self within a normative matrix—there is no 'doer.' By contrast, Deleuze suggests that there are powers as such, possibly incarnated and actualized, possibly not. Once something like a stable subject is formed, these powers can take on some axiology: 'only the subject that incarnated it in the midst of things that made it good or bad.' But it is possible to think outside this 'good or bad' for the subject who is given through action and decision. If one were to consider powers beyond the purview of the normative subject of 'good or bad,' one might open a counter-normative plane of *inclusive* disjunction: 'I want to recognize the values of subjected polities *and* do away with the very concept of 'the' political'; 'I want to demand women's rights and autonomy *and* say that gender is a false problem'; 'I want to argue for women's reproductive rights *and* refuse the notion of self-deciding individual rights, along with the concepts of reproduction.' I want to refuse normativity—refuse the notion of the constitutive domain or matrix that grants me my subjective being: and this, indeed, is what the very notion of 'becoming-imperceptible' demands.

As long as I am a subject for whom there is 'good or bad' then normativity is the inevitable and non-negotiable presupposition for being an 'I': I am nothing other than the subject of my actions, and without that ongoing decisive power I would have no subjective ground for recognition. However, were I to imagine the powers of becoming—'a' life—beyond how they are figured as good or bad *for me,* then something like a counter-ethics would be possible. Rather than an ethos of my own habits and practices, or an ecology where there is one system of interconnected life, or 'the' political where decisions are examined from the point of view of 'a' polity, the concepts of 'becoming-imperceptible' and '"a" life' enable us to pose problems that are adequate to twenty-first century horizons. Should we really be asking about normativity, values, identity and self-maintenance in an era of climate change, when this very *self*-furtherance and myopia threatens not only human existence but life in general? Surely now is the time not to ask how 'we' decide to maintain who 'we' are, but whether there might be questions, powers, problems that are not of our own choosing, that affect us not as doers or performers but as barely adequate witnesses.

Notes

1. It is correct to say, as Paul Patton does, that Deleuze and Guattari's ontology is normative: that is, their approach to the ways in which we account for the formation of the world of beings is tied to decisive values and commitments. That is, their theory of 'being' is not some neutral, value-free or purely scientific theory. This is true so long as one wishes to talk the language of normativity, I would argue that one ought not talk this way: normativity has no sense, or should have no sense, unless we assume that there are things that are not normative (facts? brute matter? chaos?). That is not the case. Anything that 'is,' or that makes a claim to being occurs through processes of force, interaction, inclusion and exclusion; there is no realm of what simply is, and then a normative domain that adds value.

Chapter 3

Post-Phenomenology's Evil Cartesian Demon

There is a doctrine about the nature and place of minds which is so prevalent among theorists and even among laymen that it deserves to be described as the official theory. Most philosophers, psychologists and religious teachers subscribe, with minor reservations, to its main articles and, although they admit certain theoretical difficulties in it, they tend to assume that these can be overcome without serious modifications being made to the architecture of the theory. [...] the central principles of the doctrine are unsound and conflict with the whole body of what we know about minds when we are not speculating about them.

The official doctrine, which hails chiefly from Descartes, is something like this. With the doubtful exception of idiots and infants in arms every human being has both a body and a mind. (Ryle 2000, 11)

If I am right in thinking that Descartes' badly argued hunch, the one which made him able to see pains and thoughts as modes of a single substance, was that indubitability was the common factor they shared with nothing physical, then we can see him as working his way around toward a view in which indubitability is no longer the mark of eternality, but rather of something for which the Greeks had no name—consciousness. Whereas previous philosophers had more or less followed Plato in thinking that only the eternal was known with certainty, Descartes was substituting 'clear and distinct perception'—that is, the sort of unconfused knowledge gained by going through a process of analysis—for 'indubitability' as a mark of eternal truths. *This left indubitability free to serve as a criterion of the mental.* For although the thought that I am in pain does not count as a clear and distinct perception, it can no more successfully be doubted than the thought that I exist. Whereas Plato and the tradition had made the lines between confusion and clarity, dubitability and indubitability, and the mind and the body, coincide, Descartes was now rearranging them. The result was that from Descartes on we have to distinguish between the special metaphysical ground for our certainty about our inner states ('nothing is closer to the mind that itself') and the various epistemological reasons which ground our certainties about anything else. (Rorty 2009, 58-59)

I will begin with the most general and attenuated axis of continuity, the one that begins with Plato, winds its way to its most lurid expression in Augustine, and finally becomes metaphysically solidified and scientized by Descartes. I am referring, of course, to our dualistic heritage: the view that human existence is bifurcated into two realms or substances: the bodily or material, on the one hand; the mental or spiritual, on the other. Despite some fascinating historical variations which I will not go into here, the basic imagery of dualism has remained fairly constant. Let me briefly describe its central features; they will turn out, as we will see, to comprise the basic body imagery of the anorectic.

First, the body is experienced as *alien,* as the not-self, the not-me. It is 'fastened and glued' to me, 'nailed' and 'riveted' to me, as Plato describes it in the *Phaedo*. For Descartes the body is the brute material envelope for the inner and essential self, the thinking thing.... (Bordo 2004, 144)

There has, in philosophy and popular culture, been a turn to 'mindfulness' that is perhaps best defined by understanding the problem that mindfulness has been designed to solve. We suffer from mind, from the imprisonment in our own Cartesian theatre (Dennett 1991, 106), or what Raymond Tallis refers to as the 'Cartesian prison' (Tallis 2004, 49). Somehow, somewhere along the line we forgot that mind was a part—not even a part, a process—of engaged embodiment. We forgot that we emerged from an entire ecology of living processes, all of them mindful in their own way. We bifurcated, disenchanted and calculated the world to the point where there was a great divide between mind and world. In addition to the plethora of self-help books on the topic, that claim to amalgamate Buddhist mindfulness with Western therapeutic methods, the notion has also been consecrated by 'legitimate' philosophy and theory, most notably the systems theory of Maturana and Varela, and the solution to the hard problem of mind put forward by Owen Flanagan:

> Eudaimonia (Buddha) = a stable sense of serenity and content (not the sort of happy-happy-joy-click-your-heels feeling state that is widely sought and promoted in the West as the best kind of happiness), where the serene and contented state is caused or constituted by enlightenment (bodhi)/wisdom (prajna) and virtue (sila, karuna) and meditation or mindfulness (Samadhi). Wisdom consists of deeply absorbed (intellectually and meditatively) knowledge of impermanence, the causal interconnectedness of everything, that everything (buildings, plants, animals, stars) lacks immutable essences (emptiness), and, what follows from these, that I am a man, a passing person, a person who passes, a process or unfolding that is known by a proper name, but that changes at every moment, until it passes from the realm of being altogether. (Flanagan 2011, 95)

We somehow thought that there was a blank material nature on the one hand that then had to be grasped by a valuing and representing mind on the other. This, according to Bruno Latour, was the great project of modernity and one in which we are still imprisoned. Even though Latour is in line with a great deal of his contemporaries who seek to put mind and world back together, by undoing the great modern separation of nature on the one hand and its mental mirror on the other, Latour is quite trenchant: we do not need to reunite mind and world. We need to see that it is the separation that should appear puzzling. How on earth did we come to think that there was this thing—nature—that could be the object of science and that would be divorced from some other human, moral, political domain?

> In suspending the critical gesture, we begin to understand retrospectively the oddness of the definition of nature to which critique had been wed. It had two surprising features: the discovery, revelation, unveiling of what lay behind the subjective fog of appearances; and what ensured the continuity in space and time of all beings in their inner reality. It has long been realized by science studies, by feminist theory, and, in a much wider way, by all sorts of environmental movements, that this era's character was precisely not the long-awaited taking into account of nature, but rather the total dissolution of the various notions of nature. (Latour 2010, 466)

Here is the story: at some point in the history of Western thought the notion of disembodied and distinct mind took hold of reason. The usual culprit for this maneuver is Descartes, the thinker who came and doubted and established 'the subject' as the one point of certainty, and the point from which the rest of the world (as extended rather than thinking substance) would need to be deduced (Flanagan 2003, 58). The literature on mindfulness is clear on this point: 'Descartes' infamous *Cogito* has, arguably, been responsible for more philosophical wrong turnings than anything else in Western thought' (Hyland 2011, 19). There are other villains in this tale: Plato, who set up a world of separate ideas or truths that would leave this world as a pale and second-rate shadow, or—more generally—modern science with its disenchantment of the world and its striving to establish the world as so much manipulable and calculable matter. What would be lost in this Cartesian turn to the subject, certainty, extended substance and the world that needs to be known or represented by mind is the original connectedness from which the subject was detached. The concept of mind is an effect—the outcome of a history of calculation, practices of logic and intellectual abstraction—that mistakes itself for a cause, seeing itself as the point from which the world unfolds. What would be required, today, is to re-narrate the emergence of 'mind' (as reasoning subject) from a more practical, historical, embodied and dynamic life: Cartesian subjectivity, or the impoverished conception of 'mind' would be but one aspect or capacity of a broader domain of life and would need to be recognized as partial, dependent and (possibly) pernicious. For Bruno Latour, postmodern constructions of reality are no less Cartesian than any of the previous elevations of detached mind:

> Who can avoid hearing the cry of despair that echoes deep down, carefully repressed, meticulously denied, in these paradoxical claims for a joyous, jubilant, free construction of narratives and stories by people forever in chains? But even if there *were* people who could say such things with a blissful and light heart (their existence is as uncertain to me as that of the Loch Ness monster, or, for that matter, as uncertain as the real world would be to these mythical creatures) how could we avoid noticing that we have not moved an inch since Descartes? That the mind is still in its vat, excised from the rest, disconnected, and contemplating (now with a blind gaze) the world (now lost in darkness) from the very same bubbling glassware. (Latour 1999, 8)

It would seem that this anti-Cartesian story, told so widely today, would be supported by contemporary insights from neuroscience, cognitive archaeology, artificial intelligence and evolutionary theories of mind. Andy Clark, the philosopher who has done so much to bring insights from artificial intelligence research into theories of mind, approvingly quotes (the widely-quoted) John Haugeland:

> if we are to understand mind as the locus of intelligence, we cannot follow Descartes in regarding it as separable in principle from the body and the world[...]. Broader approaches, freed of that prejudicial commitment, can look again at perception and action, at skillful involvement with public equipment and social organization, and see not principled separation but all sorts of close coupling and functional unity[...].

> Mind, therefore, is not incidentally but *intimately* embodied and *intimately* embedded in its world. (Haugeland 1998, 236-37 quoted in Clark 2010)

Perhaps the most significant integration of a pseudo-Buddhist 'mindfulness' with a diagnosis of the fall into Cartesianism comes from Maturana and Varela, whose work on embodied cognition claims to draw from philosophy, Eastern thought and contemporary science:

> The revolt of the rationalists—Descartes, Spinoza, Leibniz—began from a principle of 'methodical doubt.' But they became lost in mechanism, dualism and more and more categorization; and they ended in denying relation altogether. But relation is the stuff of system. (Maturana and Varela 1980, 63)

But this story would also seem to have a decent philosophical pedigree, ranging from Nietzsche's general criticism of the enslavement of a once masterful and active life of forces to a miserable reactive slave consciousness, to Foucault's Nietzschean criticism of an 'ethics of knowledge,' and then to the entire phenomenological tradition that sought to render the subject transcendental (and not as some distinct substance). Husserl's *Cartesian Meditations* criticizes Descartes' process of doubt for saving some 'tag end of the world'; had Descartes doubted more radically he would have seen that the psycho-physical subject or individual mind presupposes some event or life-world from which the 'mind' of man is disclosed.

> It must by no means be accepted as a matter of course that, with our apodictic pure ego, we have rescued a *little tag end of the world*, as the sole unquestionable part of it for the philosophizing Ego, and that now the problem is to infer the rest of the world by rightly conducted arguments, according to principles innate in the ego.
>
> Unfortunately, these principles were at work when Descartes introduced the apparently insignificant but actually fateful change whereby the ego becomes a *substantia cogitans*, a separate human *'mens sive animus'*, and the point of departure for principles of causality—in short, the change by virtue of

which Descartes became the father of transcendental realism, an absurd position. (Husserl 1977, 24)

Husserl's criticism of Cartesian error—of assuming rather than accounting for a subject—is intensified with Heidegger, for whom the question of epistemology (or how we know the world) can only occur if we forget that in order to ask the question of knowledge we must already have a world. If phenomenology is anti-Cartesian in its inception then it appears to become even more intensely so as the tradition continues and starts to embark on self-critique. Was not Husserl, for Heidegger at least, still too Cartesian in keeping a transcendental subject as opposed to a thought of Being's disclosure, of which the subject would be nothing more than a site for revealing? And is not deconstruction continuing this counter-Cartesian gesture when it insists that Being, too, would act as one more presupposed foundation that would necessarily efface the dispersed, never present, process of tracing that allowed something to appear as present? Perhaps, though, anti-Cartesianism reaches its zenith in the work of Gilles Deleuze, for whom the task of philosophy would be to reverse Platonism and arrive at thought without an image (Deleuze 1994, 131). Not surprisingly, there have been those who wish to align Deleuze with a neuroscience of distributed cognition, with a nature of living systems and with a broader 'turn' to naturalism (Lauwereyns 2010, 159).

The implications of this counter-Cartesian gesture, along with a certain self-understanding of a false turn or error taken in philosophy, are also significant for whatever is left of aesthetics. If the Cartesian story is correct and mind is primarily or properly logical, then mind's first task is knowledge, and it would be from knowledge that something like art (as a handmaiden to cognition) would follow. Certainly, this is how one strand of thinking about the relation between the brain and art has proceeded. Today, continuing this primacy of cognition (with art as extension of the survival-oriented brain) various forms of literary Darwinism have sought to ground the acknowledged complexity of art in the artwork's capacity to stimulate those problem-solving capacities that are the mark of practical knowledge (Ramachandran and Hirstein 1999; Boyd 2009; Carroll, 1995). Such approaches are anti-Cartesian in their rejection of mind as disembodied and as a separate substance and wish to see mind as emergent; the seemingly 'Cartesian' emphasis on aligning art with the primacy of cognition is countered by an insistence that cognition is not a distinct faculty, but one evolving natural activity among others. But a dominant motif has been the dethroning of cognition and logical reasoning in favor of a primarily affective and aesthetic comportment. Literary Darwinism can begin to indicate the problem of being anti-Cartesian: if one rejects the autonomy of the aesthetic, and aims to return art and the mind to life, but then does so in favor of survivalist logics, then one is both anti- and hyper-Cartesian at one and the same moment. The rejection of 'mind' seems at once to be post-subjective and even posthuman, returning all processes to one survivalist logic, and yet the grounding of all life on a logic that can be discerned through human reflection on its own practices takes on the very structure of the subject, of a single discernible ground for all emerging systems.

Heidegger, criticizing the very idea of 'logic' as the proper and universal system through which we know the world, retrieved a more original *logos*—or speaking about—that would still remain discernible in today's poets, for whom *poiesis* was the bringing into being of an event that was *not* simply the unfolding of a blueprint. (And it is this primacy of a poetic bringing into being of the world which is continued by Giorgio Agamben for whom we need to rethink 'the political' not in terms of a life that can be known and managed but in terms of an 'open' that is the very possibility of any world at all.) One strand of anti-Cartesianism would seem to involve a turn away from mathematical certainty and formal logics in favor of a broader and living *logos* that would emerge first creatively only then to be reified into fixed systems. One would then view systems insofar as they extend the living, imaginative, social and affective body, not the detached and judging 'mind.' Much of the anti-Cartesian rhetoric today consists of a rejection of a computational model of thinking and instead grounds thinking in life, including—as in many supposedly Darwinist models—a life oriented toward the organism's ongoing survival. (The problem with that anti-Cartesian counter logic is of course that it is possible because of something like the Cartesian gesture: a refusal to accept the given as given and instead to question its genesis. And even though one might want to think of this question of genesis as philosophical in general rather than Cartesian, it is possible to note a tendency in

Cartesian doubt that prompts many of the anti- and post-Cartesian war cries: separation. The Cartesian subject does not just question but also doubts and subordinates the world and then finds something like the act of thinking that possesses an indubitable certainty and privilege. Question: given some of the smug self-certainties of the twenty-first century, including the notion that thinking is natural and world-oriented and that it would be scandalous not to see 'us'—we humans—as world-oriented or world-embedded, perhaps some form of Cartesian doubt might open us up to the thought that the link between mind and world is not as symbiotic as all that. And, further, given some of the dismissive readings of what has come to be known as 'theory'—that theory was too textualist to think the material or scientific conditions of the world—it might be worthwhile to at least pose the question of just how certain we are about connectedness to life. Here one might want to think the double claim of the Heideggerian legacy: in addition to being the philosopher of being-in-the-world, Heidegger also suggested that something like *Angst* would prompt us to question just how it is that we are 'in' the world and that this question has been closed off too readily.)

Apart from a general appeal to Heidegger in claiming that the world that is given in a primarily creative and conversational—rather than logical—manner, there is a more general sense that approaching the world and life aesthetically is more mindful. Either we think of something like 'mind' that mirrors or pictures its world and then adds creative frills, *or* we think of a general creativity: a world in which aesthesis or sensation, feeling or being affected is primary. It would be from that latter interconnected, affective, attuned and mindful comportment that something like Cartesian man would be an unfortunate detachment, an error or illusion. Not only has there been a widespread 'affective turn' where cognition is deemed to be either a late and partial add-on to a life that proceeds primarily through sensations and creates its social, embodied and dynamic attachments, more specifically Deleuze and post-phenomenology seem to privilege the primacy of aesthetic perception. One introduction to Deleuze's thought—despite defining affect as mental activity—sees Deleuzian affect as an 'attack' on Cartesian subjectivity:

> According to Deleuze affects are basic components of mental activity. Now the concept of an affect does not entail the

> concept of subjective self-awareness. To understand an affect is to see it as a *force*, a particular type of energy and this energy does not presuppose self-consciousness[...]. What affects is the mind capable of? What thoughts are generated by affects? In this philosophical perspective, the mind is a site of thoughts rather than a centre of consciousness. These thoughts are not defined by the fact that someone can say: they are my thoughts. Thoughts, in other words, are not defined as *belonging to a subject*. Deleuze's books on Hume, Nietzsche and Spinoza each develop a particular aspect of this affect psychology and attack a specific dimension of the concept of the subject in its Cartesian or Kantian versions. (Due 2007, 10)[1]

This enlistment of Deleuze and affects—against Descartes, the self and consciousness—is typical of a broader notion of continental philosophy as either properly opposed to Cartesian truth and certainty, or lamentably irresponsible in retreating from the claims of truth and reason. We do not need to follow Richard Rorty's notion that deconstruction reduced philosophy to a 'kind of writing,' (Rorty 1986, 90) or Habermas's less charitable but similar account of French thought as having rejected reason in favor of a celebration of literature (Habermas 1987, 102), for there is a more tempered and nuanced theorization of thinking after Heidegger that would suggest that philosophy (and approaches to mind more generally) would do well to begin with the processes that are disclosed in art, rather than logic. Art, too, seems to have taken up this turn to mindfulness, not only in the general advent of installation art that is interactive and is oriented less to detached viewing than it is to walking, touching, feeling and contributing, but also in a new mode of inter-artistic analogy.

> The artist's mindfulness might be said to display fidelity to phenomenological happening in its originary richness. [...] we find a recovery of agapeic astonishment before the aesthetic equivocity of becoming: this stuns us into mindfulness of charged and expressive presence. We may even find a rapport with the primal 'It is good' which celebrates the giving of creation. The neutralization of creation into an indifferent, objective 'It' is overcome in terms of its originary

abundance[...]. This ambiguity is intolerable to the heirs of Descartes and modern science who would be the masters and possessors of nature. (Desmond 1995, 94-95)

Perhaps everything will approach the condition of music, moving towards a non-semantic register, abandoning narrative modes—to the degree that such a mode is at all possible. How else could one escape the Cartesian prison of logic and self-consciousness other than by way of something like a pure affect that does not turn back upon, constitute, affect and touch itself? This would seem to be the task of the twenty-first century, an annihilation of the self-gathering subject and a becoming-one-with a broader inhuman ecology.

But here is another story: Heidegger argued that the story of Descartes as a philosopher who came and doubted was nothing more than a 'bad novel.' And it appears—in true postmodern style—that Heidegger has become a character in his own bad novel. For many now read Heidegger as the philosopher who came to reject man and the subject in order to put the world together again. But here is another possible account: Heidegger's point was that Descartes could not be seen as a simple lapse or error, and that this seemingly unfortunate Cartesian accident had something to do with the very possibility of thinking. Husserl, also, thought that taking the figure of mind seriously—asking how and why we possess a 'natural attitude' in which there appears to be something like 'mind' or substance as a thing in the world—would require us to be more or hyper-Cartesian. The problem was not that Descartes came up with this unique substance 'mind' and thereby destroyed the lived unity of the world: the problem was that this 'mind' was still too worldly, still too similar to all the other objects with which we live and work (and still too close to older concepts of the soul or psyche as privileged or special type of thing). The Cartesian error was not some break with an otherwise unified, enchanted and mindful world. Indeed, the problem with Cartesianism is not mathematical separation and disenchantment but an excessive commitment to some special magical substance or 'res cogitans'; there is an insufficiency of calculus, for Descartes still relies on turning back to some living thing that will explain the separate world; he will not begin with *separation, even though that is exactly what the Cartesian project promises*. The world is not given, nor is relation; it is from some presence without any assumed relation whatsoever that Descartes must turn back upon himself and establish the one indubitable relation from which all other relations would be possible. For Heidegger, *this* was the scandal of Cartesianism—not the *subject,* but the failure to really account for relations by assuming some self-relating special thing. Metaphysical philosophy had always had the goal of establishing some ultimate ground, *hypokeimenon* or subjectum. With Descartes that 'subject' becomes the self. What ought really to have occurred—had Descartes been truly radical with doubt and beginnings—is not the unfolding of the first relation from self back to self, but a realization that the self is an effect of relation; in the beginning is the relation, a being-in-the-world that precludes anything like a 'pre-relational' subject. At the same time, that being-in-the-world is always 'a' world for some thrown *Da-sein,* and so establishing the world of relations and projects as first or originary is no better than establishing 'a' subject. There is no thing that is primordial, only an equi-primordiality: both sides of the relation have a certain firstness.

For Heidegger, there had always been a tendency towards subjectivism, or the establishing of a single ground that would underlie and explain all beings and events. (We might ask, today, whether shifting this underlying ground to 'life' really changes things that much, and whether grounding all that we know, do and feel in one affective and interconnected life does not partake of a *simple* Cartesian logic of a unified knowledge at the expense of a radical Cartesian detachment of a mind that is its own place.)

So I would pause at this point to make a minor conclusion: in terms of intellectual history it is inaccurate to see a straightforward anti-Cartesianism in the very tradition that is often appealed to, today, to make the case for 'Descartes' error.' Even Nietzsche—who would seem to be *the* philosopher to whom one might wish to appeal in order to get beyond the Cartesian prison and think a life of forces—was not so clear in attributing the blame to Descartes. Nietzsche even suggested that the modern 'assassination' of the soul was actually counter-Cartesian and, for that very reason, utterly pious. Nietzsche saw a religious fervor in modern philosophy's extirpation of the soul, and a pseudo-Christian self-abnegation in a tradition, after Descartes, of ridding the world and life of anything like the soul. Not only was it inaccurate, then, to think of Descartes as the father of modern philosophy; there was also something reactive in certain destructions of the self:

> What is the whole of modern philosophy doing at bottom? Since Descartes—actually more despite him than because of his precedent—all the philosophers seek to assassinate the old soul concept, under the guise of a critique of the subject-and-predicate concept—which means an attempt on the life of the basic Christian doctrine. Modern philosophy, being an epistemological skepticism, is, covertly or overtly, *anti-Christian*—although to say this for the benefit of more refined ears, by no means anti-religious. (Nietzsche 1989, 66)

Nietzsche suggests both that there is something religious, or will-destructive, in the ongoing assassination of the soul, and that this 'modern' gesture is not at all Cartesian but occurs despite Descartes. Noticing this inaccuracy is important for philosophical (rather than just historical) reasons. If Cartesianism occurred what does this tell us about life? What is life such that it gives birth to Cartesian man? Most importantly, why are we so insistently anti-Cartesian? What are we willing away? Is it not the most Cartesian of errors to think that an event might simply be dismissed, deemed to be erroneous and separate, with proper life having an entirely different nature? One of the arguments of phenomenology is that the Cartesian subject—that fragment of the world that takes itself to be the representing ground of the world—evidences a transcendental capacity, *as well as* the potentiality of that capacity to fail to actualize itself. It is the very nature of life, as relational, to be always oriented towards what is not fully present or given: this applies as much to conscious life as it does to any living form that is not self-sustaining. Consciousness is not only in relation to what is not itself; it has a sense—or anticipation—of what is not fully present.

Consciousness is intentional or related to what is other than itself via *sense*—an anticipatory orientation. I see something *as* something, having—in advance—some mode of relating in a certain way, with the expectation of certain outcomes. Because of this I tend to imagine the world's separate and independent existence as a realm of objects with certain determined features, and from there I also *naturally* assume that I too am one object, as a mind, among others. When Descartes doubted the world, and found the subject, he also assumed that the subject would be the most certain substance we could know: he was continuing a tendency of thought to find certainty in some privileged thing or substance that could be known apodictically. For Husserl and Heidegger the problem of Descartes' positing of the subject was not its specialness, its implied human exceptionalism, nor its tendency to separate the world of complex materiality from processes of knowing or thinking. On the contrary, the problem is Descartes' residual humanism; the cogito defines subjectivity as a special type of thing, as a distinct substance. The real, properly Cartesian question is how this appearance of something like a subject is possible: how did a certain type of living relation, a relation of knowing or sensing, come to appear and come to have a sense of itself?

Descartes' answer is, for Husserl and Heidegger, not the best path to pursue, but his *question* is the question of philosophy. How does appearance appear, and how is it possible that we started to ask this question? How is it possible for life not just to be *in relation* but to ask questions about relations? As long as we assume that there is some thing in the world—man or subject—that would be the site from which relations unfold then we fail to ask about the relation (or question) that 'we' have to such a privileged site. It is *that* question that Descartes started to answer when he doubted even this body, here and now, which might (he thought) be mere appearing. When Husserl and Heidegger turned back to that point what they sought to do was render Cartesian doubt or questioning more radical: what is appearing, *and how does appearing become questionable?* End of minor conclusion: back to the argument.

It is possible to read post-phenomenology as a rejection of the Cartesian remnants in phenomenology: supposedly Husserl wanted a truly transcendental subject, not another substance but an absolute ideal condition that would be the ground from which time (as the condition of substance) would unfold. Heidegger, too, in aiming to think the disclosure or presencing of being really repeated a mode of subjectivism, establishing an ultimate ground or foundation. Accordingly, Derrida would use words like 'trace,' 'écriture,' 'text,' or différance to indicate that any supposed site of emergence could only be *known* after some process of presencing, in which a temporality of before and after, and a spatiality of distribution has taken place; more radically, not only is such an origin only knowable after difference, the origin is itself differential. This strikes to the heart of Cartesianism and to any Heideggerian or phenomenological attempt to rethink genesis. Not only could there not be a subject as some fully self-present substance that subsisted and persisted before and beyond all relation, for the very self as identity must refer back to (and therefore be different from itself); but also, any supposed ground from which relations would unfold must itself be effected from relations. Self-presence is always given and achieved through relation, the self that recognizes itself as itself, must turn back towards itself through time. Identity or sameness, can only maintain itself, through time, by repeating itself, reiterating a quality through time, not being the ground of time. In the beginning is the rhythm. Deleuze, seemingly different from Derrida in his insistence both on the possibility of legitimately undertaking a history of the emergence of thought and systems of writing, and on the power of intuition to discern the differential forces or tendencies from which relations unfold, nevertheless seems to be even more insistently anti-Cartesian. Philosophy, despite its beginning in doubt and questioning, nevertheless always questions from an assumed 'image of thought,'— a figure of good sense and common sense oriented towards that which can be recognized, legitimated and established through time as the ground of sound thinking. In that respect, philosophy has never truly been immanent and has always fallen back upon an already given image of thought—which would include Descartes' cogito, but also Heidegger's Being, the transcendental subject of phenomenology and the seemingly post-metaphysical domain of communication.

Deleuze and Guattari's claim that relations are external to terms does, apparently, insist that the actualized world of constituted terms does not exhaust what can be said to be: actuality emerges from virtual tendencies, and those tendencies could always create new systems and new terms. But that appeal to 'the virtual' is not another foundation, despite the full reality of the virtual. Not only do we only know the virtual as it is differentiated into actual relations, it is also the case that the virtual 'itself,' unlike a supposed pre-existing world of possibilities, is real as a force for differentiation. The unfolding of the virtual is not the choice from among a collection of possible paths. This is why Deleuze places so much emphasis on the differential calculus: the creation of ever finer differences, producing ever more complex relations among differential powers, is infinite. This infinitely differential power theorized first in mathematics is nevertheless possible because of a broader truth of the differential: there cannot be 'a' subject or 'a' ground from which differences unfold, for difference is not a unity that is then disturbed or placed into relations. Unity and relations come into being from differential powers or forces—pure quantities or potentials to differ—that create points of relative stability. One way, then, of reading the tradition of post-phenomenology would be to read thinkers as diverse as Derrida, Deleuze, Foucault, Irigaray, Kristeva, Agamben and even thinkers who seemingly assert the subject such as Alain Badiou as united in the anti-Cartesian project: if there is a subject it occurs not as substance but as event or act, known only after the event.

I would suggest, though, that it is possible to produce a counter narrative in which post-phenomenology, like phenomenology, revives the Cartesian question in the spirit of Descartes. Doubt is more radical and does not leave subject as substance, but something is created in the Cartesian event, or what Derrida refers to as hyperbolic doubt. This Cartesian 'something' is what Deleuze refers to as 'sense.' It is helpful to see sense as at least in part Cartesian for two reasons: first, sense occurs as separation, when a thought or apprehension of an event detaches itself and takes on an autonomous power. Second, sense possesses some of the force of Descartes' evil genius: we experience this world, here and now, as our own, as unfolded through our projects, our meanings, our bodily comportments, our affects and emotions—and yet it is entirely possible for this world of sense to be other than it is, for the world to have been different from what it is. To think of sense as akin to the evil genius is to see it as not the world itself, as establishing a world for us that may well not be what the world or the real exhaustively *is*. To think of sense is to open the possibility of counter-actualization. As we, today, are confronted by more and more of the sense of our utter contingency—that there might have been a world without humans and there might soon be a world without humans again—perhaps being shrilly anti-Cartesian and insisting on the intimate bond between mind and world is a profoundly rigid instance of self-important subjectivism.

In many cases Deleuze will chart his way through philosophical history siding with other philosophers, such as Kant, Spinoza or Leibniz—against Descartes, but the issue is usually ontological and will still insist on the fracture of the subject, rendered more intense because the subject is not just another subject but a temporal torsion that will crack apart any notion of being as actualized substance. Deleuze will criticize any equivocity that posits two substances, for 'mind' is another expression of one expressive substance that *is* only in its all plural expressions, without any mode acting as ground for any other: MONISM = PLURALISM. And yet the incorporeality of sense that is different from states of affairs has a full reality and force that, in turn, has implications for what philosophy can do. Post-phenomenology is not anti-Cartesian, but it is post- or hyper-Cartesian, enabled by the thought or sense of separation. The potentiality of Cartesianism and the genesis of sense offer imperatives for divergent faculties.

Once thinking is considered to be a problem, and a non-natural problem (if 'nature' is taken to be a single domain of self-maintaining life) then we are well and truly on Cartesian soil. What if thinking were discordant with what has taken to be life? To take thought and its capacity for separation seriously is at once simply Cartesian, but also demands a different thought of life: what is thinking life such that it can diverge from causal and efficient modes of reasoning? What is thinking such that it can ask the world-destroying question of Descartes' evil genius, the question of the *non-being* of this world? This divergence of faculties is generally attributed to Kant who separated the capacity to think beyond the given world from the capacity to know the world as given: if it is possible to think what cannot be known or given then even though this 'not knowing' places limits on theoretical knowledge it nevertheless opens up the possibility of acting as if something like pure Ideas were possible. When Derrida writes about forgiveness, hospitality, democracy or justice 'to come,' or follows such concepts with the qualification, 'if there is such a thing,' he might appear to be taking up a Kantian notion of the Idea. When Deleuze and Guattari write in *What is Philosophy?* of the separate powers of science (creating functions), art (creating affects and percepts) and philosophy (creating concepts), and when they write of the various syntheses of universal human history they would be seem to be indebted to Kant's contesting faculties and distinct modes of understanding. But I would insist on Cartesianism, at the very least in addition to Kantianism, as a radical and hyperbolic thought event for two reasons: first, ontologically, it is Cartesianism that poses the separation of thought; second, tactically, one needs to read all the shrill and repetitive narrations of our fall and redemption from Cartesian subjectivity as reaction formations, where the insistent denial evidences a failure to recognize the naïve or vulgar Cartesianism of the present. If Cartesianism had two tendencies or sides, one turned towards a complacent humanism, the other to a hyperbolic distance from the actual world, it is the former that seems to have taken hold in the anti-Cartesianism of the present. And it is here that I would seek to align the modern figure of Cartesianism with a certain theology of evil.

If there has been a normative image of life, as creative, fruitful, dynamic, relational, self-maintaining while other-directed, then this has marked all figures of the good norm of thinking from the Christian God who creates otherness from expansive expressiveness to the man of post-Cartesian life who is always attuned to his milieu and is nothing other than an ongoing receptivity to the sense of the world. Similarly, evil has always been figured as a refusal of life: as a contingent, inert, destructive, non-relational and utterly *unbecoming* force unto itself. In this respect a certain image of Descartes' cogito stands as the modern equivalent of a radical evil that refuses any form of ongoing principle, relatedness and a certain understanding of sense (where sense is the capacity to understand, order and synthesize one's world). But there is another understanding of sense, one that runs through phenomenology and beyond that embraces this radical evil, and is perhaps best described in Derrida's response to Foucault and the defense of hyperbolic doubt.

Foucault, with more sophistication than marks the usual criticisms of Descartes, argued that the Cartesian subject was constituted by doubting all possible physical experiences (including the body, including even the state of wakefulness) while nevertheless dismissing the possibility of madness. For Descartes the very act of thinking presupposes some organizing self-presence. In this move, according to Foucault, something occurs within history: madness had once been considered to be one mode of thought among others. In pre-modern distributions of knowledge and its assumed limits madness could grant insight or enigmatic illumination, and was deemed to be a different style of thought, for a thought that possessed a certain density. With Descartes there is no longer a continuity between reason and unreason, for thinking *is* self-presence. Any mad (or unworked) thinking would not count as thinking at all. Anything that did not present itself to itself, have a sense of itself, would not be a lesser or different style of thinking but would not be thought at all. If I am thinking then I am thinking myself thinking, gathered and present to myself. One way of reading this moment in Foucault is—as Derrida will do—to read Foucault as anti-Cartesian. Foucault, Derrida argues, wants to place the relation between reason and madness *within* history, as though one might look back at history and see the point at which reason violently refused all modes of 'unworking' or disordering; and then observe the internment of madness into a separate and other space. For Derrida such a maneuver is (especially on Foucault's own account) itself Cartesian. Foucault does not accept reason as a given or constituted norm, but questions reason by assessing its history. As an aside, Derrida challenges Foucault's reading of Descartes. According to Derrida, Descartes does indeed include madness in the process of doubt; for even if he were mad, here and now, he would still be thinking and would still (insofar as he is thinking) be a self-present subject. But the crucial point is what Derrida takes to be the force of Cartesian doubt. The capacity to ask about reason *in general* or 'hyperbolic doubt' is neither something Foucault can avoid in any genealogy of madness, for the *question* of madness or problem of madness places one in the domain of sense. To ask what madness *is*, necessarily creates a distance from any constituted definition, or—to shift to Deleuze—any extended set. If we do not accept that madness is defined by all those bodies designated or collected as mad, and instead ask about madness *really* then we engage (for Derrida) in a problem of sense that is at once historical and untimely. It is historical precisely because sense is history, or the constitution of a power to designate what would be the same for me here now, and for an other not yet present. Sense is a futural bet or wager on what Derrida will later refer to as the 'to come,' and it is Cartesian hyperbolic doubt that detaches itself from sense as given (as ostensive or even stipulative definition) and—in a process that is almost mad—questions reason as such. If I ask what reason really is then I make a claim to some notion of what reason would be; if I challenge a certain 'internment' of madness as that which thought was once able to encounter, then I make some trans-historical claim regarding thought and its proper or potential sense. I have already detached myself from the simple positivity of the present and the given.

I would suggest that when Foucault reads Descartes he is, to some extent, doing what Derrida describes: placing Descartes' reason on trial, distancing himself from that enclosed definition of reason as self-presence, and then suggesting *another thought* that would not be at odds with what Descartes interred as a certain mad unworking. Rather, then, than include Foucault in the more general anti-Cartesian axiology of good and evil, where the Cartesian subject closes man off from a world of which he is properly a dynamic, attuned and affected being, it is possible to see Foucault's creation of madness as 'absence of work' as radically Cartesian. It is only by reading Descartes in a certain way that Foucault creates a genealogy of another thinking, finding in Descartes' refusal of a mad, dispersed, non-self-present delirium a point outside reason as logic. There is something radically Cartesian in the tradition of re-opening the Cartesian question, at least as that tradition runs from Husserl to Deleuze (but possibly also back to Kant). And there is something of a Cartesian domestication at work in the general late twentieth and early twenty-first-century counter-Cartesianisms.

If one reads Descartes' subject in psycho-physical terms, with *res cogitans* providing a specific 'tag end of the world' (as Husserl put it), then one could criticize Cartesianism for the following error: one part of the world accounts for the world in general. Cartesian doubt both fails to doubt in a profound manner and does, indeed, enclose thinking in a way that must deny, repress or moralize certain rogue and untamed forces that could not be accounted for by separating the world into a simple opposition between thinking things and extended things. I want to conclude by considering a positive Cartesianism of sense that would not only go beyond Cartesian dualism, but would also allow us to read today's ostensibly anti-Cartesian positions as modes of vulgar Cartesianism. (Following Derrida and Deleuze I would also suggest that such a fall or lapse into vulgarity is not something that is external to thinking.)

Derrida: it is not only in his debate with Foucault that Derrida insists upon a Cartesian potential in thinking that cannot be reduced to a moment *within* history. In his reading of Husserl, Derrida argues for an impossible relation between sense and history. On the one hand sense is intra-worldly and historical. In order for a science or language or practice to be possible it must constitute some repeatable system that views the world here and now as it would be for any subject beyond me. In this respect the sense of the world, or viewing the world coherently through time, requires not only a perception of the here and now but an anticipation of what would be true for something like humanity in general. In his reading of Husserl it is the status of that 'humanity in general' that (I would argue) opens onto a Cartesian hyperbole in Derrida. Husserl wants to account for the 'origin of the world.' Resisting the psychological tendency to locate all meaning within something like 'man' as a specific substance, Husserl argues for a transcendental subjectivity that could not be reduced to physical humanity; humans appear as psycho-physical in the world because of sense. It is sense that allows the world and 'us' to appear *as one unified human world continuing through time.* History—the world as it appears—is possible because of historicity, or a process of synthesis that cannot take place within time. Husserl's problem is the relation between humanity as a concrete psycho-physical species, humanity as constituted through time in this world, and humanity as an Idea, or humanity as a project of sense. In order for this 'man' here and now to (for example) pose a logical or moral truth he must imagine what would be the case for any subject whatever. He must, to some extent, annihilate all assumptions, all givenness and ask what remains. That question must always take place in the world, and yet posit a sense *of the world.* What makes this movement Cartesian, rather than Kantian, is the strange status it grants to the subject and sense. Kant, already criticizing Descartes for placing the subject *within* space and time, argues that the subject to whom the world appears must already be the result of a synthesis. The problem, for Husserl, Heidegger and Derrida is that, while the worldly human subject is thereby no longer seen to be the origin of sense and the world, Kantianism does not ask the question of the genesis of the transcendental subject. The origin of sense is left unquestioned. Descartes' doubt begins with what appears, and far from positing a transcendental ground (as Kant will do) insists that all we have is appearing. The movement of doubt then introduces the gap between appearance and the event of appearing; insofar as I doubt I establish this relation to appearing.

It is not surprising that Kantianism has enabled a 'post-metaphysical' suspension of the subject, and a move towards pure formalism and anti-foundationalism. For Kant and Kantianism we are always already within a world of constituted relations, with the origin or ground of those relations never in itself being a possible object of knowledge or appearance. Politically, this leads to a mode of liberal formalism in which the absence of law or foundation requires an ongoing process of deliberation and legitimation without any appeal to a ground or substance. It might seem that Derrida maintains this Kantian suspension when he insists on various terms such as 'justice to come' or 'democracy to come': there can never be an absolute experience of justice that can exhaust the process and deliberation of justice. It would follow that 'deconstruction is justice' if deconstruction were a commitment to potentialities released by the formal structure of experience that were themselves always beyond experience. Derrida will adopt certain modes of the Kantian conditional, where we can think or act *as if* there might be justice (or democracy, or friendship or forgiveness): how would such ideas open or deconstruct the present by indicating that which cannot be reduced to current structures? And yet I would suggest that the positive dimension of Derrida and deconstruction lies in Cartesian hyperbole, where we do not accept the formal limits of legitimation and possible consensus. No givenness or formal system in the world can silence the question that would ask about the genesis or appearing of forms and systems. Appearing cannot be reduced to a substance (res cogitans), precisely because substance emerges from an unfolding of appearances. Refusing to interrogate, or remain open to, what Heidegger referred to as Kant's 'hidden source' cannot tame the Cartesian question. In many respects Derrida regards this Cartesian movement of hyperbolic doubt as not only internal to philosophy, but as operating in any possible experience (except perhaps for literary experience, or at least operating differently in literary experience). Insofar as I experience anything before me as present, as being *there,* then I have already gone beyond the putative pure self-presence of what is given; I have already anticipated that this present here and now would also appear in the same way for any subject whatever. This is why Derrida locates a structure of mourning in the given (for I am already oriented beyond what is given to me towards what would be there beyond my existence). How is it that 'mere appearing' presents itself as the appearing *of* what would be there for me and for any subject whatever; from where does this givenness unfold? What is being, really? If we suspend any supposed ground that would be the source of all appearing, what remains, *what can be said to be?* Philosophy occurs in this question of sense, in this movement from what appears as present to what we can assert, say or posit as having true being. This is why literary experience as a 'saying' that is that of text itself freed from any claim to being would be quite different in its relation to presence. The movement of doubt is at once negative—ruling out any presuppositions regarding what we assume true being to be—but also positive. What is philosophy such that it can move from the world as given and then ask what is *truly* given and what might truly be?

I would suggest that Deleuze is a more Cartesian philosopher than either Derrida or Heidegger. First, Deleuze and Guattari make a formal or essential distinction between the tendencies of art/literature and philosophy. In *Difference and Repetition,* Deleuze re-opens the Heideggerian question of what it is to think, and in this respect Deleuze (and later with Guattari in *What is Philosophy?*) takes up Heidegger's criticism of Descartes. The question of thinking is short-circuited if one imagines a substance oriented towards a correct picturing of the world; a specific being is then assumed to provide a ground for the thinking of being in general. Against this error of transcendence (one being as the distinct ground for others), or this error of equivocity (one being as a different thinking substance in relation to another extended substance), and against this error of good sense and common sense (where thinking is given as the same for all in relation to a common world), Deleuze poses the challenge of thought without an image. In so doing, like Husserl and Heidegger, Deleuze takes doubt or the question to a hyperbolic level, not content to stop with any supposed being *who questions.* Indeed, the question no longer characterizes the subject but acts as a way of releasing thought from any ground whatever. For it is not only philosophy that questions; it is not only the subject, Dasein or man who exists at once in relation while also not being exhausted by the relations through which becoming is actualized. Deleuze writes being as '?being,' indicating not that we cannot know what being is, but that being exists in a mode of relation in which the relations that occur are not determined in advance. More positively, this then allows for a way to think about the different relational potentials of thinking: art, philosophy and science. If Heidegger insisted that truth was not something that thinking may or may not bear a relation towards, this was because the relational nature of thinking—its comportment—*is truth*. Even the most erroneous or seemingly accidental event expresses something about thought's possibility. Deleuze, too, does not dismiss error, illusion, stupidity or malevolence as distinct from thinking: there is one being that gives itself in multiple expressions. Deleuze and Guattari distinguish various orientations, tendencies, styles or temporal distributions of the question of ?being, and their distinction among philosophy, art and science gives us—I would suggest—a positive Cartesianism.

In some ways it might seem to make more sense to see the diverse lines of thought's potential as Kantian: there are modes of thinking, such as philosophy's creation of concepts, that indicate an opening of new relations and temporalities (such as the notion of thinking *as such*, that would be different from the reference to actual thinking individuals). But I would stress a certain Cartesian dimension. First, Deleuze stresses the significance of both malevolence and stupidity, as though thought's resistance to alignment—its errancy and capacity to detach itself from good sense and common sense—does not accord with Kantian notions of thought's conditions as oriented to world-forming and coherent synthesis. In response to Descartes, Kant had insisted that insofar as one thinks and doubts, then there is already a form of time and space that would enable this doubting *by me, and of this world* to take place. The self who doubts a world beyond itself is already synthesized into a continuing unity in relation to a spatially distanced world. But it is just this already present transcendental and conditioning form that Deleuze questions. In *Difference and Repetition* passive synthesis is not presupposed (and not subjective) but opens the possibility that there may be various and divergent orientations—*not those of a spatial world set over and against a subject*. Deleuze refers to 'contemplations' or 'perceptions' that are neither human nor organic, and so the world's syntheses could also be attributed to rocks, waves and particles. In *What is Philosophy?* Deleuze and Guattari argue for philosophy *not*, as Kant had done, as a critical procedure to draw thought to its limits in terms of an experience that must be given *to* a finite subject, but as the creation of potentials and tendencies that do not presuppose a subject-object relation. Although it is Descartes who is widely accepted to be the author of (not surprisingly) 'Descartes' error,' or the mistake of separating the subject from the world, it is Cartesian doubt—doubting even the body that appears to be mine, even that the self I experience and the entire world might be a dream— that destroys the transcendental form of an already given time and space. If there are no transcendental conditions, then it follows that we could have philosophy in which concepts might be created that do not refer to objects of possible experience (such as time in its pure state), and also that we could have art in which the expressiveness of matter appears as such, and not as it is *for me*.

Even though Deleuze's thought is quite fairly and accurately deemed to be a form of realism in its Bergsonian commitment to intuiting durations and rhythms as such, and not as they would be from the point of view of the practical subject, there is a strong Cartesian drive in the affirmation of thinking as a power to create a realm of sense—a plane of orientations, relations, ideas and concepts—that are not reducible to the world's functions (which have their scientific legitimacy and organize a world that is distinct from, but related to, observers). *Sense* is not the Kantian Idea, whereby I recognize that I cannot experience or know the law as such, but nevertheless act *as if* I were a being whose will might be pure law. *Sense* is not the self that wills itself *as if* it were nothing other than a pure form of willing, unimpeded by any desire or motivation other than itself; sense is the creation from experience of something like a pure predicate, released from subject-object relations, opening the idea of the appearance as such, in itself. Sense is separation, taking the form of what—theologically—has been deemed to be evil: cut off from ecological life, without the assumption of a body or mind to whom the appearance is given, sense is a world in which the mind is its own place.

This, also, is the force of Deleuze and Guattari's various formations of becoming-animal or becoming-imperceptible or even becoming-woman: such maneuvers are Cartesian because they do not (like today's supposed anti-Cartesians) insist on the world as always the world *for* this or that body, existing in history, contexts or in terms of the *meaning* that the world would have for this always oriented body. Instead, these operations of becoming, especially becoming-imperceptible, do not assume a body, a lived world, a connectedness and certainly not a constituted or even constituting time and space. These becomings are movements of sense in which what is perceived is not located as an object within time but becomes a pure predicate, what it is in the animal that 'animals.' It is as if we could, indeed, annihilate the world, not accept the given, including even my body here and now that seems to be the condition or point from which the world unfolds.

Notes

1. One might offer a reading of Deleuze that reversed this quick account of the subject, psychology and affect. The world is composed of multiple self-consciousnesses, well beyond the human being and psychology, and well beyond thoughts. Indeed, one might say that the world is multiple self-consciousness or self-enjoyment, plural subjects, beyond thinking and beyond psychology. Or in Deleuze's Leibnizian voice: [...] the subjective form is the way by which the datum is expressed in the subject, or by which the subject actively prehends the datum (emotion, evaluation, project, conscience ...). It is the form in which the datum is folded in the subject, a 'feeling' or manner, at least when prehension is positive (Deleuze 2006, 88).

Chapter 4

Queer Aesthetics

Perhaps no notion has been more normative than that of becoming. Perhaps because of Gilles Deleuze and Félix Guattari, with their concepts of 'becoming-animal' or 'becoming-woman,' or perhaps because of a now-institutionalized poststructuralism that appears to have privileged process over stability, creation over system and singularity over universality, becoming appears at first glance to be *the* notion that would free us at once from moralizing normativity and rigid identity politics. What I want to suggest in this chapter is that the contemporary valorization of becoming over being *repeats* rather than destabilizes a highly traditional and humanist sentiment of privileging act over inertia, life and creativity over death and stasis, and pure existence or coming-into-being over determination. Indeed, all the forms of anti-essentialism that marked the late twentieth-century could only have force because essence—or that which is, as such, beyond its actualization—was deemed to be necessarily (or essentially) impeding. Becoming, thought in its opposition to normativity and essence, has always underpinned standard liberal notions of the political, the ethical, and the aesthetic. The political: a good polity is a polity that does not merely follow rules and order automatically but gives a law to itself freely.[1] The ethical: a subject is not a mechanism that unfolds in time to realize what he was always going to be, but becomes what he ought to be by realizing his self-creative freedom.[2] The aesthetic: art is the minimal distance or deviation from perfectly clear, accepted, and rule-bound communication; art works *as art* only in disclosing once again that the world is not fully seen and said, but is opened through seeing and saying.[3]

To get a sense of the ways in which this concept of becoming has presented itself as a self-evident good, we need only ask whether it would be possible to speak *against* becoming. Would it be possible to assert simply that one *is*: that I am the being who I am and have always been; that I do not expect or hope to change? Or, would it be possible—this time not referring to oneself—to affirm a world or nature that is fully actualized, and that bears neither a potentiality for change nor a tendency to change in ways that are not determined in advance by some norm? Does not the very insistence on the importance of *the political*, from Plato and Aristotle to the present, presuppose that 'we' —the polity—do not accept a closed and completed state form but consider human collective life to be creative of itself? When there is talk of a loss of politics today, this is usually a way of referring to widespread passivity and the consumption rather than production of images. If one can distinguish a power of mind and life from matter and inertia it is to the degree to which the former is active and self-creating. Well before Henri Bergson distinguished between matter and memory by arguing that the former is fully actualized and can only vary mechanically through the redistribution or reconfiguration of what is already given, while the latter will properly lead to a spiritual becoming that will free itself from fixed and rigid units, there had been a long history of privileging a living and dynamic becoming over the stasis of an unthinking matter that has no potentiality or relation beyond itself. Theologically, it is chaos that simply 'is' while *being* is creative, dynamic, fruitful, and multiplying. Even if, as Giorgio Agamben notes in *Homo Sacer*, there would be a problem of considering how natural generation would be accommodated in a redeemed world, there is a long history of justifying a properly divine creativity. Agamben articulates the problem this way: if there is a heaven then everything would be complete and redeemed, so how would the blessed deal with the problem of such activities as eating (with the concomitant acts of digestion and waste)? And this is the problem that marks Agamben's project of potentiality today: could we imagine a becoming that is *not* constrained in advance by some aspect of already actualized life? Our imaginations of heaven, after all, have tended to take human bodies and simply resituate them in an eternal domain, not asking about the potentiality or becoming of those bodies. Agamben recognizes that heaven, traditionally conceived, could not accommodate waste, growth, and regeneration; but this opens the problem of dynamic action. Would a godlike power *do anything, would this not impede completeness and perfection?* Could there be a divine becoming? Such a problem has haunted theology that at one and the same time wants to grant dynamic creativity and life to God, while also recognizing that divinity would not need to become. Milton, for example, maintains that the angels—like Adam and Eve before them—will be involved in the production of hymns of praise. But what makes such production divine is that it is unprompted and unnecessary. Like Agamben four centuries later, Milton recognizes the problem of human potentiality: a world without becoming would be *mere life*. Even a redeemed humanity will never remain in itself but will create further, expressing itself as nothing more than this creating spirit (Schwartz 1998).

We can chart this highly normative anti-normativity of becoming by working back, genealogically, from Bergson. Bergson's attack on dualism was preceded by a series of anti-Cartesian attacks on mind as a thing within the world. Cartesianism was targeted from its inception as a dangerously mechanistic reduction of the world and a godless detachment of man as substance (Israel 2001). Bergson's attack on Cartesianism (and other representations of mind as a substance within time and space) needs to be distinguished from the contemporary appeal to becoming. There is a difference between affirming—as Bergson did—that all life bears tendencies both towards explosive difference and inertia, and simply affirming that the subject is nothing other than its pure relation to what it is not, a pure becoming. That is, there is a difference between a metaphysical objection to positing one substance—such as mind—as the point from which time and movement are perceived, and the existential objection that man or humanity is distinguished by its *not* having any essence other than its capacity to become. Bergson did not treat mind as becoming, rather than being, without thoroughly challenging the notion of a simple opposition between being (what simply is) and becoming (processes of change that those beings undergo). What Bergson radicalized in his vitalism was a failure to think the difference between being and becoming appropriately. That is, Bergson will not—as later affirmations of becoming would do—celebrate 'life' or political subjects as mobile and self-creating in opposition to a supposed essential or timeless nature or 'bare life'; he will remove 'man' from his privileged position of *homo sui faber* and describe *all* life as bearing (at least in part) an explosive capacity to destroy its bounded and self-same identity. In this respect, Bergson is at once the queerest of philosophers, regarding all life as deviation or disturbance (Grosz 2004), and the most normatively humanist of philosophers, placing the power that had always elevated man—dynamic becoming—at the heart of all life. But Bergson is not alone; his work evinces a more general problem of the relation between becoming and *man*. There has *always* been an anti-humanist privileging of becoming that would set itself against 'man' as nothing more than an animal with special qualities, such as reason (Derrida 1969).

Kant had insisted that for both ethical and metaphysical reasons one could not consider the world as an object in itself that is then pictured by the mind. The relation of mind to world is itself the outcome of an active synthesis: mind is not that which can be known as a being or substance, for transcendental subjectivity is the process of synthesis itself, knowable only after the event, in its effects. It follows, ethically, that mind cannot be a thing or nature *from which* one might establish certain norms. Instead—because it is nothing other than a synthetic power—mind is that which gives a norm to itself (Korsgaard 1996).

In some ways, then, one could read Kant as a vitalist; and this was, indeed, how Deleuze and Guattari chose to figure Kant—as an active vitalist, privileging a subject who is nothing other than *pure act*. In contrast to Kant, they set another tradition of vitalism, running from Leibniz to Raymond Ruyer. That second, passive, tradition is not that of a subject but of a 'pure internal awareness' : 'Vitalism has always had two possible interpretations: that of an idea that acts, but is not—that acts therefore only from the point of view of an external cerebral knowledge […] ; or that of a force that is but does not act—that is therefore a pure internal Awareness […] . If the second interpretation seems to us to be imperative it is because the contraction that preserves is always in a state of detachment in relation to action or even to movement and appears as a pure contemplation without knowledge' (Deleuze and Guattari 1994, 213). In the conclusion of this chapter, I will look at this passive vitalism in relation to D. H. Lawrence's poetry, but for now we can note that such a tradition of vitalism would enable us to consider different modes of becoming and different modes of aesthetics. Aesthetics does not, of course, begin with Kant, as there has always been some conception of art or beauty at the heart of philosophy, with beauty in turn being linked to a proper and normative mode of becoming. This occurs most obviously in Plato's *Symposium*, where it is the beauty of the beautiful that explains its desirability. Desire should, in its apprehension of the beautiful, move beyond the delighted perception of any beautiful object and arrive at the understanding that insofar as there is apprehension—*insofar as there is perceiving*—one ought to direct oneself to that which makes apprehension in general possible. This possibility is the form or Idea as such. We perceive beautiful things only because they actualize a potential *to be beautiful* that is never exhausted in any single being: it is that eternal potentiality, or Idea, that knowledge ought to attain. This attainment occurs through becoming: not simply accepting passively what is true or good or beautiful, but realizing it for oneself, through dialogue, education, and reason. This *good becoming* is liberation from the passively received and an activation of proper potentiality: one sees, through the beautiful, the beauty that makes perception possible, and one realizes the potentiality of oneself, becoming what one ought to be by activating dynamic perception.

We can contrast Platonic perception, desire, and Ideas, where perception is drawn to that ultimate ground or condition which makes it possible, to Deleuze's notion of a desire that bears a potential for Ideas only *in relation*. Desire is the capacity to create relations through encounters, relations that are *external* to the potentialities or differential powers from which they emerge. Drawing, among other sources, on the passive vitalism of Raymond Ruyer, Deleuze posits that the development of a body occurs *not* just as the unfolding of a form from itself, but as an orientation to what Ruyer refers to as 'transcendental forms' or what Deleuze refers to as Ideas. For Ruyer, the becoming of an embryo is neither self-determined from the beginning nor caused by the environment; instead, there are virtual powers towards which development tends. In the case of camouflaged animals, becoming makes sense only *in relation* to a field that is beyond the animal's body-world relation (Ruyer 1958). This passive vitalism is one in which 'life' is not some force that actualizes itself in single bodies, but a 'field of survey' that places any body's becoming in relation to the forces of its milieu, and never as active *self-creation*. Becoming-woman and becoming-animal, for example, are not the becomings of women or animals, which is why, notoriously, in *A Thousand Plateaus* Deleuze and Guattari distinguished becoming-woman from the women's movement and also saw becoming-woman as the starting point for all becomings. There would no longer be man as subject, the being who is nothing more than his own self-becoming, for becoming-woman suggests that becoming is oriented, or tends toward, a term beyond the process of becoming. Becoming-woman and becoming-animal are also tied to *writing*: for Deleuze and Guattari, writing is rhizomatic insofar as it possesses a force and field of its own, beyond the self, mastery, or becoming of the writer. There is not a self who affirms its own becoming *as* a woman, nor a self who writes about animals to uncover animality as such. For there are no terms or points—no human or animal—outside of encounters; and neither term becomes *for itself, from itself or without inflection from without*. There is no woman as such or animal as such toward which one becomes. But there are styles of becoming, such that any becoming-woman will both encounter something other than itself, and rewrite just what that 'other' (or woman) is.

Deleuze's reversal of Platonism is not an elimination of Ideas but a creation of a new concept of the Idea: one does not become toward the Idea in order to realize oneself, for Ideas are created attractors that violate thought's self-sameness and transgress any internal or proper becoming (Deleuze 1994). Plato's Ideas are transcendent: they are potentials towards which thought might direct itself. Deleuze retains this aspect of the Idea, while refusing to place the outside of thought beyond life.

When Kant rejects any notion of Ideas that are transcendent to thought, and instead argues that the Ideas toward which thought strives are consequences of extending thought's own potential beyond any given object, he liberates becoming from any end outside itself: 'Against rationalism, Kant asserts that supreme ends are not only ends of reason, but that in positing them reason posits nothing other than itself' (Deleuze 1984, 2). The subject is now elevated to becoming both an ethical being who gives a law to himself (because he is pure power of decision and does not proceed from any decided norm) and to an aesthetic subject whose capacity to perceive *form as such* allows him to feel his own harmonizing and synthesizing activity.

Is it surprising, then, that today theory appears to be enlivened by the concepts of potentiality, becoming, and the experience of the work of art that would be liberated from any norms or figures—any meaning—other than that of perception feeling itself perceiving, art feeling itself as art? The most explicit exponent of such a potentiality freed from any body, norm, or organism other than its own power of the pure act can be found in the work of Agamben, who, in *Potentialities*, explicitly turns back to Aristotle to think a potentiality that is not governed by an already given end. And, despite his criticism of vitalism in *Deleuze*, Badiou's emphasis on the subject, as a pure event facing the void, without any prior or determining body or transcendence, could also be read (as Badiou himself will do in *Manifesto for Philosophy*) as a subjectivism of a specifically Platonic mode. The subject is nothing other than an apprehension of a universal that it brings into being. This universal for Badiou demands a certain fidelity beyond any worldly or already individuated point of view. For all their differences, and they are many, both Agamben and Badiou regard the work of art as an experience that is irreducible to the cognitive or predicative statements of philosophy or science. For Agamben, the work of art demonstrates that, before there are subjects who have proper and determined ends, there is the opening of the world *as such*. For Badiou, the work of art's experience of a world is not (as Heidegger would have it) the proper mode of thought qua thinking as disclosure; rather, it is because a world is unfolded poetically that philosophy can argue that there is no world in itself outside its disclosure, no throbbing, pulsating 'lived,' only a void.

The 'aesthetic,' then, has—at least since Kant—been a way of returning the subject from its captivation with the given and known world to the subjective conditions through which any such world is given. In Kant, it is in the work of art that one feels, but does not know, the synthesizing power of the subject. For Kant, the aesthetic is that mode of presentation that does not simply give the world but presents the world in its event of presentation.

Kant's vitalism of a subject who cannot submit to a norm precisely because he is the power from which any possible normativity might be generated, has its pre-modern and theological precursors. For Aquinas, God is not a being who acts according to an essence, for his essence is nothing other than that of pure being; God is existence as such, the power through which any determined form can be brought into actuality (Gilson 1994). This scholastic definition of God derives from the Aristotelian concept of potentiality, which (as I have already suggested) forms the focus and basis of much of today's 'theory,' especially as theory gives itself the task of finding, from within life, something like a power of life transformation that is not that of annihilation or negation For Aristotle, a living being has a proper and living potential: a being lives in order to actualize what *it ought to be*. To say that such and such a being is *good* is to say that it realizes what it can be in the fullest way possible. In the case of human reason, its highest power (of reason) is the capacity to intuit this principle of becoming as such, and then to create itself according to its sense of its power of self-determination (Irwin 1988).

When contemporary writers, such as Agamben (who refers explicitly to Aristotle) or Judith Butler (who adopts the more general notion of performativity), seek to liberate the self from any *proper* end that would govern its becoming, they at once react against the traditional definition of human potentiality as teleological, while also repeating the idea that the human animal has a peculiarly special end: that of having no end, of being oriented to nothing proper.

To say that becoming, today, is normative is to make a twofold claim. First, becoming presents itself as a self-evident good, not as one norm among others, and not as one good among others, but as the underlying or a priori condition that allows for anything like *the* good. If there were no becoming, there would be no decision or value, and nothing could be apprehended as what one ought to do, rather than what one simply is. Second, if we accept that there is becoming, or that any constituted and decided being is the outcome of a dynamic and constituting power, then we are impelled to be self-normativizing; if the subject is nothing other than the power of its own becoming, then it must take this becoming upon itself, liberate itself from all the illusions of a given nature or normality, and become nothing other than self-becoming. If the subject were not to give itself to itself, not affect itself and realize itself, then it would have abandoned its proper potentiality *to act and become*.

It is in contrast to this normativity of becoming, or becoming as normative, that we can place the *queerness* of Deleuze's concepts of becoming-animal, becoming-woman, and becoming-imperceptible. Here, becoming does not realize and actualize itself, does not flourish into presence, but bears a capacity to annihilate itself, to refuse its *ownness* in order to attach, transductively, to becomings whose trajectories are external and unmasterable. Thus, if we refer to Deleuze as a vitalist, it is not because he insists on the becoming of *life as such*, in opposition to the terms that are effected from an act of becoming. Rather, any becoming is always localized; it is a force of a particular quantity, in relation to another quantity, producing a point of relative stability, or a field. In terms of 'the aesthetic,' it is not a question, then, of art practice returning the subject or creative potentiality to the sense of its own forming power. Rather, the art object would be the result of a collision not intended or reducible to any single life.

Another mode of vitalism, running from Ruyer to Leibniz, entails also another mode of aesthetics, one that does not rely on *the* work of art as a condition in general that would bring the subject back to its acts of perception that constitute its world. As Deleuze suggests in *The Fold*, this form of vitalism does not see life as a constituting power that flows forth and recognizes itself after the event of creation. It is a vitalism of divergent series in which every power to perceive creates its own opening to the infinite, its own series of perceptions passing from finitude to an open whole. For Leibniz, there are not selves who perceive, nor subjective powers that synthesize the given; for the harmony of the universe follows from the fact that there is only one universe, perceived differently by every one of its components. The universe is not some single object that is then perceived or synthesized; there are events of perception, each of which is an unfolding of an infinite series. There is no conflict in these series precisely because there is no outside as such, or life as such, beyond all the points of view that compose the harmonious whole. This doesn't mean that truth is relativized, that we don't get to the truth because of perspectives; rather, truth is composed of relative series, not located in 'a' point, but effected from an open whole of converging *and diverging* points. Life just is this quantity of divergent worlds. As a more modern form of this line of thinking, Ruyer's vitalism simultaneously entails a resistance to mechanism—to the idea that one might determine in advance the various lines of becoming that compose the universe—and a radical passivity, as in his concept of 'absolute survey.' As Ruyer argues in *Neo-finalisme*, every perception is a feeling *of* the whole of being, a sense or orientation that is productive of a located viewpoint, a viewpoint that can be located only because it bears its own sense of a whole or relation of which it is also an effect (Ruyer 1952).

Thus, the concept of becoming, far from being a radically new turn in a twenty-first century vitalism that has broken with normalizing metaphysics, is the normalizing concept par excellence. It has always been the case that anything resistant to dynamism, fruition, creation, and a flowing forth of open and productive life has been demonized as a death or inertia that tarnishes life from the outside. A subject must be nothing other than the event of its own performance, acting, or unfolding. If, following Butler, we recognize that performance is enabled by prior norms (for one must always perform *as* this or that specified being), we nevertheless take heart in the power *to perform* that will introduce a certain nonbeing or undecidability into the rigidity of the very identity upon which we must unfortunately rely. Butler's success as a theorist lies in her capacity to maintain a tradition of theory as *theoria*: as a looking or perceiving that activates itself in a resistance to that which would be merely given and immune to the becoming one takes upon oneself as an ethical subject. Against this Butlerian retrieval of a relation between norm and performance, one might suggest that, rather than rely on something like becoming in general, a power of creativity or dynamism that is different and distant from any norm, one could always see becoming as having a relation to what is not itself. Becoming-animal, for Deleuze and Guattari, is not the becoming *of the animal,* just as becoming-woman does not proceed from women as a group (even a group formed for the purposes of action alone in some decision of strategic essentialism). Indeed, becoming occurs *not* as a retrieval of the life, dynamism, or vitality that has fallen into reification and substantivism, but as an encounter between 'a' life—always *this* power of difference—with another. Deleuze and Guattari insist that 'pluralism is monism' because if there are a thousand tiny becomings or awarenesses, there is no transcendental ground or subject—no life in general, and therefore no one ground that would be substantially different from the grounded. Deleuze and Guattari's celebrated monism is of one power of difference expressed multiply and not a single life that differs.

Vitalist Aesthetics

In order to make this more explicit I want to contrast two modes of vitalism and aesthetics, the first from Ezra Pound and the second from D. H. Lawrence. An aesthetics tied to active vitalism privileges impersonality (as distance from personae), defamiliarization, and negation. Usually, such an aesthetics presents itself as a strictly formalist endeavor. It matters less what one says in a work of art, than the disjunction one manages to achieve between represented content and the forming power that synthesizes materials. In general, then, the modernist techniques of fragmentation, disembodied voices, allusion and parataxis preclude a subject being presented and instead intimate a power of presentation that is never given as such. Consider Ezra Pound's modernism, which began with the presentation of personae *as personae*, but which developed into the epic venture of the *Cantos*, a work that quoted Western culture from Sappho to the present as so much dead, circulating, passively repeated and atomized content devoid of animation. Pound's relatively early 'Hugh Selwyn Mauberley' presents a voice that answers, in a passively craven manner, both to the markets of consumption ('the age demanded an image') and to the desire for a synthesis of the past in the present ('the classics in paraphrase!') (Pound 2003, 549-50). Pound began with translations of the Chinese poetry of Li Po and fragments of the Western poetic tradition before the latter fell into what Pound saw as a weak and flabby dependence on the propulsions of rhyme and meter. Often, what Pound borrowed, though in another voice, was quoted in such a way as to create a disjunction with the present, so that the voice of the past is reanimated to speak as if from the point of view Pound himself *would have* sought. So the opening of 'The Seafarer' that Pound 'translated' from early Anglo Saxon presents the distanced singing voice, detached from its own culture:

> *May I for my own self song's truth reckon,*
> *Journey's jargon, how I in harsh days*
> *Hardship endured oft. (236)*

Pound's use of the past, here in his drawing upon Anglo Saxon sources, and elsewhere in his use of Sappho, Greek epic, Dante and even (as in 'Hugh Selwyn Mauberly') earlier phases of his own work, despite its seeming passivity enables a mode of active vitalism typical of high modernism. By taking up already given fragments and voices of the past the implied modernist artist is (to quote Joyce after Flaubert), 'like the God of the creation, remain[ing] within or behind or beyond or above his handiwork, invisible, refined out of existence, indifferent, paring his fingernails' (Joyce 1922, 252). It is because the artist remains indifferent that he is never determined by any specific or finite position within the world, remaining as pure creation liberated from any of the points of view that he adopts. Pound's use of fragments, personae, translations, voices and historical periods—for all its implied absence of authorial intervention—enables a position of *pure* act or creative force, untainted by the substance or finitude of an action or creation. The mode of quotation is crucial: the author is at once not speaking, not present, and yet able to summon materials that speak about a world in which speaking is no longer possible or at least distanced and difficult. The present has been rendered so passive as to preclude the possibility of speaking authentically. One can only repeat the fragments of the past, yet never be at one with that lost past. In Pound's translation of Li Po, the poetic voice is not that of Romantic interiority or self-expression, but perception reduced to its relation to the world, a simple 'I' that is nothing other than its present: 'While my hair was still cut straight across my forehead / I played about the front gate, pulling flowers' ('River-Merchant's Wife' 251). In his imagist phase, Pound also tries to present language as an object, standing alone, presenting an imaging as such. This 'making new' of language is directed towards reviving the force and energy of language and also—and Pound was explicit about this—reviving the imagination that would no longer be enslaved by conventions and ' easy' listening, nor by bourgeois 'taste.'

Pound's poetics was one of anti-commodification, where commodification is counter-vital both in its mass-production of things (rather than created works) and in its tendency to produce lulled and passive consumption that could only be broken by the difficulty of modernist poetics. This governing intention later led him to criticize his own imagism for producing yet one more fashionable and easily digested vogue:

> *The age demanded an image*
> *Of its accelerated grimace,*
> *Something for the modern stage,*
> *Not, at any rate, an Attic grace ('Hugh Selwyn Mauberley' 549)*

Yet, it was his final project, the *Cantos*, that yielded an aesthetics that was far more explicitly vitalist, sexually normative, and fascist. Vitalist: through processes of fragmentation, cutting, juxtaposition, parataxis, and the insertion of untranslated elements, culture could be presented as lacking any already given synthesis, forcing the reader—and culture in general—to confront the machinic, atomized, lackluster, and incoherent nature of modern life. Sexually normative: not only did Pound present figures of a fallen sexuality that were variously diagnosed as homosexual, promiscuous, effeminate, and (therefore) infertile, he also created a direct association between sexuality and artistic production. Modernity suffers from a compulsion towards a restricted economy: in its corrupted and fallen mode, life, like art, must be measured through capital. What is lost is expenditure that has not determined its productive end in advance. At a formal level, this meant that Pound aligned proper artistic experimentation with a fertile, productive, and living expenditure that would produce ends that were not already determined. At the level of content, Pound placed journalists, homosexuals, Jews, and bankers in an excremental hell: journalists merely allowed language to circulate for profit, rather than generating genuine poetic creation; homosexuals were guilty of a same-same sexuality that could know no genuine fertility or life; bankers (and, by extension for Pound, Jews) were responsible for the institutions of usury which would direct all money into the creation of further money, precluding any excessive expenditure that might allow for genuine artistic excess:

> *The stench of wet coal, politicians*
> *... ... ... e and ... .. n, their wrists bound to*
>   *their ankles,*
> *Standing bare bum,*

> *Faces smeared on their rumps,*
> *wide eye on flat buttock,*
> *Bush hanging for beard,*
> *Addressing crowds through their arse-holes,*
> *Addressing the multitudes in the ooze,*
> *newts, water-slugs, water-maggots,*
> *And with them... ... . r,*
> *a scrupulously clean table-napkin*
> *Tucked under his penis,*
> *and ... ... m*
> *Who disliked colloquial language,*
> *Stiff-starched, but soiled, collars*
> *circumscribing his legs,*
> *The pimply and hairy skin*
> *pushing over the collar's edge,*
> *Profiteers drinking blood sweetened with sh-t,*
> *And behind them ... ... f and the financiers*
> *lashing them with steel wires.*
>
> *And the betrayers of language*
> *... ... n and the press gang*
> *And those who had lied for hire;*
> *the perverts, the perverters of language,*
> *the perverts, who have set money-lust*
> *Before the pleasures of the senses (Pound 1956, 61)*

Pound associated proper, fruitful, excessive, and creative spending with a pre-modern form of patronage, where art was not yet subjected to markets, commodified language, effete styles of pleasure, or the homogenizing blandness of democracy.

Finally, Pound's effort turns fascist: by emphasizing art as a decisive break with the circulation and system of production, for the sake of a higher, productive, and creative end beyond already actualized life, Pound justified a violence of the present for the sake of a future that would return life to its proper, active, and expansive creative potential. Indeed, it is just in this respect that one might consider fascism to be tied to a certain privilege of *becoming*. Radically futural, fascism acts for the sake of a singularly violent decision and act over the meandering and undirected or unfruitful pleasures and affects of the present. Fascism, at least in its modernist form, was tied to a horror of static, inert, reifying and lifeless infertility of twentieth-century democracy, or—more specifically—a diffuse, inhuman (because animal-like) dispersion of a people who would be devoid of decision, self-identity, striving and vigorous assertion. Pound's work is complex, and its tendencies to fascism—to the privilege of the single decision and productive force of the future—cannot be unequivocally separated from a revolutionary impulse that would not be enslaved to an axiomatic of production and directed force. One needs to consider the ways in which an active vitalism of self-constituting life that produces itself from itself is distinguished ever so subtly from a passive vitalism that enables life to be thought of from divergent, dispersed and infinitely divisible points of difference. That is, whereas Pound's response to the horrors of modern democracy—its rendering equivalent of all forces, its general tendency towards a reduction of intensity and distinction to vague uniformity and single quantities—was to assert the life and force of art as decision, another passive vitalist potential opened thought to vibrations of life and thought beyond act and decision.

When Deleuze and Guattari consider the tendency of the Body Without Organs to develop a cancerous or fascist mode they confront two of the major problems of modernist aesthetics and its relation to politics. First, the vital productive forces of life cannot be deemed to be good *in opposition* to the evils of undecided, animalistic, machinic and squandering forces of death. For this moral opposition between productive, bounded, formed and self-asserting life and a diffuse and squandering dispersal of forces is a moralism of the organism, where bounded living forms are opposed to the dissolution of death. Second, fascism is an internal possibility of the vital order, not an accident that befalls an otherwise good life from without. Pound's work is worthy of attention precisely because it gathers revolutionary forces that would break with bourgeois humanism and normalizing stasis and yet reterritorializes those same forces on a normative image of life, life as pure becoming that encounters no event other than itself and its own production. If, as Pound did, one fragments the syntax that normally allows the reader to pass from one term to another, if one places usually opposed and contrasted terms alongside one another without connectives, then the reader is forced to compose an order that is not given, or at least confront a disorder that would foreground the arbitrariness of any system. Reading is not consumption but production. We do not, in everyday and efficient language, recognize language and syntax as the connective and normalizing systems they are. By removing connectives, we are forced to relive order *in its ordering*. Perhaps not surprisingly Pound will associate the passivity of imagery—the lack of vitality in thinking—with the loss of a fertile ground of artistic production outside the system of capital.

By contrast, we can think of the ways Deleuze and Guattari do not want to break with capitalism's tendency to take the movements of bodies into inorganic flows and systems, but want to release that movement from capital. Their immanent and passive vitalism would not be a return to a force before capitalism and syntax, but a move *within* capital and relations: not a grounding of syntax, relation, and systems on some anterior life force or spirit above and beyond systems, but an intuition of the powers of relation and proliferation within, between, and among bodies. Pound's reference back to a force that would not be submitted to the system of circulation—the references in the Hell section of *Cantos* to Renaissance patronage of excess and a spending without calculation of return—reveals a (sexually) normative image of life at the heart of active vitalism. Opposed to the fruitful, and expansive relation between productive force and a production that can be released into the open, Pound's banker-Jew-journalist-homosexual-necrophiliac closes production in upon himself (as redundant language, dead money, or nonactualizing flows of putrid bodily fluids):

> *skin-flakes, repetitions, erosions,*
> *endless rain from the arse-hairs,*
> *as the earth moves, the centre*
> *passes over all parts in succession,*
> *a continual bum-belch*
> *distributing its productions. (Pound 1956, 65)*

Desire is caught up in itself, bearing no distance from itself. Pound's aesthetics valorized the distances between terms and sounds without an overarching unity or reason. The productive excess of terms without subordination to a recognizable, consumable, or syntactical sense demands that the reader *work* in relation to the poem: rather than follow some natural order of sense, he has to reawaken the creation of order before the efficient, reified, systematized, and jejune order of commodity production.

Pound's form of vitalism is anticapitalist in its opposition to a world reduced to so much already formed circulating content: art should always be *other than* the ready-made. This entails either taking the ready-made and presenting it *as* already formed (through quotation and repetition out of context and order) *or* cutting into the ready-made with radically external, alien, and unreadable matters. As the *Cantos* proceeds, the typeface takes over the voice (with the intrusion of dollar signs, Chinese characters, ancient Greek, diacritical marks, numerical calculations); the poet, as grand absent artist, is not one whose voice extends itself into speech and content, but can only be assumed (after the event) as that which would be other than any of the presented fragments.

We can contrast Pound's active vitalism with Deleuze and Guattari's notion of the art of the ready-made, which has two features. First, art is inhuman. In *What is Philosophy?* Deleuze and Guattari describe a bird's selection of materials for its territory as the beginning of art in the form of the ready-made. This is not a process of defamiliarization, or decontextualization but a selection of a matter that has a quality or 'thisness' that allows a body to form a territory, to create relations, and to produce a body-world coupling (Deleuze and Guattari 1994, 184). Second, the ready-made does not refer back to the gesture or selection of an absent artist, for there is no self who selects; from selection and relations, or the encounter of forces, something like a body or milieu is formed. *This* is art as the house or dwelling, a certain detachment or 'standing alone' of matters.

The passivity of Deleuze and Guattari's vitalism has been associated (often critically and negatively) with capitalism. If Pound's vitalism (and active vitalism more generally) always threatens to fall into a mode of fascism in its elevation of a decision or force outside social circulation,

Deleuze and Guattari are wary of the microfascisms and the 'cancerous Body without Organs' that would follow from an insufficiently rigorous political movement of deterrirorialization. That is, if the taking up of movements, potentialities, and forces from within capitalism liberates itself from the capitalist axiomatic only to proliferate by turning back in upon the self—the affirmation of one's own especially queer becoming, or the simple affirmation of becoming as such, liberated from all relations—then one has left the grand system of capital without creating a positive line of flight. Queerness defined negatively—as *other than* any given syntax or system, or as the negation of the ready-made—would be insufficiently vital, if one takes vitalism in Deleuze and Guattari's sense as the creation of 'a' body without organs. The imperative is, then, not a return, retrieval, or revitalization of the already existing synthetic force that has become alienated or reified: vitality occurs with a line of flight, a becoming, or an event that is not the expression or extension of an already existing force but the outcome of a genuine and positive encounter.

Here we can link Leibniz's passive vitalism to Deleuze and Guattari's concept of becoming-animal. For Leibniz, the body's being or individuation is not a consequence of it being synthesized or recognized as this determined being; what something *is* is not defined by the way in which it is recognized, nor by the way in which the being affirms itself. A being is not the being it is because it is recognized *as* this or that type. A being is individuated by all the relations it bears to other relations; a monad is absolutely unique in its occupation of a point in time and space, as well as the way it perceives and is affected by all the other relations and affections of time and space. Identity does not refer back to a subject who is perceived only through the world it constitutes. On the contrary, Leibniz's world is composed of affections, which expand inward infinitely. A body is its susceptibility to relations, and 'I' am nothing other than the perceptions, events, encounters, and vibrations that produce a certain feeling of oneself or 'self-enjoyment.' For Deleuze, following Leibniz, it is possible to intuit the singularity and difference of the tiny souls of which we are composed, which surround us, and which constitute our individuation: I am those souls I feel as my own (so that we can say that the soul that feels the other souls—the mind that contemplates—exists at a different level) while the feeling I have of the souls that compose me enter into relation with souls from without. I can feel hunger, fatigue, confusion—all working divergently: I am tired, but need to eat, but puzzled as to whether eating will stop me from sleeping; my body is composed of these souls that I can observe, but that can be observed in turn. All this confusion, fatigue and hunger is felt by the body next to me, whose sadness I can only dimly feel so caught am I in my own contemplations. And yet, I can feel another's sadness as their sadness, affecting me in my own being, while not perceiving their world and their duration. One does not become 'oneself' by living *as* this or that normative being imposed from without but from which one always differs. Identity is not difference *from*, nor a negative becoming in which one destabilizes or subverts a given norm. Rather, identity is distinct but unclear; each being is distinctly individuated by being composed of only its own encounters and affections, and yet one feels certain of those affections clearly (my own sadness) and others dimly (your sadness).

This, in turn, has consequences for the politics of images and its problems. It is not a question of either creating images that would be less stringent in their production of norms, or of producing an active, critical, and negative relation to images. On the contrary, micropolitics and schizoanalysis regard any image as ensouled, composed of thousands of affections. Every normative image—such as the 'mommy-daddy-me' of *Anti-Oedipus*—is not imposed upon an otherwise radically open or undifferentiated life in general. The image does not impose difference on disorder, but covers over distinction with generality. The Oedipal 'daddy' is made up of racial, historical, sexual, and political desires. And it is here we can discern another mode of passive vitalism, one in which forces not of the subject are not taken up and reactivated, but contemplated in their power to destroy subjective syntheses and coherent, as opposed to articulated, identity. We recognize the force of the Oedipal triangle—still, today, with repeated emphases on family values. Rather than negate the image we open up its souls and contemplations—how the figure of the good work-at-home mother is possible because of a series of mid-twentieth-century technologies creating the modern household, and because of civil rights battles granting women identity and one universal gender regardless of race. The twenty-first century television series *Mad Men* at once presents perfectly Oedipalized individuals, but does not posit some rebellious 'becoming' against the images of familial life but instead displays life as a war of images, as a field in which bodies create and are created by perceptions of other bodies. Such twenty-first century works would seem to be post- or counter-modern in their refusal of the grand gesture of modernist refusal. Art is not the distanced negation and fragmentation of images but the proliferation of images, showing that social fields are not stereotyped or negated by mass-produced images, but emerge from images. There is not a self above and beyond the fixity of the image, for the self is a thousand tiny images. But there is one way in which *Mad Men* continues a modernism of passive vitalism, in which the image industry is not countered by a more active and willing life, but opens out onto more and more images. Of course, one way of reading *Mad Men* is to see gender and sexuality as performed; the series would denaturalize the Oedipal family and capitalist individual by demonstrating all the ways in which the self does not have an identity prior to performance. The central character—Don Draper—takes on his proper name and identity after being mistaken for another individual during the war, and he goes on to live his life as Draper by performing the role of father, husband and wage-earner. But the series' setting of advertising agencies and the emergent tele-visual culture marks a subtle difference: selves do not occur through subjection to images from which they posit themselves as having been. Selves *are* warring images: the battle on the television screen to establish a brand or mark as desired is coupled with selves as images at war, including the war between older models of familial gender, and emergent images of gender as allure, as resistance, *as becoming*. Advertising deploys the images of freedom, choice, self-fashioning and unique identity in order to create territories of viewers. This way of reading contemporary image production allows us to look back at modernism and read its texts in terms of passive vitalism: selves are relations to images, perceptions, and temporal intervals between desire and desired, and this would be different from performativity, where the self is always at odds with the various voices and roles that she takes up.

D.H. Lawrence's prose, often criticized for privatizing or mystifying class politics by presenting social relations in terms of sexuality, can be seen as the creation of just such a sociopolitical field. The Oedipal triangle, in *Sons and Lovers* for example, opens out onto a social field. The mother turns her affections to the son precisely because she is disenchanted with the limited education, worn spirit, alcoholism, and resentment of her miner husband. The son, in turn, perceives other women through the figure of his mother, but again in a broadly political field: the cramped and restricted world of his first lover, Miriam, emerges from a desperately declining rural mining milieu, where marriage is the only form of possible social expansion (and where the son sees his mother as similarly folded into a field of historical, social, and class restrictions); the more educated and expansive world of the son's other lover, Clara, is tied to a bourgeois marriage market. But Lawrence is more than a sociological writer who ties the personal and sexual to the political; he also transforms the very style and syntax of literary point of view to create a mode of perception that is neither sexual (in some private and personal psychological sense) nor political (where self-sufficient bodies relate to each other in some community or *polis*).

Similarly, in Lawrence's poem 'Snake,' the observing voice is all too human, feeling himself invaded or overtaken by desires to destroy or master the animal; but alongside the affects of the human, there are also counter-affects that allow the snake to be viewed as noble, stately, more alive than the body of speech and reason. The poem presents a composition of competing perceiving selves in the one speaking body; this fracture is not a negation of the self, but its expansion. Directly thematizing the relation between human and animal, 'Snake' relies not on the fragmented and juxtaposed quotations and allusions of Pound's modernism, but on an encounter between two temporalities or durations expressed at the level of form and content.

If active vitalism presents a field of parataxis that must presuppose some absent cause that, as Deleuze and Guattari observe, 'acts but is not' (Deleuze and Guattari 1994, 213), Lawrence maintains an 'I' viewpoint that is a localization of received impressions and affects. But the 'I' is not only contrasted in terms of content with the snake, it also yields to stylistic poetic variations. According to Deleuze and Guattari, we can distinguish between form of content and form of expression. Not only does this allow us to think about the relations of bodies and the relations of language; it also gives Deleuze and Guattari a way of describing the 'higher deterritorialization,' which occurs when a work of art renders the relation between form of content and form of expression undecidable.

Lawrence's poem begins with propositions that describe the snake as a subject completing actions: 'A snake came to my water-trough.' The snake is contrasted with the I as observing subject: 'I came down the steps with my pitcher / And must wait, must stand and wait, for there he was at the trough before me' (217). The 'before me' that concludes that lengthy line of verse (a line that itself 'waits') gives two senses to 'before.' The snake is 'before me' temporally: its presence imposes a sense of another duration. The snake is also 'before' the 'I' spatially. We are given a spatial proximity of two bodies, with an intense temporal distance. The snake is described with adverbs and adverbial phrases: 'softly,' 'silently,' 'vaguely,' 'dreamily,' 'slowly.' The 'And' that frequently begins the poem's lines ties the form of expression to the form of content. Because the observing 'I' increasingly finds himself captivated by the snake's movement, desire, duration, and milieu, his waiting is expressed not in a syntax of subordinate clauses and consequences, but simple connectives: 'And I like a second comer, waiting.' Giving us a 'second coming' of the 'I' that is radically counter-messianic (for the second coming here is one of being late, redundant and without revelation), the poem begins to open up the field of the human: to be this highest point of evolution, progress, and rational development is to come second, to be without any existential priority; it is to be belated. Thus, instead of regarding the human—with its expansive point of view, instrumental command of nature, and subjective self-awareness as a point of culmination towards which life is directed—'Snake' moves in the opposite direction. The snake is 'one of the lords / Of life' (219) whose earth is 'secret' (218); the animal opens onto a time and sense well beyond the 'I.' The poem describes a waiting where the 'I' arrives at 'my' water trough, only to be dispossessed by an intrusion which is perceived in a double sense. On the one hand, the human milieu regards this animal as an interfering body to be eliminated. Education, action (described as 'paltry' [219]), human voices (that are 'pett[y]' [219]), myth, and even masculinity pull the 'I' towards command and destruction: 'And voices in me said, If you were a man / You would take a stick and break him now, and finish him off' (218). At the same time, and on the other hand, another aspect of the 'I' is drawn away from itself towards a fascination with or perception of, not the self-awareness and active mastery of the human, but the snake's divinity that lies in a *not* seeing, in a godliness of being 'adream':

> He drank enough
> And lifted his head, dreamily, as one who has drunken,
> And flickered his tongue like a forked night on the air, so black,
> Seeming to lick his lips,
> And looked around like a god, unseeing, into the air,
> And slowly turned his head,
> And slowly, very slowly, as if thrice adream,
> Proceeded to draw his slow length curving round
> And climb again the broken bank of my wall-face.
> And as he put his head into that dreadful hole,
> And as he slowly drew up, snake-easing his shoulders, and
>   entered farther,
> A sort of horror, a sort of protest against his withdrawing into that
>   horrid black hole,
> Deliberately going into the blackness, and slowly drawing himself after,
> Overcame me now his back was turned. (218-19)

It is the snake who becomes *one of* the 'lords / Of life,' who is 'like a king, / Like a king in exile, uncrowned in the underworld.' The description of the snake as 'like' a king, or as one who 'seemed' like a king, draws attention to the event of encounter as perception: another duration appears, yet remains—like the snake writhing back into the earth—always hidden, secret. At the level of *form of content*, the poem takes two bodies—snake and human—with the snake presenting itself as secret, hidden, unselfconscious, and vital precisely because of its radical passivity, its distinction from the 'I' viewpoint's 'horror' at that which cannot be brought beneath its own command. At the level of *form of expression*, the poem oscillates between a poetic voice of a reflective 'I' that recognizes itself as a fragment of a history and humanity of domination—'I despised myself and the voices of my accursed human education'—and another that in its fascination can follow movements, allowing an affect ('horror') to become the grammatical subject:

> *A sort of horror, a sort of protest against his withdrawing into that horrid black hole,*
> *Deliberately going into the blackness, and slowly drawing himself after,*
> *Overcame me now his back was turned. (219)*

Both at the level of expression, where the grammatical 'I' recognizes its own limits precisely insofar as it is self-aware and human, and at the level of content, where the poem describes the encounter between the time of human history, burdened with myth and education, and the duration of a snake that forces us to wait, Lawrence's poem expresses a passive vitalism that is also positively queer. It is not the critical negation of man but the intuition of other durations that can open up a genuine event of encounter. (Queerness is neither the anti-normative, simply different *from* the dominant, nor is queerness the reiteration of the norm to achieve destabilization: queerness occurs in the encounter between two disjunct temporalities.) This is neither an event of recognition, nor of defamiliarization. The inhuman, or the powers of time and movement that do not serve recognition and command, are expressed here as a certain capacity to live the earth not as one's own. The snake's earth is a 'dark secret': not a matter or ground that we synthesize in order to recognize ourselves as *subjects* of truth, nor is it a milieu or world that is given in terms of some meaningful horizon of projects. The 'I' finds itself to be a second coming in a negative sense, as one who can only perceive from afar what it might be to live without a commanding and educated past, without the imperatives of recognition: how might one live if one could free oneself from the conditional: 'If you were a man'? Such a question is answered positively by a perception of the animal as another style of perception and duration *and* one of the lords of life in its liberation from mastery.

Notes

1. When Giorgio Agamben writes of the need to 'return thought to its practical calling' as part of the project to retrieve *the political*, he at once betrays the thoroughly *proper* notion of politics as emerging from creative action; at the same time he also laments a present in which the becoming of politics through speech and praxis becomes attenuated in managerial systems of biopolitics that will regard life as being nothing more than mere matter for

political proceduralism. Agamben's (1993) 'coming community,' which would break with present states of bureaucratic management, retrieves the active praxis of becoming and potentiality that had always been (rightly, he argues) foregrounded in premodern political theories, but that have been occluded with the modern attention to mere life; such potentiality, he continues in *Homo Sacer*, might (finally) be freed from all taints of becoming oriented to some proper actuality, some orienting end.

2. In his *Ethics*, Alain Badiou contrasts the *act* of the subject over culturally relativist claims to identity. Badiou is highly critical of a world in which 'ethics,' rather than affirming the capacity of subjects to seize events that are not already calculated within modern procedures, appears to do nothing more than save human beings from becoming victims. While he presents his work as at once a radical break with metaphysical affirmations of an ultimate ground or 'One,' he also ties his thought to what he deems to be a philosophical tradition of truth and universalism, which can neither be reduced to facts, nor decided once and for all, nor located in any domain other than that of the act. Whatever else it is, *ethics* cannot be that which follows from nature: from Plato to Kant and Badiou, the good is not an object from which action follows. Rather *action* can be ethical only if it decides the good from itself.

3. One of the ways in which modern art has been defined and celebrated has been in its radicalization, renewal, or destruction of convention; but this 'making new' is linked closely with ethical and political celebrations of difference and becoming. If scientific and technological procedures reduce the world to so many already quantified, lifeless, circulating, and mechanistic units, it is the task of art to reawaken the subject to the world not as so much mere matter but as that which is given to the subject through syntheses that art will reanimate. According to a lazy received reading of Plato's expulsion of the poets from the republic, the philosopher rejects the secondary and mimetic qualities of art in favour of the originary ideas of reason; even here, though, there is a privilege of all the features that will mark art and the aesthetic. It is art, in its proper mode, that yields form in its original, creative mode of becoming; it is scientific language that is passively received and manipulated for efficiency. The valorization of art as the active bringing into being of form goes back at least as far as Plato, for it is the sophists who merely manipulate terms in contrast to Socrates, who will form himself as an active character through dialogue (see Nehamas). When art is devalued—as that which is passively received—it is always in favor of an art of active creation, dialogue, and *becoming*.

Chapter 5

Queer Vitalism

This essay is about vitalism and the apparent ethical urgency of returning to the problem of life. This urgency of the turn to life, I will argue, far from being a recent, radical and necessarily transgressive gesture, has always underpinned (and presupposed) highly normative gestures in philosophy, literature and cultural understanding. Indeed, the very notion and possibility of the normative, or the idea that one can proceed from what is (life) to what ought to be (ways of living) has always taken the form of vitalism. For the purposes of this essay, then, I will define vitalism as the imperative of grounding, defending or deriving principles and systems from life *as it really is*. (This is why many posthuman or anti-biopolitical models can be vitalist: it is life beyond humans, or life beyond the bourgeois subject of production, that is often appealed to in order to open a new horizon.) From this it follows that there will be two forms of vitalism, for there are two ways of understanding this notion of 'life as it really is.' For the most part 'life as it really is' is defined through actual life: here, vitalism begins from living bodies (usually human, usually heterosexual, usually familial) and then asks what it means to live well. We could refer to this, following Deleuze and Guattari, as an active vitalism because it assumes that 'life' refers to acting and well-organized bodies. However, there is another way of understanding 'life as it really is,' and this is to align the real with the virtual. For Deleuze and Guattari this leads to a passive vitalism, where 'life' is a pre-individual plane of forces that does not act by a process of decision and self-maintenance but through chance encounters.

By understanding life as virtual we no longer begin with the image of a living body, and are therefore able to consider forces of composition that differ from those of man and the productive organism. Those queer theories that account for the self as it is formed in the social unit of the family (with the self taking on *either* male or female norms) fail to account for the emergence of the self and the genesis of the family; in so doing they remain at the level of the actual and of active human agents. Passive vitalism is queer, by contrast, in its difference and distance from already constituted images of life as necessarily fruitful, generative, organized and human. It is not just different or distortive of those images, but comprises a power of imaging that is not oriented to the eye of recognition, the eye that views the world according to its own already organized desires. For this reason such a vitalism would also have implications for aesthetics, especially if aesthetics is understood as a consideration of sensations. Indeed, it would reverse the relation between perceiving body and synthesized sensations. On an active vitalist account the subject synthesizes a world according to its own point of view, and then is able to reflect upon that synthesizing activity when artworks draw attention back to the world-forming power. A passive vitalism would be queer in its transformation of how we understand the work of art, perhaps less as work—as that which would expose the subject's formative capacities—and more as monument. On a passive vitalist account there would be qualities or powers *to be sensed* from which something lie a body that senses would emerge, a body being formed through the sensual forces it encounters.

For Kant, the work of art is to be judged only in its capacity to enliven the subject's capacity to give order and synthesis to the world. Beauty is the experience of intuited material as perfectly harmonious with the subject's conceptualizing or forming powers, while the sublime refers to an experience that allows the subject to feel its own striving for form and order. The work of art returns us to the subjective and constituting power from which the lived world unfolds. This emphasis on art as disclosing the active power that originally forms the world as this meaningful world for 'us' is maintained in all forms of post-Kantian aesthetics that take us back to the structure, language or matrix that gives sense to 'our' world. This would include queer theories of performance or defamiliarization that seek to present the performance of gender *as performance,* allowing the active body to appear as that which becomes through its own self-forming actions.

(At Least) Two Vitalisms, Two Histories, Two Philosophies

In *What is Philosophy?* Deleuze and Guattari argue for a tradition of passive vitalism (beginning with Leibniz and extending to Ruyer) which counters the dominant tradition of vitalism, which runs from Kant to Claude Bernard:

> Vitalism has always had two possible interpretations: that of an idea that acts, but is not—that acts therefore only from the point of view of an external cerebral knowledge ... or that of a force that is but does not act—that is therefore a pure internal awareness ... If the second interpretation seems to us to be imperative it is because the contraction that preserves is always in a state of detachment in relation to action or even to movement and appears as a pure contemplation without knowledge. (Deleuze and Guattari 1994, 213)

Before looking in detail at what the aesthetics of such a passive vitalism might be, and how such an aesthetic might open a way of thinking beyond modernist norms of art, we would do well to define the dominant vitalism mentioned in the above quotation that 'acts but is not.' Deleuze and Guattari suggest that this vitalism begins with Kant. This would already make it different from the vitalism or normative figuration of life that has always been Western philosophy's spontaneous gesture. We can discern a vitalist normativity in the very ethic of philosophy's definition of itself against sophistry, dogma and opinion. Philosophy refuses to accept the ready-made and received judgments of gossip and chatter and instead strives to legitimate truth by tracing its genesis, whether that be from Platonic ideas clearly intuited, categories of universal reason, or by reflecting upon the subjectively constituted structure of the world. If language circulates without justification, or is repeated without an animating and intuiting intent that would ground what is said in an ongoing and truth-oriented experience, then language falls into an automatic, inhuman and merely technical repetition. The doctrine of Platonic Ideas is, after all, an ethical and political maneuver that would aim to ground assertions, identities and claims in an originating and animating force: the Idea which grants each being its proper form allows us to decide what any being is, and the ways in which it ought to become, according to its preceding and governing essence.¹ Not surprisingly, Neo-Platonism will render the vitalist potential in Platonic ideas more explicit. Neo-Platonism regards every being in this world as an emanation of the One, and in so doing neither detaches a world of matter from a divine transcendence, nor denies any being a full participation in holiness. In contrast with a strict Platonism, Neo-Platonism tends to suggest that the One is not above and beyond its emanations, but is given only through each of its expressions. Thus vitalism in its most general sense would be a commitment to the animation or spirituality of everything that lives, and would be contrasted both with forms of atomist materialism that reduced matter to that which operates only through mechanical and external relations rather than its own immanent force, and with Cartesianism, which separates mind from body, regarding the latter as devoid of any inner life.

Both of these modes of vitalism—an anti-atomism and an anti-Cartesianism—were prevalent in the seventeenth century, and could often take on a quite revolutionary strain (Rogers 1996). Rather than seeing order as necessarily imposed from above on an otherwise chaotic and unruly world, vitalism granted each aspect of the world its own striving potential directed to order and relations. Against Cartesianism and the disenchantment of the world, modern vitalism drew on Neo-Platonism to argue for each being's tendency towards the expression and fulfillment of the divine. It is possibly requisite to correct, then, one notion which dominates the history of ideas: that modernity is governed by a Cartesianism which places mind and matter as distinct worldly substances, seeing matter as operating mechanically and mind as being a power to represent and organize the relations of the rationalized matter. Instead, there is an (at least) equally prevalent continuation of an emphasis on the world's immanent spirit, its striving towards the good, and the contribution of every living being in its difference and specificity towards the efflorescence of the whole. It is this expressivist tradition that Deleuze draws upon throughout his diverse corpus in his references to Leibniz and Spinoza. However, Leibniz and Spinoza stress a univocity—or one life—that expresses itself in both mind and body, rejecting any Cartesian substance that would be simply, distinctly or merely mechanical. For that expressivist tradition the world of distinct and separate entities flows from the one expressive life which becomes what it is only in its production of diverse and emanating bodies, all of which have their origin or true being only as expressions of a prior animating One. For Deleuze, though, this ultimately expressive virtual life does not provide a grounding unity, substrate or single substance but a power for differentiation. It is Nietzsche, according to Deleuze, who will radicalize the expressivism and univocity opened by Spinoza and Leibniz. The latter philosophers refused to posit any substantial distinction between emanating life and its dazzling array of expressions, but it was Nietzsche who regarded the emanating life as a plane of forces effecting itself through styles and dramas.

We can make a first note towards the distinct contribution of Leibniz's passive vitalism in contrast with the general doctrine of Platonic and Neo-Platonic emanation. Leibniz, like Deleuze after him, will not posit two distinct substances. For Leibniz, the reasoning, perceptive and 'singing' monad is what it is only in the passions, affections, and perceptions that it expresses. Reason, mind or spirit are not the same as matter, but the relations of material bodies are like the ground bass upon which each monad unfolds its own melody, each of which contributes to the overall harmonious symphony of the world. The world I perceive is the same world that you perceive, but our different perceptions unfold a different line of the infinite, each perception having its own zone of clarity. Whereas Neo-Platonic emanation posits each individual being as deriving from and expressing a One, Deleuze (like Leibniz) refuses to posit a unity that would be other than each perceiving and affected point of view; the world is just this multiplicity of viewpoints, each of which composes a truth of a whole that is nothing other than this expressive multiplicity. To refer to Deleuze as a Platonist in a de-realizing or unworldly sense— as a philosopher who wishes to overcome the gritty actuality of this world in favour of some mystical unity (Badiou 2000)—is to fail to take into account what I will refer to as the *queer* nature of Deleuze's vitalism. Every body in this world is possible as an individual because it gives some form and specificity in time and space to a potential that always threatens to destabilize or de-actualize its being. This is what Deleuze refers to as real conditions of existence and allows us to think of his philosophy as offering a positive sense of queer being, or what Deleuze also refers to as '?being' (Deleuze 1994). That is, in addition to the actual bodies that populate this world in time and space there is also the virtual plane that is thoroughly real and that is infinitely different; it exists in each body as its potential for variation, a potential that is actualized (but not exhausted) not by the decisions that body makes but by the encounters it undergoes.

In concrete terms, to see what difference this might make for thinking about this world, we might begin by thinking of gender. Active vitalism, at least in the form that Deleuze and Guattari trace back to Kant, regards all concepts and categories as originally imposed by the subject upon an otherwise meaningless life. Active vitalism might regard gender as one of the ways in which life or the social 'constructs' categories that differentiate an otherwise general or undifferentiated humanity: the criticism of stereotypes (as clichés or rigid forms imposed upon life) would lead to an overthrow of rigid categories in favor of what we really are (as unique individuals) or would expose that there are no such things as individuals, only effects of gender as it is represented or performed. Genders and kinds are known in the vague and general opposition between male and female, distinctions that are imposed upon life and that need to be reactivated by being traced back to their social and familial origins. By contrast, for Deleuze and Guattari's passive vitalism, genders, kinds and stereotypes are not categories imposed upon life that might be overcome or criticized in the name of a universal and self-aware humanity; instead, it is life as a multiple and differentiating field of powers that expresses itself in various manners. Differentiation is not a false distinction imposed on an otherwise universal humanity. On the contrary, every female is an individuated actualization of a genetic potential for sexual differentiation, and every aspect of that female body—ranging from chromosomal and hormonal composition to the stylization of dress and comportment—is one highly individuated way of actualizing a potentiality. Deleuze and Guattari's concept of 'becoming-woman' could be read as a residual humanism in their work, as their attempt to keep some form of sexual identity in an otherwise posthuman corpus: but if they say that 'becoming-woman' is the key to all becomings, and is a 'key' insofar as it opens out towards becoming-imperceptible, then this indicates that gender is a difference that needs to be more rather than less differentiated, moving towards a 'thousand tiny sexes' (Grosz 1993). Every woman is an actualization of a potentiality to be female, while the difference between straight and gay gives further specification or distinction, and this would continue on and on to the smallest of differences, marking out not only each body, but also all the events, souls and affections within bodies. There is, then, no opposition between sexual difference and queerness. And it is not the case that one would see a contradiction between affirming sexual difference, and also acknowledging that difference goes well beyond its human form. (Elizabeth Grosz's position is perhaps the clearest form of this, at first puzzling, account of difference: it is at one and the same time legitimate to affirm the distinction of two sexes, *and* to argue for a sexual difference beyond humans and beyond binaries [Grosz 2011]). It is not the case that causes, such as feminism that would aim to affirm the possibility of women's becoming would—as gender differentiated—be opposed to movements of queerness that would strive to liberate bodies from gender norms. The key to Deleuze's passive vitalism and the aesthetics that it mobilizes lies in thinking difference beyond the kinds and generalizations of a politics of active vitalism. Whereas active vitalism would seek to return political processes to the will, intent and agency of individuals or subjects, passive vitalism is micro-political: it attends to those differences that we neither intend, nor perceive, nor command.

Again, to return to a seeming tension between queer politics and gender politics, we might consider movements of trans-sexualism, cross-dressing and the politics of sexualities. On an active vitalist model the very identification of oneself as, say, 'woman' or 'queer' would be internally contradictory (even if politically radical or strategic). In order to achieve political recognition I must at once be recognized as this or that being participating in some movement of identifiable collective will, but I must also realize that the demand for recognition by way of the normative matrix compromises my claim as a subject. The vital, on this model, is the spirit or subjective act that is always belied or compromised by actuality. It follows, then, that there would be a conflict between the vitality of political claims and the intrinsic compromise of political actuality. It also follows that those selves who would embrace certain kinds or distinctions—men who want to be regarded as naturally homosexual, women who want to be recognized as masculine, and bodies who regard their individuation as possible only outside or beyond gay, lesbian or gendered kinds—would have competing and exclusive political agendas.

What is presupposed is a distinction between the active enunciating self of politics—the active subject whose claims must be heard in opposition to normativity—and the enunciated or represented individual defined by sex, gender, sexuality or other terms such as race, ethnicity or belief. Such an opposition is captured in what Gayatri Spivak refers to as strategic essentialism: on the one hand we acknowledge that politics requires kinds or essences, but we also see such terms as the effect of strategies, or activist decisions made for the sake of political efficacy. Such a term creates an ongoing problem and contradiction for any political movement that undertakes an overthrow or revolution in terms of transgression, for acting in the name of a subordinated term must begin from the already determined and subordinated field of positions. Catherine Malabou has recently stated this problem in the following form: 'the feminine' provides a thought of difference beyond the simple generalizing logic of man and generic humanity, and yet—because of this—one would not want to align 'the feminine' exclusively or exhaustively to actual biological women (Malabou 2009). But what if there were a virtual and fully real femininity that expressed or actualized itself in woman, and that accounted for the biological and actual difference between men and women, but was not exhausted by that binary, allowing all the mutations, variations, differences and becomings among (and beyond) women? The thought of passive vitalism, or a vitality that exceeds bodies and their actions means that we can at once recognize difference among the actual entities of this world, acknowledging that these terms organize a broader potentiality that could also positively have yielded a different (but not just any) plane.

The same problems and tensions apply to the tired dialectic between philosophies of rights on the one hand, and multicultural and racial political claims of difference on the other. That is: there are those who would defend a 'subject,' universalism or radicalism opposed to all constituted identities (and would therefore reject any multiculturalisms or relativism that merely allowed competing bodies to exist alongside each other). At the same time there are those who oppose any such appeal to the subject, philosophy or critique as such insisting that one only knows the subject as this or that specified, individuated and socially determined form. In the first mode of critique that opposes actualized terms to the subject's constituting decision we could place Alain Badiou and Slavoj Žižek, both of whom insist that there is no intuitable domain of life in itself, for being is just that void that is given only in its disappearance. But for every insistence on the subject as an absent power (known ex post facto) that must be inferred as that which gives birth to the decision there are also a range of political debunkers who regard such appeals to an originating act as one more ideological obfuscation or mysticism: all we have is an actual political field of determined bodies, always already given in terms of race, sex and gender. It is no surprise, perhaps, that today a series of 'philosophers' berate the ways in which multiculturalism (or the claim for difference) precludes an ethics of decision and the subject. For Alain Badiou subject events occur not through processes of inclusion and the allowance of any lifestyle whatever, but through acts that decide—with no prior justification in actuality—that a new situation has occurred; subjects are nothing other than such decisions (Badiou 2001). The entire possibility of ethics is not grounded on life and actuality, but on a subjective decision or break. Badiou's ethics of the subject is ostensibly an anti-vitalism, insistently opposed to the grounding of political claims on some already existing actualization of being or life. But it is just the vibrancy of the subject's difference from the world as already actualized, the radical distinction of the subject as negation of an already lived order that places Badiou in stark contrast both with the undifferentiated and generalizing inclusiveness of a weak multiculturalism that would seemingly appeal to differences among individuals, and the passive vitalism of Deleuze and Guattari who would regard the subject of identity politics and activism as not yet fully individuated. Far from seeing the subjective event as occurring in a break with the world of differences, as Badiou would do, and in a manner that is quite distinct from regarding the profusion of different cultures and bodies as the very force of life, Deleuze and Guattari put forward a vitalism that is neither that of the decision nor of the differentiated body. Their vitalism is passive in its attention to the barely discerned, confused and queer differences that compose bodies.

Deleuze and Guattari's insistence that there is an active vitalism that one can discern in Kant alerts us to a long-running privileging of the decision and the re-awakening of the subjective act in the face of a fall into everyday normality and normalization. Active vitalism strives to overcome the imposed norms that reduce an individual's autonomy, but also takes into account the vitality of traditions, cultures and practices that constitute bodies as individuals and agents in the first place; and form of theory that operates as a constructivism—whether it is art, language, society or culture (or Kant's categories) that gives form to the world has the same problems as active vitalism. Life, for any form of active vitalism, is equivocal: there is the forming power on one hand, and that which is formed on the other. Because of this equivocity we are granted an immediate ethics or moralism: that which is formed ought not overtake the properly forming power; we should resist any passifying captivation or enslavement to what is not ourselves, and if we do grant life and worth to what is not ourselves (others, animals, ecology) it is only to the extent that these 'others' are granted the same vivifying power. A passive vitalism, by contrast, is one of re-singularization or counter-actualization: every differentiated political claim, whether that be in the name of the human, a sexualized or gendered individual, or a racial minority may begin with a molar politics, but has the potential to become minoritarian, and it is this potentiality of queering that is 'properly' vital. This is to say that the 'property' that marks queer vitality is an impropriety; what something *is* resides in its magnitude of deviation. We might say that becoming-woman is a queer predicate because it would be the capacity of what counts as 'woman' to enter into variation: it makes sense to have a category such as 'becoming-woman' because in addition to all the actual instances of women, one can imagine more and more difference and mutation. Marilyn Monroe was a successful icon, not because there could be Marilyn Monroe impersonators but because there could be a Madonna or a Lady Ga Ga (who repeated the Marilyn-effect, the power to make a difference in a style of becoming).

Individuation

Both vitality and queerness are crucial to Deleuze's philosophy of individuation. First, vitality: a body is identifiable or individuated not because it takes the undifferentiated potentiality of life and then subjects itself to a norm. It is not the case, as Judith Butler would have it, that in the beginning is a radically undifferentiated becoming that can become an autonomous being only by being recognized as this or that generality in some social matrix (Butler 2005). Butler's notion of the performative self is directly opposed to a simple active vitalism: there is no grounding and pre-social 'sex' which is then represented in language or signification. There is no subject or proper self who then acts and speaks; instead, in the beginning is the act or performance from which we conclude or posit that there must have been a pre-linguistic subject. Sex, then, is not some materiality or ground that issues in or is belied by gender; for it is only through gender that we can conclude that there must have been some instituting act. Further, and more importantly for Butler, genders or social norms cannot simply be removed or destroyed in order to reveal the true and real subject; a subject exists and has being only insofar as it is performed as a relatively stable and recognized social kind. And if the self is constituted as recognized then it requires some reference to the heterosexual matrix of normativity, even if it marks its own being as a negation, mourning or refusal of that matrix. For Butler, then, social differences are at once the means through which subjects are constituted as recognizable performing, speaking and acting selves; at the same time as the subject is also a potentiality for destabilization or unsure repetition of the normativity that is its founding condition. Queerness then lies in the difference between performance and performed; the social differences we recognize would be stabilizations or reifications of a performative power that is nothing other than the capacity to destabilize differentiated kinds:

> In this sense, if vulnerability is one precondition for humanization, and humanization takes place differently through variable norms of recognition, then it follows that vulnerability is fundamentally dependent on existing norms of recognition if it is to be attributed to any human subject.
>
> So when we say that every infant is surely vulnerable, that is clearly true, in part, precisely because our utterance enacts the very recognition of vulnerability and so shows the importance of recognition itself for sustaining vulnerability. We perform the recognition by making the claim, and that is surely a very good reason to make the claim. We make the claim, however, precisely because it is not taken for granted, precisely because it is not, in every instance, honored. Vulnerability takes on

another meaning at the moment it is recognized, and recognition wields the power to reconstitute vulnerability. We cannot posit this vulnerability prior to recognition without performing the very thesis that we oppose (our positing is itself a form of recognition and so manifests the constitutive power of the discourse). This framework, by which norms of recognition are essential to the constitution of vulnerability as a precondition of the 'human,' is important precisely for this reason, namely, that we need and want those norms to be in place, that we struggle for their establishment, and we value their continuing and expanded operation. (Butler 2006, 43)

Difference, then, is negative (Butler 2004A, 198): both the difference between kinds, and the difference from social kinds; but there is no difference in itself as some intuitable power.

When Deleuze argues for a mode of passive vitalism he insists that life tends towards difference, creating further and further distinctions. This is so much the case that he follows Leibniz in seeing the world as composed of souls that descend infinitely. My body is a soul or monad because it is capable of perceiving and being affected in an absolutely singular manner: no other body has the same unfolding of time and space, the same perceptions and affections as mine. And within this body are a thousand other souls: a heart that will beat according to all the hormonal, nutritional, climactic and nervous perceptions it endures (and so on with every organ, and so on with every organ's cells, and so on with every microbiological event). Far from a body being individuated through subjection to norms, a body is absolutely individuated above and beyond (or before) any of the generalizing norms that the laziness of common sense applies. This vitality is therefore essentially queer. The task of thinking is not to see bodies in their general recognizable form, as this or that ongoing and unified entity, but to approach the world as the unfolding of events. Take an encounter between two bodies: you, a straight man, consider your sexuality to be properly vital, contributing as it does to heterosexual reproduction. I, however, as a lesbian female regard my sexuality as properly vital: not subjected to rigidifying norms of biological reproduction, I am capable of creating myself in ways far more imaginative and varied than any social norm might dictate. The dispute between two such bodies would concern a proper image of life (as biologically reproductive, or imaginatively productive) and would be disjunctive: either I answer to the norms of social reproduction as they exist, or I create other norms and ideals. And one could go on adding other bodies to this terrain: I might be a gay man, assured that my homosexuality is genetically determined, or a trans-gendered individual considering myself to be capable of living a gender while maintaining a sex. One could see such a dispute as devolving upon just how we determined the relation between life and norms: either we regard life as having a genetic reality that would determine sex regardless of social performance, or would see social performance as the determining and decisive force that makes possible any individual body. Determining sexual political disputes in this way—as rejecting the norm of the heterosexual nuclear family but doing so in favor of some more radical determining force—merely substitutes one normative image of life (familial, productive) for another (genetic, socially constructed, performatively constituted). Either life is and ought to be oriented to reproduction, or life is capable of variation, or there are genetic determinants that preclude a realm of pure decision.

What such a way of thinking depends upon is what Deleuze and Guattari (1983) diagnosed as an exclusive use of the disjunctive synthesis: *either* one subjects one's desire to social norms *or* one falls back into the dark night of the undifferentiated. They opposed this transcendent, exclusive and illegitimate use to their own immanent, inclusive and vitalist disjunctive synthesis. Here the relations between terms are neither exclusive (either male or female, either social/political or genetic, either real or constructed) nor transcendent (where such terms organize and differentiate life, and do so on the basis of some grounding value, whether that be genetics, reproduction, liberty or the human). That is to say, we could argue that queer politics in one of its dominant forms remains committed to a transcendent and disjunctive use of the synthesis and is therefore profoundly Oedipal: either you recognize yourself as a being within the familial order of male-female or you risk falling into psychosis. It is the family as the basic unit that also relies on an active vitalism: in order to become individuated 'we' must recognize ourselves as part of a symbolic order, for we have no self or being outside the human and self-governing world of father-mother-child, and political action must proceed from a desire that begins, initially, from a relation between self and other that can then open onto a broader political field of historical, racial and social forces. Judith Butler, for example, reads Antigone's rebellion against the State as at once familial, negative and activist: the very possibility of making a claim, of speaking and being heard, requires that Antigone be situated as a sister and daughter, but it is just that positioning that is rendered negative, impossible and activist by Antigone's speaking for the claims of her brother. She at once speaks as a familial subject, dutifully promising to bury her brother, while also negating or perverting that subjectivity, by speaking against her father who would refuse her that sibling bond: 'If kinship is the precondition of the human, then Antigone is the occasion for a new field of the human, achieved through political catachresis, the one that happens when the less than human speaks as human, when gender is displaced, and kinship founders on its own founding laws' (Butler 2000, 82). One could extrapolate from here, as Butler does, to the structure of political speech in general: in order to speak and be recognized I must be situated in a social body, but 'I' have being only in my negation or queering of that recognized normativity. The subject is active when it takes up, and then destabilizes or negates, a norm that is at once its condition for being and its condition for not being. To be is to be disobedient, acting and speaking only within the frame of a presupposed obedience against which one is defined:

> The claiming becomes an act that reiterates the act it affirms, extending the act of insubordination by performing its avowal in language. This avowal, paradoxically, requires a sacrifice of autonomy at the very moment in which it is performed: she asserts herself through appropriating the voice of the other, the one to whom she is opposed; thus her autonomy is gained through the appropriation of the authoritative voice of the one she resists, an appropriation that has within it traces of a simultaneous refusal and assimilation of that very authority. (Butler 2000, 11)

Like Freud, Butler's conditioning matrix of obedience or subjection is familial (even though she uses the ambivalence of one's familial relations to argue for a necessary mourning and melancholia in one's object choice); to take on a gendered body as one's object choice both creates one's own sexuality in relation to an other, and entails a renunciation of other gendered and sexual potentials.

For Butler the socio-political world extends from the initial coordinates of the family. Deleuze and Guattari reverse this order; the Oedipal family is not the frame from which the self moves out into the political world, and the political world is not sexualized on the basis of the family (the king or president is not a father figure). Rather, there is an initial collectively sexual field, a group investment in a body—such as the despot who terrorizes the social field through public displays of sexual excess and consumption—and from that broad sexual field there is a gradual contraction to the modern nuclear family, the father coming to stand in for the larger historical figures of history. The gender binary, considered in terms of the young child either lining up on the male or female side of the divide, is not a differentiation of a pre-Oedipal indifference, but the diminution of far more complex differences: how did all the complex figures of race, history, myth, spectacle and politics come to be contracted onto the either/or of the male father or female mother? Deleuze and Guattari insist on a schizoanalysis that sees the family as a stimulus for historical political coordinates, and sees the 'global persons' of the family as possible only through a process of historical, political and racial contraction. The father is not the basis from which the political figure of the king, the despot or the dictator is extrapolated; on the contrary, it is only possible for us today to understand ourselves as individuated through our relations to our mothers and fathers because an entire history of domination has increasingly displaced its complex, political and collective desires onto private familial images.

Micropolitics

For Deleuze and Guattari, schizoanalysis reverses this process: we need to see the ways in which our seemingly familial and Oedipal conditions—the child constituted as a gendered individual in a family dynamic—is a compression of historical and political forces. In practice this would require opening any relation among bodies to the historical, political, 'micro' and vital (or infinitely small) potentials from which they are composed. The attention shifts from persons and norms, to the thousands of souls from which we are effected. So, the heterosexual man who defends his being on the basis of reproductive norms only lives and feels this normativity because his body is composed of passions, affections and orientations which it is the task of Deleuze and Guattari's 'schizoanalysis' to break into its various components. We would need to analyze the composition of each of 'man's' defining souls: images of the nuclear family, which have a figurative (Christian, bourgeois, popular science) dimension; notions of life which are also inflected by theology ('be fruitful and multiply'); political discourses (the family as economic unit); and racial notions of man as the rational, democratic and white individual towards which all human civilization is 'progressing.' In order to form some notion of 'the human' one needs to take all the capacities for genetic variation and assume some underlying unity. This 'man in general,' according to Deleuze and Guattari is achieved historically and politically by unifying complex differences into some single figure. The same applies to 'woman,' 'lesbian,' 'trans-sexual' or—in some cases—'queer.' If the latter term denotes a group of bodies who seek recognition on the basis of their relation to, or difference from, other bodies then 'queer' forms a majoritarian mode of politics: a political force that reduces difference for the sake of creating a political subject group. If, however, 'queer' were to operate vitally it would aim to signal the positive potentialities from which groups were formed: there could only be lesbian women because certain differences are possible (such as sexual difference, and difference in orientation), but that would then lead to further and further difference, not only to each individual but within each individual.

Minoritarian politics moves in the opposite direction from recognition and aims to maximize the circumstances for the proliferation and pulverization of differences. In terms of policy and representation this would have concrete consequences: one would not strive to attain a representative polity—include more women and gays in parliament—but would see politics not as representation (of women's issues, gay rights, minority values), but as mobilization. What processes could operate in the absence of any ideal image, figure or grouping of human normativity?

As a concrete example, we might look at reproductive rights, and the question of whether same sex couples should be allowed access to IVF or other forms of assisted reproduction technologies. One way of approaching this would be through rights, access and—perhaps—broadening notions of what counts as a family. Such an approach could also take into account pragmatic considerations about distribution of resources, the quality of life for children of same-sex couples given the prevailing norms, and might also have to deal with the competing rights of religious and ethnic groups. 'Queer' in this context would count as one variable among others, and questions of life would be considered in terms of relations among persons: how do we compare and negotiate the competing demands for, and quality of, various notions of what counts as a good life? How do we balance the claims of one group—those bodies who affirm their right to be queer—with another, such as those Christian agencies who have requested exemption from equal opportunity law when it comes to dealing with adoption by gay couples? How do spiritual rights compete with sexual rights? Such questions and problems negotiate interests, already constituted political positions that mark out and, according to Butler, enable political agency. By contrast, a Deleuzo-Guattarian approach would consider life beyond the concept of the person, and would therefore define its vitalism as queer, as having to do with all those potential differences that exceed and infinitely divide each body. Desire, Deleuze and Guattari insist, is both pre-personal and necessarily revolutionary; so one would take any political interest such as the demand by a gay couple for a child, and then look at its multiple constituting desires. These may be in part revolutionary—a destruction of the family unit as the sole site for reproduction, a refusal of the norms of social recognition, and even an affirmation of life beyond one's own body—but also in part reactionary, in the desire for inclusion in the social field as it currently is, in the maintenance of the family, now as a sexually diverse unit of social production, and in the racial commitment to one's own kind. Desire is essentially revolutionary precisely because it is the force from which social relations emerge; even if all social forms emerge from desire, desire also exceeds the systems that it has generated. We may have a fascist body politic because desire has been captivated by the body of the leader, but those same desires—*as desiring*—are not exhausted by the body they have invested. Even when desires are reactionary—such as the racial deliriums that underpin the manifest political interest of having a child of one's own—they are nevertheless distinct from the social machine that takes up those desires into its own workings. To say, as Deleuze and Guattari do, that we are composed of a thousand tiny sexes is to place race, politics, history and sexuality within, not between or among, individuals. Any body's desire, and therefore its relation to other bodies' desires, is composed of multiple and divergent series. My relation to other sexes may have familial determining points; one might relate to something like 'masculinity' through the image one has of one's father. But every father, in turn, presents a certain racial, economic, political and sexual complex. The father who comes home complaining about all the migrants who have taken away his employment, all the single mothers who are destroying the welfare system, who then treats his successful upwardly mobile son with resentment, while fearing his daughter's relation with her black schoolmate gives the child an entire racial-cultural-economic field through which sexuality is negotiated.

There is no such thing as 'a' life, or if there is it is sub-individual for we are composed of many lives; and a vitalist queer politics is a micro-politics that negotiates the multiple affections and attachments that compose any field. We would have to add to any consideration of same-sex couples and reproductive rights a critical approach to family as such: questioning the prima facie value of a child of one's own, of family units, of reproductive medicine as a form of bio-capital. The same would apply to any issue of queer politics, which ought not be considered as a negotiation among competing political groupings, nor as a 'pragmatic' relation between the necessary accession to norms and the desire for autonomy.

Micropolitics is a form of pragmatism insofar as it focuses on life, but this is a life of passive vitalism where we attend to all the minor, less than human, not yet personalized desires that enter any field of social relations. Desire is not, as it is in the Kantian tradition, the capacity for an individual to bring what is not already actual into being; desire is pre-individual. It is because there are desires—pre-human desires, such as the genetic, political, social, biological, metabolic and fantasmatic forces that enter into relation—that individuals are formed (and this includes individual humans, as well as individual social systems.) A post-Kantian form of pragmatism would negotiate the social field accord to competing desires and interests of individuals: on the one hand we recognize social groups by granting rights (such as marriage or reproductive rights to same-sex couples); but on the other hand, we negotiate the contingency and force of the rights tradition, or the ways in which Western conceptions of rights enable political and colonial hegemony. If pragmatism refers questions of truth and right back to the life that is maximized and enabled, the pragmatism of micro-politics considers the lives of which we are composed. This different passive form of pragmatism would not refer claims back to competing interests but would de-compose claims, looking at the forces from which they are composed: how is desiring a child or a marriage possible, what social, political, sexual, fictional, genetic, institutional forces do marriage and reproduction entail. We would need to take something as general and majoritarian as the right to reproduction and look at the desires from which it is composed, some of which would be 'sad' or reactive (my desire to be like every other normal family, and which diminish my power by referring my body to what it is not yet and may never be); but other components would be joyful (if I imagined an other life as creating potentialities beyond my own imagination, perhaps also compelling me to feel different affects beyond those of autonomy and self-management). Every body is queer, not because there is no body that actually attains the ideal embodied in any norm (say, where there is no woman who fulfills the figure of 'woman'); rather the queerness is positive. No body fully knows its own powers, and can only become joyful (or live) not by attaining the ideal it has of itself—being who I really am—but by maximizing those potentialities in ourselves which exceed the majoritarian, or which are not yet actualized. Counter-actualization or re-singularization takes bodies as they are, with their identifying and determining features, and then asks how the potentials that enabled those features might be expanded. If I identify myself as having a certain gender or sexuality then I can either regard this (in active vitalism) as a form of strategic essentialism, where I decide to adopt an identity for the sake of political efficacy while remaining aware that who I am as a subject is radically different from any identifying term; or (as in passive vitalism) I would recognize that gender, sex and other defining features emanate from histories, passions and relations that I have not lived but which might be retrieved:

> For if every individual is distinguished from all others by its primary singularities, the latter fall short of extending themselves as far as the primary singularities of other individuals, according to a spatiotemporal order that makes the 'subdivision' of an individual be continued into the nearest subdivision and then into the subdivision following that, all the way up to infinity. The comparative extension and intensity of these subdivisions—favored zones that belong to each monad—even allow species of monads or souls to be divided into vegetal, animal, human or angelic traits, 'an infinity of degrees in the monads' in continuity. (Deleuze 75)

From the position of passive vitalism one would need to look at the composition of bodies as themselves encounters. Deleuze's book on Leibniz cites a seemingly politically and sexually neutral example:

> I hesitate between staying home or going out to a nightclub: these are not two separable objects, but two orientations, each of which carries a sum of possible or even hallucinatory perceptions (not only of drinking but the noise and smoke of the bar; not only of working but the hum of the word processor and the surrounding silence...). And if we return to motives in order to study them for a second time, they have not stayed the same. Like the weight on as scale, they have gone up or down. The scale has changed according to the amplitude of the pendulum. The voluntary act is free because the free act is what expresses the entire soul at a given moment of its duration. (Deleuze 2006, 79)

A body at a desk is at once composed of inclinations towards a drink in a club (anticipating the hum of the surrounds, the coolness of the drink, the conviviality of the atmosphere) competing with the desire to continue writing (the anticipated sense of a job done, the interest in solving a problem). What is required in such a situation is a 'differential calculus' for it will always be the smallest imperceptible inclinations that lead to a decision one way or the other. The same idea can be extended politically. Our sympathies, affects, desires and acceptances as social and political beings are composed of micro-perceptions that barely come to awareness. It is true that for the most part our desires follow the paths of least resistance, perhaps accepting what has always been deemed to be acceptable; but at some point the souls rise up: cortisol and seratonin levels rise and suddenly Rosa Parks refuses to sit at the back of the bus. What had been actual and what had been 'our' world is no longer all that one perceives or is affected by. One of the key ways in which Deleuze and Guattari see such counter-actualization coming into being is through art.

The Aesthetics of Vitalism

In many ways the link between art, vitalism and political renewal is rather tired and seems to run directly against everything that might be revolutionary in Deleuze and Guattari's political theory. Particularly dominant in the broad understanding of Romanticism and modernism, vitalism appealed to a life force that would be capable of destroying or enlivening the reified categories of the understanding. Vitalism, in its Romantic and modernist modes was also an appeal to various forms of defamiliarization and impersonality. That is to say, for the purposes of everyday efficiency and action we cannot afford to live the intensity and complexity of life, and so we create concepts and languages to manage and diminish the forceful chaos of existence. Art, however, by using language or figures in unfamiliar or unworkable combinations can reawaken us to the creative force from which such systems emerged. In its Romantic form vitalism was active and subjective: whereas everyday understanding reduces us to being so many socio-political and atomized individuals, the work of art intimates a creative power or genius that is given only after the effect, intimating the subject who must have been the author of a synthesis. This was how Kant described beauty in nature, where the delight in form prompts us to posit some notion of design, even if that creating power is felt reflectively, rather than known. The work's harmonious order enables me to feel the concord between me as peceiving subject, and world perceived; reflecting on that feeling of order I recognize myself as one who does not merely (or passively) receive the world. I also feel myself as a world-forming power. This self that I feel is not my worldly bodily or identified self; it is the *subject* though whom all worldly forms are given. In modernism, the vital power that was reawakened by art was achieved through impersonality, with the work of art suggesting a creative spirit behind the created form—a spirit given only in its not appearing. Modernist uses of language, for example, broke with standard and easily consumed modes of syntax, and by the breaking of forms forced art consumers to create and order the received material, once again experiencing language and art as created rather than simply given. Such high modernist or Romantic modes of defamiliarization and renewal that would reawaken the creative force from which our lived world has been synthesized are essentially normalizing insofar as they refer back to the subjective or grounding conditions from which works must have emerged. These conditions can be retrieved, recognized and re-lived as our own. The human in general, or the transcendental subject, is just that spirit or power that must be felt, but not known, above and beyond any work of genius.

By contrast, Deleuze insists on real and immanent conditions, and also on the virtual or vital, not as an active underlying ground but as a 'swarm' or chaos that, far from grounding or returning life to its animating power, deterritorializes life beyond any of the seemingly proper forms that we know. What I hope to demonstrate is that vitalism in its active form has dominated general concepts of the aesthetic at least since Kant. This active form of vitalism, which refers systems and identities back to a constituting power, is also highly normative: life has a proper trajectory towards fruition and the realization of its proper form; art is the process whereby deviations, failures or corruptions of the vital power may be retrieved and re-lived. Deleuze and Guattari's passive vitalism, by contrast, challenges the idea of a single, unifying, productive and fertile life force whose proper trajectory is fruition, expansion and revelation. In a number of contexts Deleuze describes the deterritorializing vitality of life as 'sterile,' 'divergent,' 'self-enjoying,' and 'surveying.' That is, the vital is not that which springs forth from itself to synthesize, unify and produce its world; it is receptive in its feeling of that which is not itself, often yielding nothing more than the isolated or punctuated affect of encounter.

To summarize so far: there are two ways in which we might think about vitalism and personality, both of which involve dissolution. First, in the tradition of active vitalism personality is that which remains the same through time, allows us to be recognized as this or that individual being and which also (*as socially enabling*) is existentially or virtually disabling.

I become human by subjecting myself to the system of recognition, but that same system belies my unique individuality. Personality, or recognizing oneself as human, is required and enabled by seeing oneself as an instance of humanity in general, but this requires a certain sacrifice or even mourning for one's singularity or specificity. Kant insists that one must have a sense of one's phenomenal personality but must also recognize a free noumenal, supersensible and moral personality that we cannot know or perceive but can only think after the event of decision. In contemporary discourses of the subject, such as Judith Butler's, there is a similar 'ex post facto' logic of the subject—it is, as Deleuze and Guattari define active vitalism, a subject that acts but 'is not.' For Butler, one must subject oneself to enabling and recognizable norms. To be recognized by, and with, others requires some determined personality. But those necessary norms and figures of personhood are at odds with the act, performance or event that brings them into being. On this account, personhood comes into being through moments or decisions that are perceived only after the event as the outcome of a performance that must be posited as having been. We do not see, live or intuit performativity itself, only its effects. A politics and revitalizing imperative follows: do not be seduced by normativity. Recognize that the self who is performed and recognized is at odds with the less stable—one might say 'queer'—vital self who acts (who 'acts but is not').

I would suggest that this form of active vitalism, as critique and negation of norm, image, figure or stereotype is not only the dominant in theory, but also characterizes most of the approaches to selfhood in popular culture and public policy. That is, there is today a widespread suspicion regarding the passive reception or incorporation of images; indeed, we might even say that capitalism is just a continuous production of 'images,' a constant destruction of any definitive, transcendent or external quality in favor of an incessant process of newly consumable images. One is always defined, on the one hand, as either male or female, while also experiencing oneself as that consuming subject who is neither male, nor female: a unique subject as point of consumption. Against that negation of the image we could posit Deleuze and Guattari's positive use of the conjunctive synthesis: I am girl and woman and lesbian and masculine and effeminate and ...; here the self is not some radical alterity before and beyond images but a potentiality to include, transform and vary all the races, sexes and peoples of history.

In its active vitalist form the self is always, ideally, a purely formal principle of decision irreducible to any image. The good citizen is not seduced by rigid norms, does not passively allow himself to be imprinted by pre-given figures, and relates to social and representational systems critically. In policy, for example, governments increasingly express concern regarding negative and pernicious images, whether these concern the representation of the acceptability of certain practices—binge drinking, smoking, the sexualization of children—or the direct war on life-impeding images, or the image as life-impeding per se. In the UK, the Body Image Summit of 2000 sought to police the overly stringent body ideals imposed upon girls and women; this summit led to later campaigns to ban the promulgation of overly thin or 'size zero' models. The assumption that an image or model is a norm, or an image of what the viewer ought to be, is unquestioned; such an assumption relies upon a definition of the self as at one and the same time determined by the consumption of images, while properly being other than the generality of the image. Only if the representational and normative sphere is *achievable* by the bodies it organizes will we have a healthy body politic. If the model, ideal or imaged persona is radically at odds with actual bodies then individuals either diminish their own being through submission and subjection or are not recognized as subjects at all.

What has been lost is the fictive, virtual or incorporeal power of the image: is it not possible to see a body of 'heroin chic,' of androgynous subtlety, or even childlike frailty not as an ideal self, but as ideals that float freely from actual bodies, varying the imaginative range of what counts as human. Would the problem then be not that body-images are insufficiently normal—not like real women—but are insufficiently queer, too close to actuality? One might imagine a higher degree of inclusion and disjunction, with more bodies that are increasingly less realistic, yielding more of a sense of the model or image as image/model, not as some active representation of a life that must know and recognize itself and always remain in command of the production of affects. The war on reified and passively-ingested images leads to, and presupposes, a vitalist ethical imperative that would aim to re-awaken the sense of the produced status of the image: one ought not regard any actuality—be that the heterosexual matrix or humanity in general—as a final or essential form. (Indeed there are no essences, only existence.) The true self is not the subject who is recognized so much as the act, performance, decision or 'lived' that is other than (although only known through and after) the norms which give it being.

If this form of active vitalism demands a becoming-impersonal it does so only in recognizing that while we may require personality to live and speak socially and politically, we are always irreducible to (and other than) such ideals. This mode of active vitalism has specific consequences for activist politics, and results in a certain style of problem: where there is always an 'on the one hand / on the other hand' structure. The very notion of 'queer' is always a queering of some norm: on the one hand I say 'no' to normativity, while on the other hand I demand recognition from the very matrix of recognition whose system allows me to speak. This structure of compromise (or negation and recognition) also plays out in concrete issues: are demands for civil partnership (for example) ways of enlivening social bonds, or are such appeals for inclusion negations of one's non-heterosexual status? Do movements of sexual or gender re-orientation inject an instability or performativity into the norms of male and female, or are we not seduced too easily into already defined gender roles? Such problems concern the degree of act in relation to the image: is our relation to the norm properly productive (introducing or exposing a potential deviation or queerness) or are we not, in remaining activist at the level of sex/gender/sexuality passively obedient to already constituted categories? Such a structure is theorized by Butler as a necessary acceptance of recognition and submission, alongside an instability or excitability internal to those very normalizing procedures. But such structures are not unique to queer theory (a fact which should give us pause for thought: for Alain Badiou a subject is just this decision or event who breaks from an enumerated scene to institute a new mode of numeration. For Slavoj Žižek the subject is an impossible, barred, excluded and negative remainder that occurs in the failure of any image or object to capture desire.) By contrast, as I have already suggested, the Deleuzo-Guattarian approach differs in its very style of problem, which is not to interrogate the relation between body and norm according to the appropriate degree of its vitality (whether the relation really issues from a proper force of decision or is not further subjection). Instead of seeing the self in relation to perceived norms (a self which is defined as other than any of its perceptions), Deleuze and Deleuze and Guattari make two key interventions.

First, for Deleuze there are not bodies, selves or subjects who perceive, for the self is composed of perceptions, each of which *is* its imaging of other perceiving souls: the heart has its life by responding to the hormones, rhythms, flows and movements that create it as a point of view, while the body is at once a perception of all those barely perceived durations within, and the affectations that it encounters without. Instead of subject-norm relations, we deal with multiplicities and singular points: networks of perception and imagination that create points of view, and that can—at singular points—produce entirely different relations and configurations. Second, once bodies—all bodies—are no longer bodies with organs (the eye that sees in order to negotiate a world mastered by the hand, relating to other subjects through the voice of reason), we can take the image beyond organic and centered thinking to look at the power of micro-perceptions: not just the domain of body-images and imposed norms, but all those barely discerned perceptions that compose all images, and that exist and insist beyond the human.

Notes

1. In *Difference and Repetition*, Deleuze argues that there is a radical potential in Platonism—where Ideas are pure potentialities from which differentiated beings are actualized—that is lost in Aristotle's criticism of Platonism. For Aristotle, rather than Ideas, it is categories which define each being; and these categories are referred back to a (human or at least subject's) good sense and common sense that identifies common and repeatable features (Deleuze 1994).

Chapter 6

Difference, Time and Organic Extinction

How, today, might the question of time and sexual difference be articulated? It might appear, at first, as though the mode of this question has always been sexual (or at least gendered) and that this engendering of the question of time has impeded any fruitful understanding: time has been regarded either as the time taken for forms to come into being and pass away (a pre-modern Aristotelian notion) or time is the neutral abstract 'container' within which changes occur (modern Cartesian time) (Deleuze, 2005, 4). In both cases, one could argue that time has been conceived organically and anthropomorphically. Either the world is composed of proper forms that will take time to unfold: the earth would be one bounded whole, reaching fulfillment through time, with time as a delay in the realization of an end, while 'man' would be that being blessed with reason capable of intuiting the forms of time. Man is not only a historical animal; he also forms himself through time, becoming the being who he is by having a conception of his life as a whole, as a self-formed narrative. Or, on the modern conception of time, there is one general substance in extended space, and time measures the movement from any one point to another. Time is the series of equivalent 'nows' and man, no longer analogous to (or a lesser form of) a God who sees the reason of the world, charts movements from a point of view that is purely calculative. This is the modern, formal, linear time of equivalence.

Such a modern understanding of time as the abstract container within which movement takes place, where time is a general substrate that is not man's own, marks a certain understanding of human sexuality and sexuality as human. 'Man' is a being whose sense is determined by a general temporality of life: because he is a historical animal, going through the time of evolution, cultural developments and linguistic formations, his being in the present bears a density that is not immediately transparent to his own intentionality (Foucault, 2002, 139). It is this conception of a general time of life that enables the modern motif of sexuality, where my present sense of self emerges both from the evolution of human sexuality in general, and then the formation and self-narration of ourselves as familial; on one conception at least, contemporary time is therapeutic. Only if I understand the sense of my emergence will I be able to take command of my future. For psychoanalysis, this meant that there would be the sense of a lost (maternal) plenitude that the subject would be able to read within himself. All our objects of desire would be substitutes for a constitutive loss that follows from being human, from being thrown into a life, history, language and Oedipal scene that is never one's own. Woman would figure as the lost pre-linguistic origin, an origin that can only be fantasized, ex post facto, as that which must have been abandoned in order for man to enter a communal, rational history (Brennan 1993).

Even if we no longer hold to such psychoanalytic mythographies, it is possible to discern this gendered figuration of time today in various critical reactions to man's own modernity: in the Gaia hypothesis of James Lovelock, for example, the Cartesian notion of the world as extended and external matter is corrected in favor of the figure of a single organism of life (Lovelock 1988). Supposedly we should overcome a modern technocratic and disenchanted conception of time, in which there will always be more earth as usable resource, and instead we should understand human life—especially creative and productive human life—as having emerged from and being in symbiotic relation with one earth conceived as 'Gaia.' Man is no longer an active (historical, temporal) subject set over against a passive and lifeless matter; there is one web of life, with all beings connected through a non-linear temporality. Time is no longer a series unfolded from some theological (humanoid) origin, nor a series mapped by man, but the real condition in which life generates life. Such an understanding of time has, for all its claims of breaking with human chauvinism, reinforced rather than annihilated the traditional humanization of time. Supposedly, if 'we' wish to live on, we need to become aware of a time—ecological, geological—beyond our own, paying our due to an existence that we failed to recognize as our own. In no movement is this more apparent than in eco-feminism. Queer theory may have remained within the Oedipal and human axes of recognition (albeit critically, with Butler (2004A, 161) arguing for self-constitution and mourning processes devolving on the face), but eco-feminism has sought to retrieve a time and spirit beyond man and calculation, beyond the human reproductive cycle of time, towards a time of a broader organic and spiritual wholeness (Warren 2000). But is extending the figure of organic time beyond human bounds—to the point where life in general becomes one unified, self-creating, auto-poetic and fruitful whole—the most thoughtful way of approaching what, with further thought, we might consider to be the question of the present? How might we, today, confront the increasingly insistent though increasingly foreclosed question of the temporal short-circuit of man's existence? In the most literal terms, the more overwhelming the evidence that human life has shortened the time of the planet, the greater the degree of denial: climate change appears to be irreversible and catastrophic, but as its seriousness increases so does its repression. More generally, as temporality discloses itself as less and less human, and less and less gendered—not following the model of man's imposition of temporal mapping on a passive nature (in the manner of subject/object, active/passive, male/female)—figures of the organic and human nature of time appear to be resurgent. One may cite here not only the already mentioned redemptive figures of life as Gaia (a goddess whose being man may now recognize for the sake of his living on), and not only the rhetoric of climate change policy that supposedly deals with the anthropogenic shortening of time by asking questions of 'sustainability,' for this rhetoric only addresses man's living on through time by adapting and mitigating his own being. In addition to these reaction formations, where the increasing sense of the inhumanity of time is reconfigured in terms of our climate, our ecology and the saving of our earth, the concept of time and becoming in its supposedly radical forms has worked to save the most anthropocentric of figures: man as the being who gives himself his own time through self-formation in which the self is nothing outside its own becoming. There has been a broad imaginary re-humanization of time in contemporary theory, concerned increasingly with the sense that any life or world we have must be considered only from the point of view of the reproductive and self-productive organism. (This retrieval of time is discerned in the return to living systems and in the emphases—following

Agamben and others—on the redemption of the political, via acts of historical memory, precisely when the polity is not the site in which conflicts take place so much as that which precludes us from thinking the very conflict of a time that takes place beyond human and organic frames.) That is, we imagine that temporal analyses will disclose to us the meaning and genesis of something like 'the political' or 'the world' as it is *for us,* and that historical genealogy will in turn place us once again in an active position of mastery and meaning. What needs to be considered, I would suggest, is a sexual time, where sexuality is taken in its non-organic and truly sexual sense, as that which drives beyond the organism's needs and figurations, and as that which opens thought beyond its own command and measure. Such a time might be *engendered,* opened from all the modes of life (organic and non-organic) that produce distinct and interconnected rhythms, but would not be *gendered,* could not be figured within the norms of man or his others. Time is essentially sexual, and sexuality is essentially temporal. Yet these two intertwined essences subvert and preclude any proper thought or thought of propriety.

The Temporality of Sexuality

What makes an event or movement sexual? The answer cannot lie in reproduction, precisely because there are non-sexual modes of reproduction (in the non-human, non-mammalian world), and human reproductive futures that may well take place outside of sexual difference (including sperm production from stem cells, cloning and the possible extinction of the Y-chromosome) (Bainbridge 2003; Sykes 2003). One of the answers to this question is Oedipal, or at least has to do with human sexuality and a mediated relation to biological reproduction. The subject occurs as a gap between organic need and a desire that is tied to the signifier or language. The attachment between infant mouth and maternal breast meets the fulfillment of organic need, or at least maintains the relative stability of biological being. The organism begins in a state of coupling, with its organic integrity assured by that which lies beyond its own bounds. It is this figure of the organism before desire, language and difference that, I will argue, already ruptures the coherence of time and sexuality, and is an effect of sexuality's retroactive time. What happens, though, when the action or connection through which organic sustenance is made breaks with, or slips away from, the aim of meeting metabolic needs? That is, the mouth attaches to the breast for organic needs, but then continues to enjoy the feel of sucking, imagining or fantasizing an object; sexuality is just this slippage from organic need (Laplanche 1976). A macro (or schizoanalytic) version of such slippage may be evidenced in the life of humanity. Man is coupled with the earth for his own survival. He nevertheless intensifies the processes of this coupling (processes of consumption, production, resource depletion and capitalization) to the point where the process itself becomes the aim: capital generation for its own sake, consumption for its own sake, production so excessive that one requires advertising to manufacture needs and gaps.

This inherently sexual nature of slippage from organic need was already theorized by Freud in his *Three Essays on the Theory of Sexuality* (1905). The sucking of the breast becomes sensual sucking—the mouth enjoying its own material dynamism, feeling itself feel, establishing a relation not to alimentary goals that fulfill an economic imperative of meeting a need that can be determined quantitatively (input of fuel for so much expended energy). Sensibility occurs for its 'own' sake, even if the very possibility of 'ownness,' the self or 'mineness,' occurs only with this sensuality. The mouth that feels itself feeling can then mark itself as locus of desire, as a zone to be felt for its own sake. It is at that moment of slippage from (or propping onto) organic need that something like temporality emerges. Strangely, it is in the uncoupling of organisms that a relation to a virtual otherness opens: mouth and breast are not connected as two parts in a single process, for each organ's connection opens its own line of pleasure. In desiring what is not actually before me or present I open towards a future, anticipating. There are always three terms, at least, in any sexual relation, for part relates to part through an anticipation that exceeds determinable quantities (Lacan 1985). What occurs in the rupture of alterity, where relations are no longer determined intrinsically (by the meeting of a metabolic deficit calculable in advance) but extrinsically, is that relations become external to terms: the production of desire and events can no longer be grounded in an originating event, or proper relation. But also, the potentiality for relations is not exhausted by the actual relation that has occurred. The organism cannot master or determine those forces it encounters, or the forces by which it is transformed. There is no longer a simple unfolding of possibilities from what an organism is (as though time were grounded in natural becoming). A non-presence, or what the organism can feel but not know and command, now marks all anticipation, all futures.

This non-presence that seems to disturb the linear time of metabolic quantities—where a deficit can be restored by the input of quantities, returning to constancy—does not arrive from without, accidentally. Freud's notion of the organism desiring a return to quiescence is the myth of the organism's own world; the figure of the organism 'dying in its own way,' finding its own path *back* to plenitude is actually a futural and desiring creation. The organism's supposed origin is the effect of a body becoming bounded in time, and then imagining that an overcoming of that binding would be some sort of return. Instead, the syncopation that enables time—the pulsation that marks out a space and distribution—exposes the illusory status of the organism. The notion of the bounded body that maintains itself by meeting its needs, going through a time that is nothing more than the time taken to restore quantities to their natural and proper equilibrium: this is a myth, the sexual-Oedipal myth of the organism. It is only after the emergence of desire, whereby the mouth effects a relation to what is not present (the feel of the breast, lips, fluid, sucking) that something like a before and after, or here and there, inner and outer, self and other, can be established. There is a production of the temporal, of anticipation, retention and maintenance, only through the sexual: it is not with elements that are fully given, actualized and existing with complete internal relations, that one is given time. If a being or entity is sufficient to itself, and if its relation to what it is not is also already fully given, then there is nothing to be played out. One can think here of a certain notion of God, for whom all future events are foreknown. And it is from the possibility of a God to whom all things are immediately and fully present that one can also consider Leibniz's monad. A monad's individuation is constituted by all predicates being fully explicated; we know what a being is if we know all the events that have befallen and will befall it, and all the relations it bears to every other monad. I am who I am because of all the encounters that make up my life, including all the events that precede and follow me. This logic of internal relations is given more specifically in the familial and Oedipal figure of the organism. The organism—as in organicist aesthetics—is a bounded whole in which each part possesses the identity it does because of its participation in a living whole, and in which the whole is not a collection of disparate atomic parts but the dynamic result of interconnected, mutually self-constituting and autopoietic relations. The whole is not composed of parts, for it is nothing more than the consequence of relations that are given only in the productive activity of each part's relation to every other. The child is therefore perhaps the perfect figure of organicist aesthetics: what Freud referred to as 'His Majesty the Baby' (Freud 1959, 49). Gazed upon by the parent as an image of utter integrity and self-enclosed completeness, the child is a world unto himself, a bounded whole—not yet corrupted, self-conscious or seduced by a world of surmise and suspicion. One always imagines and mourns this child that one must have been prior to the repressions and anticipations of adult subjection, prior to the alienation, prohibition and otherness of a world of external relations (Leclaire, 1998). This figure of the child as pure presence unto itself is crucial in the imaginary of time and sexuality. (One might also say the same about a certain figure of woman, or a certain figure of the animal: a bounded un-self-conscious whole, not yet subjected to a world of contestation, not yet exposed to an outside that is anything other than its own.)

Sexuality occurs as a slippage, gap or intrusion in organic self-presence. The child's autopoeitic and organic self-maintenance is possible only through a relation to otherness that precludes any linear temporality or economy of self-regulating equilibrium. The relation to what is not the organism's own becomes sexual through a time of disturbance and nonpresence. The mouth that sucks sensually is oriented not to the aim of restoring a need, returning to quiescence, but to a contact and touch displaced from the order of organic sustainability. The look towards the other who will meet my needs becomes one of sexual desire when the other's world is neither given nor readable (Laplanche 1999). When the organism is oriented beyond itself to the signifier—or towards that which is not determined from an internal relation of the organism's own system—then temporality is truly generated as sexual. For time is not the existence of a series, but the potentiality of relations *not given in*, and not unfolded from, the present. The organism is timeless, determining relations from itself. Sexuality is time, the exposure to the non-present, the anticipated, the deviation and potentiality of an open.

Time Is Sexuality

So far, this chapter has negotiated sexuality as a deflection from organic need and plenitude, and has considered time as a radically passive synthesis of relations determined neither by the will, nor intentionality nor a sense of the living body. But can this time of sexuality, and the sexuality of time, be approached less anthropically, less Oedipally? So much would already be implied from within the Oedipal figure of the self-contained pre-linguistic infant. The fantasy of a pure presence to self in which a being goes through time (a time of its own) is generated ex post facto from the position of submission to a time of desire in which neither the anticipated future nor the retained past is present, owned or lived. That is, the timelessness of the self-contained ego can be given only after dispersed syntheses have constituted a point of relative stability. The original, pre-Oedipal plenitude of the pre-linguistic infant is the effect, not the ground, of temporal distribution. Time in general, or what we might begin to imagine as 'time in its pure state,' can be imagined only through sexuality. But sexuality, in its radically temporal mode, can only begin to be approached beyond the human and the organic.

The time of the organism, so we are constantly reminded today, is homeostatic and autopoietic: the world is always a lived world, and the lived world is the organism's own. The living body's 'outside' is given only as the disturbance of equilibrium; its range of anticipation and retention is enabled only by the degree to which the body's needs entail projection into a future and maintenance of a past. The organism itself is the effect of syntheses that are neither centered (on life) nor oriented towards maintenance. The organism is, after all, the effect of multiple series of irreversible annihilations. Literally, carbon-based life only emerges from a radical disturbance of earlier milieux in which oxygen was toxic. At the level of thought and life, the organism's bounded unity occurs at the expense of a once pre-human openness to inorganic and inhuman rhythms. Such pulsations would be sexual. Life and time beyond 'conscious' bodies pay no heed to organic demands and identities; such an inhuman time operates through a profound erotics, if eros can be thought of as a style of coupling of potentialities that *may* pass through the striving of organisms but necessarily pulses beyond the organism's interests. Time must be inhuman—a rhythm irreducible to the syntheses enabled by 'our' sensory-motor apparatus. And this inhumanity must be sexual, creative (or creatively destructive) and productive of encounters whose forces and relations cannot be determined in advance, either by the intentionality of needs or the figures—organic, human, Oedipal, communal—that render time and desire perceptible.

Sexuality and Extinction

From the foregoing it would be possible to attribute an essentially sexual quality to extinction, and an extinguishing tendency to sexuality: sexuality occurs as deflection or deviation from replicating production, the productions of sexuality are not only discontinuous with the organisms from which they emerge but open onto the non-organic in general. Consider, in this respect, the sexuality of consumption: beyond organic needs, or even within the organism's (illusory) figuration of its needs, there exists a persistent and insistent process of ingestion that is blind to the (supposedly) proper and organizing limits of the living body. This is especially so if we consider the original proper living organism to be not the located finite human individual, but life as a whole, the organism of Gaia. The very processes that originated from the striving of organic maintenance—eating, reproducing, producing—have pushed the organism to (self-)annihilation. One should not be too quick to attribute this to a distinct death drive that would have split itself off from sexually creative processes—where the forward and progressive creativity of sexual time would be deflected towards a return to quiescence. If we are prepared to admit that sexual time is creative time—opening out beyond organic normativity—then this proliferating temporality is creative and destructive at once: creative precisely in its destruction of bounded identities and normative wholes. Gender would also have this creative and destructive ambivalence. Genders act as ideals, norms or figures that are never attuned to the individuations of bodies. The ideality of 'man' and 'woman' can be understood both as deflecting life from its organic normality, creating a disjunction between immediate existence and a received notion, and also as productive of destructive modes of consumption: the libidinal investments in the figure of man as *homo faber* have alone been responsible for ecological havoc, but so too has been the figure of woman as earth mother, carer, redemptive other or attuned body. Are not human organisms and their modes of consumption tied to rhythms and motifs that are not that of their own survival? Do not the very existence and weary persistence of genders testify to a rigid death in life, or archaism, that at once precludes a pure future, yet also inserts a perverse unpredictability?

How, then, does this barely witnessed time that is not that of the body, organism or life—but that is still creative—come to intrude on our all too organic present? We live in an era of intensely organic self-maintenance, with individuals enclosing ever more around the privacy of consumption—private video screens, personal digital music players, 'radio' stations tailored to individual play-lists, fast foods designed to meal times outside communal ritual dining and cooking, personal trainers, phones that use GPS to monitor distances that we have walked, flexible worktime and technologies no longer demanding common work spaces and rhythms and, most importantly, a dissolution of any seeming distinction between consumption and production. Our 'private' consumption of television, amusement services, sexuality and leisure—even the gender-critical industries of popular feminism, identity politics, activist movements and theory—is already a market organized around the desexualization of time. Time is ever more reterritorialized not so much on a quantifiable clock time, but on a displayed media time: nearly everything we do, consume, read and purchase can be tracked and displayed by Facebook, or other applications such as 'Goodreads,' 'Yelp' or 'Map my run', all of which broadcast our private consumptions and searches onto social media. But this re-territorialization of time onto the recognizable and generalizable individual is not confined to popular culture and marketing. Theory has, after all, been one of the industries to maintain the humanism and forward movement of time, a time of emancipation, of a maintained left, of a 'we' who will recognize justice in a time to-come. Time is rendered not profligate but profitable, not dilatory but capitalizable. This increasingly privatized, localized and autopoietic time (engineered to the body's rhythms of self-maintenance) at once intensifies a broader rhythm of creative annihilation—a dissolution of humanity to make way for what is unknown—yet isolates the organism from the intensity of inorganic life. That is, these very same privatizing technologies that fold time and consumption around the individual's bounded body, are the same technologies of individual annihilation: the brain, we are told, is becoming atrophied because of the intense and private use of screen culture (from games to reality television), just as our social networking skills—some claim—lose traction when overtaken by social media applications. It is the increasing organicism and desexualization of time—the enclosure of human perceptive life into its private bubble geared entirely to self-maintenance without profligate squandering—that will lead to the end of organic time and life.

If, however, one could think about the sexuality of time in its capacity to create syntheses and productions beyond those of organic striving, two events might follow. First, even if the organism were not to alter its spatial extensive trajectory (for it may now be too late to halt the destruction of habitable earth within an already predictable time period), there might be an intensive opening to a counter-ethics. No longer focused on an ethos of abode—a morality grounded upon where we dwell—and certainly not a logic of sustaining or rendering ourselves viable, we might ask (finally) what life is, what life might do, beyond organic self-enclosure. This would be an intensive and sexual question: intensive, because it would not take life as it actually exists and seek to extend its range (by rendering animals more human, by hoping that humans might live longer), for it would take those aspects of life that are not fully actualized—problems, questions, disturbances—and seek to maximize their force. This problem would also be sexual: not grounded upon the organism's self-recognition but extending its powers of mutation (especially those mutations that occur through unintended encounters). Second, if we alter the logic of living on, of sustaining, extending, adapting, mitigating or justifying the human as it currently is, then something like a sexual life—a life open to the forces of its own destruction—might be given a chance.

Chapter 7

Ethics of Extinction

Here is the problem: faced with extinction the human species might, finally, be presented with a genuine ethics, with a sense of what it owes to place (ethos) and to those beyond its own organic life (the future). Alternatively, it is perhaps the possibility of annihilation that once and for all destroys ethics. Certainly, if ethics is a question of *how one ought to live*, of one's sympathy for others, of an art of the self, or the creation of a virtual community, then ethics would seem to be the least appropriate and perhaps least viable of projects for today. If we consider ethics to be the problem of forming oneself then it could be argued that the arts of self-formation are reaching their limit, *and* that it was precisely this conception of the ethical—as self-production, self-maintenance, ongoing self-recognition—that precluded concern for the milieu within which that self-production was sustained. Three ethical models here, in the Anthropocene era, would require questioning, if not complete disposal. It may be the case that we could apply our philosophical models to the new problems of the twenty-first century, and that these models—like all else—would need to adapt in order to be sustainable. It may also be that the new ethical problems 'we' face (including the viability and justification of who 'we' are) would require new forms of questioning. The new form of content would require a new form of expression (Deleuze and Guattari 2004, 158). Ethical theories that presented themselves as *formal* might really operate only with the form of a human life, while ethical forms of naturalism would be limited to a certain conception of nature that would no longer be sustainable.

First, a contemporary form of Kantianism insists that insofar as I am a self I am also intrinsically structured by normativity: to act without principle would be a form of contradictory and impossible suicide. Not only can I not will to extinguish myself—for any decision I take regarding self-annihilation is already bound up with a world of others and therefore with an essential respect for the human—I can also not act without ongoing norms. Christine Korsgaard has insisted, following the refutation of the possibility of a private language, that normativity is intrinsic to language: 'The private language argument does not show that I could not have my own personal language. But it shows that I could not have a language which is in principle incommunicable to anybody else. When I make a language, I make its meanings normative for me' (Korsgaard 1996A, 138). An even stronger Kantian account of an essential normativity lies in the argument against suicide (Korsgaard 1996B, 17): destroying my own being would demonstrate a disregard for humanity as such, and would be contradictory insofar as one reasons to do away with reason. I am always already a member of the human community, and therefore cannot choose to end my life without extending that desire for extinction to all other humans. As human and capable of a free act I cannot make an exception of myself; insofar as I decide I can do so only as a being *not* determined by contingency, as a being who may act lawfully, deciding for oneself. And this necessary maintenance of oneself, as human and therefore free to will, but not free to will the end of willing, extends to the relation I bear to others and my own acts. To act now in one way and now in another—to have no sense of myself as a continuous identity—is to end oneself, is to destroy the being that I am.

Now that the human species faces its own annihilation, and does so precisely because it has remained committed absolutely to its own survival as uniquely human and blessed with a duty to live that distinguishes it from other species, quite different questions from that of *self*-maintenance, normative consistency and the necessity of living on need to be addressed.

Alternatively, if ethics is taken to be tied inextricably to ethos or habitus, then this would seem to be just the sort of ethical turn required today. If we accept, following the Aristotelian tradition, that asking how one ought to live can only make sense in relation to the others through whom we define ourselves, and through the traditions that grant those relations meaning and complexity, then the confrontation with the possible loss of all narrative continuity might at once be *the* Aristotelian question par excellence, but also a question that destroys the possibility of the ethical. On the one hand, it might be argued that what we need today is a retrieval of communal narratives, along with an awareness that the world is never mere standing resource of manipulable matter but always a world *for* this or that intentional organism. The sense of place that is so crucial to Aristotelian ethics is a place of meaning: any world, any person, any event to which I am exposed is always given *to me* in terms of my own sense of personhood. And this is so even if the event is of such a nature as to disturb or refigure what counts as a person. There has recently been a widespread return, beyond neo-Aristotelian ethics, to a phenomenological argument that there is no world in general, only a world as it exists for this or that bounded form of life. There is no milieu other than the surrounding range of perturbation that prompts a body to respond and adapt. This notion of the inescapable bounds of sense is articulated in three forms: traditional Aristotelian ethics, theories of living systems or embodied mind and various forms of Gaia hypothesis or life as a global brain. In response to a widespread sense of disaffection and disenchantment, philosophy, senses of community, or religion are now proffered as practical means that enable us to give order and sense to life; they are not exercises in truth or ways of transcending one's locus. One can consider here popularizing uses of philosophy, such as Alain de Botton (2000) and A.C. Grayling (2001) and more academic reactions against a philosophy and society diagnosed as overly technocratic. Martha Nussbaum's philosophy as therapy (Nussbaum 1994), or contemporary Western philosophy's recent embrace of eastern traditions of meditative thought (Flanagan 2011), answer the present potential loss of the world with a return to a more connected relation to one's milieu. So, whether it is the return to some sense of self-creating community in Aristotelianism, an insistence on the embodied mind's coupling with its milieu, or the recognition of the interconnectedness of all life in one global brain, this widespread attention to the human organism's thorough worldliness suffers from one over-riding problem of blindness: the world in which we will be extinct, the world that 'we' have extinguished and the world that increasingly takes on forms of distinction that we cannot directly perceive is *not* the world that has had meaning for 'us.'

Indeed, insofar as ethics relies upon something like a subject of enunciation we might say that an ethics of extinction would have to be a counter-ethics or possibly an anti-ethics (working against ethos, or the sense of locatedness of self.) It was Kant who insisted that without the possibility of attributing actions to a subject whom we would hold responsible—a subject who must be free—morality would have no sense. Freedom is a practical requirement, even if it cannot be known or intuited. And similar requirements of coherence and personification characterize other ethical models: one of the neo-Aristotelian laments, against Kantianism, is that ethics is not formal but has to do with forms of life, sympathy, and the imagination of others' worlds (MacIntyre 1984); recent work on cognitive science and the embodiment of mind has, more than any other paradigm, stressed the locatedness and concreteness of human decisions (Churchland 2011). There is, in all these emphases upon the ethical and its requirements of personhood, narration and practical engagement with the world, a reaction against theory, against the perniciously distanced, impersonal and disembodied observer. Ethics is not a question of calculation and formalization but of what to do, here, in this locale, in this world with others. Ethics is praxis, not logos. But do the problems that face 'us' today have that type of *practical* requirement?

Is the situation of extinction a problem of praxis, response and sympathy? Is it not, rather, an occasion for a mode of calculation that insists neither on the freedom and openness of a radical future irreducible to the material world nor on the communicative horizon within which all action, as some form of proto-speech, would take place? It is not only the global climactic crisis that demands forms of thinking that take account of forces beyond those of human intentionality, the same could also be said for milieux as (seemingly) human as global terror and global finance. It is not only the case that such threats posed to human existence have no single, locatable agent to whom 'we' might address certain ethical demands for justice; it is also becoming increasingly clear that there has been a catastrophic attribution of subjectivity and mastery to processes that are without located agency. Consider the recent and widespread financial crises, ranging from the global financial crisis of 2008, emanating from something as seemingly humble as a series of home mortgages, to the precipice of collapse of the European Union in 2012. On the one hand, as capitalism hurtles towards its seemingly inevitable demise, there appears to be no shortage of guilty persons: those in government who failed to regulate, those liberated from regulation who failed to exercise foresight, prudence or concern, those who blindly consumed, spent and borrowed without a sense of time or consequence and, when the crisis became all too apparent, those who maintained all the old privileges of bonuses and conspicuous spending precisely when these practices were deemed to be responsible for the widespread chaos. The same follows for climate change, worsened by large corporations answerable only to shareholders, and by governments incapable of looking beyond electoral terms. Terrorism, too, for all its figuration through certain faces and types of crowds, becomes upon examination a diffuse toxin that is exacerbated by anti-terror legislation, xenophobia, resentment caused by constant surveillance, fear of terror and the panic it causes, and the fear of the panic that the fear of terror causes. How would one respond to this ethically? Is there a 'one' who, in the traditional terms of ethics is called upon to respond? One might say that we are given a hyperbolic ethical situation: it is precisely because we are at a point of extinction with the stakes not being this or that act within the political but the survival of any possible polity, that we are impelled finally to decide. But if there were any possible response to this situation par excellence would it not be, at least in part, to imagine that there is no 'we,' no agent to whom this hyperbolic demand is addressed: would it not require the annihilation of the imagination?

Early in the twentieth-century the two great philosophers of life, Edmund Husserl and Henri Bergson, conducted two different but equally provocative thought experiments. Husserl asked us to imagine the world's annihilation (and by *world* he was not referring to the material object planet earth but to the experienced horizon of that planet *as lived*, the lived planet *as world* that so many phenomenologists today regard as the *sine qua non* of all life):

> The existence of a world is the correlate of certain multiplicities of experience distinguished by certain essential formations. But it cannot be seen that actual experiences can flow only in such concatenated form.. It is instead quite conceivable that experience, because of conflict, might dissolve into

illusion not only in detail, and that it might not be the case, as it is de facto, that every illusion manifests a deeper conflict.. in our experiencing it is conceivable that there might be a host of irreconcilable conflicts not just for us but in themselves, that experience might suddenly show itself to be refractory to the demand that it carry on its positings of physical things harmoniously, that its context might lose its fixed regular organizations of adumbrations, apprehensions, and appearances—in short that there might no longer be any world[...].

Now let us add the results reached at the end of the last chapter; let us recall the possibility of the non-being of everything physically transcendent: it then becomes evident that *while the being of consciousness,* of any stream of mental processes whatever, *would indeed be necessarily modified by an annihilation of the world of physical things its own existence would not be touched.* Modified, to be sure. For an annihilation of the world means, correlatively, nothing else but that in each stream of mental processes certain ordered concatenations of experience and therefore certain complexes of theorizing reason oriented according to those concatenations of experience, would be excluded. But that does not mean that other mental processes and concatenations of mental processes would be excluded. (Husserl 1983, 110)

Bergson asked us to consider the speeding up of cosmic time. For Husserl the thought of the natural world's non-existence would compel us to imagine human subjectivity as radically altered but nevertheless remaining. Bergson asked us to imagine the speeding up of cosmic time, with all the natural material events of the globe occurring twice as fast:

Outside ourselves we should find only space, and consequently nothing but simultaneities, of which we could not even say that they are objectively successive, since succession can only be thought through *comparing* the present with the past.—That account by science is proved by the fact that, if all the motions of the universe took place twice or thrice as quickly, there would be nothing to alter either in our formulae or in the figures which are to be found in them. Consciousness would have an indefinable and as it were qualitative impression of the change, but the change would not make itself felt outside consciousness, since the same number of simultaneities would go on taking place in space. (Bergson 1913, 116)

For Husserl the lived or 'natural' world's annihilation would not alter transcendental subjectivity in its essence as pure potentiality for the synthesis of time. For Bergson, not quite in opposition, a speeding up of the world would not change its nature; consciousness, though, would be fundamentally different if it took place at a different speed. Consciousness *endures*, so that it is not just a series of events placed next to each other; each event is what it is because of all the past events, and if the rate of events were sped up then the nature of events themselves would alter essentially. Quite simply, if I were to slow down the viewing of a film I would experience a play of light, a series of small movements, and the flicker of an emotion that would not be perceived were that film played at the standard speed or sped up. I would not experience *more* or *less* of the film but would have a different experience entirely, and in turn would have a different experience of all else in my life precisely because 'I' am nothing other than my singular duration, altered perpetually by what is perceived and its speed or slowness of affect: 'duration properly so called has no moments which are identical or external to one another, being essentially heterogeneous, continuous and with no analogy to number' (Bergson 1913, 120). At first Husserl and Bergson seem to present opposite cases: for Husserl transcendental subjectivity is not bound to the world of natural time, and would even exist (though radically altered) without the world altogether; for Bergson consciousness is its flow of the world, and while matter is what it is and can be sped up in its rate of change and still remain matter, the speed of conscious events determines what consciousness will be, what it will endure.

Bear in mind before we consider these experiments any further that both these philosophers were concerned with the extinction of philosophy. For Husserl certain philosophical forms, such as historicism and psychologism, had accounted for the origin of truth and logic by placing these possibilities of thinking within human and material time: logic, mathematics and geometry were deemed to be grounded on actual human subjects who had lived in concrete time and who had either founded (in the case of historicism) or reflected upon (in the case of psychologism) truth procedures. Such explicating maneuvers were responses to scientific criteria for rigor but in their capitulation to such standards reduced philosophy to one more worldly act of observation that threatened philosophy's very life. Philosophy could only survive if it were to release itself from the grip of such already constituted modes of judgment and instead question the possibility of judgment as such:

> To be human at all is essentially to be a human being in a socially and generatively united civilization; and if man is a rational being (*animal rationale*), it is only insofar as his whole civilization is a rational civilization, that is, one with a latent orientation toward reason or one openly oriented toward the entelechy which has come to itself, become manifest to itself, and which now of necessity consciously directs human becoming. Philosophy and science would accordingly be the historical movement through which universal reason, 'inborn' in humanity as such, is revealed.
>
> This *would* be the case if the as yet unconcluded movement [of modern philosophy] had *proved* to be the entelechy, properly stated on the way to pure realization, or if reason had in fact become manifest, fully conscious of itself in its own essential form, i.e. the form of a universal philosophy which grows through consistent apodictic insight and supplies its own norms through an apodictic method. Only then could it be decided whether European humanity bears within itself an absolute idea, rather than being merely an empirical anthropological type like 'China' or 'India'; it could be decided whether the spectacle of the Europeanization of all other civilizations bears witness to the rule of an absolute meaning, one which is proper to the sense, rather than to a historical nonsense, of the world.
>
> We are now certain that the rationalism of the eighteenth century, the manner in which it sought to secure the necessary

roots of European humanity, was *naïve*. But in giving up this naïve and (if carefully thought through) even absurd rationalism, is it necessary to sacrifice the *genuine* sense of rationalism? And what of the serious clarification of that naivete, of that absurdity? And what of the rationality of that irrationalism which is so much vaunted and expected of us? Does it not have to convince us, if we are expected to listen to it, with rational considerations and reasons? Is its rationality not finally rather a narrow-minded and bad rationality, worse than that of the old rationalism? Is it not rather the rationality of 'lay reason,' [*Vorgegebenheiten*] and the goals and directions which they alone can rationally and truthfully prescribe? (Husserl 1970, 16)

For Husserl, saving philosophy from itself would also be a redemption of human life: the human subject, in its rigid or 'naïve' scientism, is extinguishing itself. But Husserl saw this self-extermination as a sign of possible renewal; it is in the nature of consciousness, as a synthesis of the external world, to mistake itself for one already existing object. The positing of the subject as one more concrete thing within the world is no unfortunate error. It is precisely because we live in a world of things that are ready and present that we also take ourselves to be similarly natural objects. Such a 'natural attitude' works perfectly well for the sciences but will not only lead to the crisis and death of a properly scientific or rigorous philosophy, it will also mark an end to responsibility. As long as we accept logic, mathematics or the sciences as self-evidently true systems we will fail to recognize the genesis of those systems and will, in turn, fail to recognize the power of subjectivity—*not* as some given term upon which truth can be founded, but as that which gives itself foundation. Bergson also thought that the intellect's capacity to manage the world efficiently was responsible for taking mind and its experiences as similarly manageable data. He, too, thought that only by annihilating man as a rational animal within the world would there be some future for a spirit or consciousness liberated from natural calculations—a spirit that did not yet exist:

> Our freedom, in the very movements by which it is affirmed, creates the growing habits that will stifle it if it fails to renew itself by a constant effort: it is dogged by automatism. The most living thought becomes frigid in the formula that expresses it. The word turns against the idea[...]. Like eddies of dust raised by the wind as it passes, the living turn upon themselves, borne up by the great blast of life. They are therefore relatively stable, and counterfeit immobility so well that we treat each of them as a *thing* rather than as a *progress*, forgetting that the very permanence of their form is only the outline of a movement. At times, however, in a fleeting vision, the invisible breath that bears them is materialized before our eyes. We have this sudden illumination before certain forms of maternal love, so striking, and in most animals so touching, observable even in the solicitude of the plant for its seed. This love, in which some have seen the great mystery of life, may possibly deliver us life's secret. It shows us each generation leaning over the generation that shall follow. It allows us a glimpse of the fact that the living being is above all a thoroughfare, and that the essence of life is in the movement by which life is transmitted. (Bergson 1911, 127-28)

So if Husserl appears to dismiss the constitutive role the world's or earth's own duration plays in consciousness, and if Bergson refuses a subject in general that would be a pure potential for logic outside any specific duration, both philosophers nevertheless thought that the way of dealing with the human capacity to extinguish itself—to imagine itself as nothing more than a mere thing among things—was not to appeal to the imagination of a common humanity. Rather, Husserl's world annihilation experiment suggested that a destruction of all that has come under the name of humanity, including the archive of constituted disciplines, would at least disclose some power of humanity that might begin to think of itself as something not already given. And Bergson's speeding up of cosmic time also tries to distinguish between a cosmos whose speeds are not its own, for the cosmos would not lament hurtling to its end at twice the rate, and a consciousness that is certainly not fully actualized as a common human species. Elsewhere, in *The Two Sources of Morality and Religion*, Bergson distinguishes between morality's reliance on a body of common interests defined against external threats, and dynamic religion that has the capacity to orient itself to no one in existence, towards a virtual other to whom I am not bound by either interest, or passion or sympathy.

> Now, a mystic society, embracing all humanity and moving, animated by a common will, towards the continually renewed creation of a more complete humanity, is no more possible of realization in the future than was the existence in the past of human societies functioning automatically and similar to animal societies. Pure aspiration is an ideal limit, just like obligation unadorned. It is none the less true that it is the mystic souls who draw and will continue to draw civilized societies in their wake. The remembrance of what they have been, of what they have done, is enshrined in the memory of humanity. Each one of us can revive it, especially if he brings it in touch with the image, which abides ever living within him, of a particular person who shared in that mystic state and radiated around him some of that light. If we do not evoke this or that sublime figure, we know that we *can* do so; he thus exerts on us a virtual attraction. (Bergson 1935, 68)

> Mankind lies groaning, half-crushed beneath the weight of its own progress. Men do not sufficiently realize that their future is in their own hands. Theirs is the task of determining first of all whether they want to go on living or not. Theirs the responsibility, then, for deciding if they want merely to live, or intend to make just the extra effort required for fulfilling, even on their refractory planet, the essential function of the universe, which is a machine for the making of gods. (Bergson 1935, 275)

Where does this leave us today? Certainly it is inadequate to turn back to Husserl or Bergson and try to retrieve a humanity or subjectivity that would be other than the calculations and interests of warring interests. These early twentieth-century gestures of appealing to a virtual spirit or transcendental subjectivity occurred in the face of philosophy's possible extinction; if humanity were a potentiality beyond the calculus of matter then it, too, would have an existence outside those disciplines and bodies of thought. Something similar occurs today with an appeal to an ethical or political subject who must, supposedly, be in existence (if only virtually) in any claim of interest; there must be an 'I' who speaks or demands and, therefore, a 'you' or 'one' from whom consensus is sought. But what Husserl's world annihilation experiment and Bergson's cosmic time experiment disclose is that questions of extinction, annihilation and the acceleration of cosmic time *destroy* a subject or humanity as we know it. Further, whereas Husserl and Bergson thought that the task that would save thought and philosophy would be the annihilation or acceleration of the natural world, and the destruction of man as a natural body within the world, today it is the possible extinction of the man of ethics and philosophy that may allow us to consider the survival of the cosmos. At the very least, it is time to question the 'we' who would subtend and be saved by the question of ethics and politics. If that 'we' is annihilated what remains is less a subject of thought, a common humanity, a proto-politics, but a fragile life that is not especially human. And once that is all that remains one might ask about the viability of living on: if humanity values life, rather than imagining itself as that which supervenes upon or survives beyond life, then that valuation would have to consider those modes of life beyond humanity, beyond ethics and politics. This would not yield an environmental ethics, for an environment is always that which surrounds or houses a living being as environs or milieu. What it might be is a counter-ethic for the cosmos.

If it is not presupposed that the only life worthy of consideration is ethico-political—to do with a sense of ethos, polity, abode or dwelling—then one might consider those modes of life that are not defined by milieu. In relation to the human one might ask whether modes of living and modes of relation could exist without the assumption of a 'we,' and without the assumption that 'we' are worthy of living on; one might ask whether the future should not be saved for another mode of life altogether. Such a question might force a consideration of what is worthy of survival, even if such survival appears, today, to be less than certain.

Chapter 8

Just Say No to Becoming Woman (and Post-Feminism)

The topic of post-feminism is neither joyous nor rigorous. The 'post' of post-feminism can either signal the redundancy of a feminist movement that has achieved about all it could achieve, implying an acceptance of gender politics. From this point of view, we can celebrate that certain things are no longer acceptable—unequal pay, sexual harassment, the refusal of reproductive rights, discriminatory language or exclusion from the public sphere—and these achievements would render feminism triumphant and redundant. Alternatively, post-feminism would be a critical stance that attends to forces that are far more complex than those that could be explicable via categories of gender (McRobbie 2004). It is obvious that feminism has made gains that 'we' (humans and the non-humans who benefited from eco-feminism) are now enjoying; and yet we might also remind ourselves that such hard-won gains are 'one generation away from extinction.'[1] It is no less obvious that for all those gains, figures of gender and tired clichés of sexual difference still organize a lot of our thinking (insofar as we are still thinking). Indeed, perhaps there is a third sense we could grant to the term post-feminism: in addition to referring to the completion of feminism, and to the overcoming of the simplicities of feminism, perhaps post-feminism might be more akin to terms such as 'post-modernism' or 'post-structuralism.' Here, to be *post*-feminist would be at one and the same time a refusal of the implicit borders of gender politics, while recognizing that any supposed era after feminism will be haunted by the figures of binary sexual difference that were exposed, criticized, deconstructed and parodied.

It may well be that we live in a time of the posthuman, where we recognize the claims of animals, technology, the planet and other unbounded forces; and yet it is precisely here, in the genre of the post-apocalyptic, that the most tiring gender narratives are repeated. One can think of Cormac McCarthy's *The Road* (2006) in which the world after the end of the world (the world after the destruction of capitalism and civility) is nevertheless ordered by a familial narrative: a man journeys with his son through posthuman wreckage, mourning the child's mother. Or, consider any number of post-apocalyptic cinematic events where the disaster narrative is typically entwined with a heterosexual romance: *The Book of Eli* (2010) is at once a reflection on a world in which the archive of Judeo-Christianity has been destroyed (with one fabled remaining copy of the Bible), and also a terrain in which a heroic Denzel Washington fights the forces of posthuman evil. Yet the narrative is still structured (as nearly all Hollywood narratives are) by a male-female encounter. The heroic Eli not only saves the world by preventing the one remaining bible from falling into the wrong hands; he also saves Solara, the young female who signifies the future at the film's close. One might say that it is easier to imagine the end of the world, and the end of capitalism, than it is to think outside the structuring fantasies of gender.[2] There must always be an active male heroism driven by a feminine fragility that appears to hold the promise of the future. Explicit narratives of this form, such as *Children of Men* (2006) in which a world that has stopped breeding is given feeble hope in the form of a young pregnant woman to be saved by the male lead, are surrounded by less overt regressions to the romance plot and its variants. *The Walking Dead* (2010), *I am Legend* (2011), *The Day the Earth Stood Still* (2008), *28 Days Later* (2002)—all these imaginings of the end of the world nevertheless remain with a sentimental Oedipal structure of the family. It might make sense to think in Deleuze and Guattari's terms that 'becoming-woman' is the key to all becomings (Deleuze and Guattari 1987, 291): gender and sexual binaries seem to be the last archaism in a world that is elsewhere happily posthuman. Finance capital has destroyed the notion of a locus of capitalism; the era of the brain and artificial intelligence has put to rest any notion of the exceptionalism of the human; research on non-human languages and cognitive archaeology has meant that we are truly post-structuralist (no longer believing in the linguistic paradigm). We are post-capitalist, post-linguistic, post-political, post-racial and yet not fully post-feminist. We have gone through the performative turn, the affective turn, the non-human turn, the theological turn and the ethical turn, and yet we seem to keep turning back to woman.

Even so, for all the rigidity of gender and notions of woman, surely the twenty-first century seems to demand that we think *beyond* woman, rather than beginning with woman as our first step to human freedom. Why, now, would we want to keep talking about a category as tired and flabby as 'woman'? And why would we want to take a philosophical corpus, such as Deleuze and Guattari's with all its energy directed at moving beyond human normality and tie it back—again—to the question of becoming woman? If Deleuze and Guattari (1987, 280) had anything to say on the issue it was to insist on becoming-woman as a moment of passage, and so—not surprisingly—they cited Virginia Woolf's claim that it would be fatal for writing to 'think of one's sex. ' Given this framing of the concept in Deleuze and Guattari's corpus, why would one ever waste thought and ink on this relatively isolated, and manifestly transient, notion of becoming-woman?

One way of defending a continued focus on 'woman,' if not 'becoming-woman,' would be strategic: even if gender and sexual difference were blunt organizing categories they nevertheless have their persistence and need to be dealt with rather than willed away. Part of the value of psychoanalysis has been in acknowledging the gap between what we may know to be true, and an archaic psychic economy that continues to operate. (Juliet Mitchell [1974] argued for the pertinence of psychoanalysis precisely because despite the women's movement's reasoned claims intractable Oedipal structures remained in place.) When Deleuze and Guattari wrote *Anti-Oedipus* they accepted the truth of the Oedipal individual at the level of the historical imaginary: insofar as we demand to be recognized as subjects we must submit to an either/or disjunction of male/female. Yet Deleuze and Guattari also strenuously insisted that *subjection* was not the sole logic. Instead, they took up a modernist notion that other forms of language, perception and embodiment would be possible, beyond the current logic of Oedipal individualism. If modernism in its literary-aesthetic mode was in part a critique of the West, and in part a critique of the subject, it was also an ambivalent critique of 'man' tied to a concept of writing. When Deleuze and Guattari quote Virginia Woolf in their plateau on becoming they are drawing upon an author whose modernism was already in dialogue with centuries of anti-humanist critique, ranging from Friedrich Nietzsche's tirade against a 'consciousness' whose interiority could only be established by severing itself from the intensity of life, to Henri Bergson's argument that the intellect had reified the life of spirit. At first glance modernist anti-humanism seems to be marked by a neo-Romantic positing of 'the feminine' as that which might operate as an exit from the Western subject of judgment. (One can think here of the 'oceanic' conclusion of Joyce's *Ulysses* with the affirmative repetition of Molly Bloom's 'yes,' and Julia Kristeva's [1980] appeal to Joyce's 'semiotic' mode pre-Oedipal poetic language.)

In addition to ostensibly 'feminist' modernisms that celebrated a redemptive power of the feminine, there was also a modernism that refused both man *and* woman. If Deleuze and Guattari's aesthetic is indebted to modernism it is not surprising that they appealed to Woolf in their description of the transition from becoming-woman to becoming-imperceptible. Just as becoming-woman is a divided concept, looking back to a seemingly redemptive figure of the feminine beyond rigid being, but also forward to a positive annihilation of fixed genders, so modernism was also a doubled movement. Modernism was in part a logic of the subject in its striving to be nothing other than the distanced observer, or nothing other than any of the personae though which one speaks (Ellmann 1987). But modernism was also an anti-subjectivism, or rather a pulverization of 'the' subject for the sake of a plural and multiplying point of view. In addition to the arched, refined and urbane distance of impersonality, modernism was also a tactic of positive and positively destructive refusal. Radically anti-humanist modes of modernism would not just be *other than* any determined subject; one would not just be posthuman or post-feminist in the sense of negating of distancing oneself from 'man.' Rather, one would take up and decompose the rigidity or stupidity of the figures that had strangled thinking, not imagining that one might simply and too quickly will away the forms, figures or 'territories' that had oriented thinking.

'Becoming-woman,' I would suggest, needs to be read as a defiant and affirmative refusal. It is quite distinct from either the Lacanian notion of imagining that there is no woman (that there is no 'beyond' that would exceed subjection, and no 'thing' that would guarantee my enjoyment [Copjec 2002]). Becoming-woman is also distinct from attempts to destabilize the 'heterosexual matrix' from within by repeating and distorting gender's already constituted figures (Butler 1993). That is, 'becoming-woman is not an authentic recognition that gender is some fantasmatic lure whose 'beyond' I need to think in the form of a radical negation (as in the Lacanian insistence that 'woman does not exist.') Nor does one take up the existing figure of woman to repeat or perform it ironically (Cornell 1991). For both these positions—that we must negate gender or perform it parodically—suffer from simultaneously over-valuing and undervaluing thinking. They overvalue thinking by assuming that one can pass from recognizing the fantasmatic status of thought's contaminating figures to adopting a distanced and critical attitude; at the same time the future potentiality of thinking is diminished by not creating or writing other modes of perception. The problem with Oedipus is both its negating stranglehold on thought, *and* its inability to imagine that thought might be jolted from its familial slumbers. For the Oedipal structure is just that, a style or mode of perceiving: one views the world as a subject, as a point of view opening onto a world that is structured and differentiated according to a certain common logic. The broader claim and project of Deleuze and Guattari's *Anti-Oedipus* is to destroy that style of subjectivism by creating a mode of thought that is not that of a world differentiated by 'a' system of signification for 'the' speaking subject. Becoming-woman is one of the ways in which they imagine a different mode and temporality of perception: not a world that I can only live as always already differentiated, a world to which I am subjected, with only a fantasmatic or negative 'beyond.'

I.

I would suggest that the problem of considering the worth of political or tactical concepts such as 'becoming-woman' opens onto the broader terrain of human stupidity and the relation between stupidity and time. Is it sufficient for us to look back across the philosophical or literary corpus, spot the moments of racial, gendered, sexual, ethnic or historically embedded bias (where thought has allowed itself to be captured by cliché), and then proceed to separate the dynamism of ideas from the stupidity of unthinking inertia? If this were so then one could see modernism as an attempt to rid thought of its opacities in order to arrive at a moment of renewed vision. One would overcome thought's limits and all its reified points of inertia to arrive at a pure becoming. (And one would apply the same criteria of pure becoming to Deleuze and Guattari, reading certain aspects of their corpus as suffering from subjection to a form of 'little Oedipus,' where they remain too faithful to their Marxist forbears [De Landa 2003].) By contrast, an acknowledgment of something like a transcendental stupidity (Deleuze 2004, 187; Ronell 2002, 20) would require us *not* to see 'becoming-woman' as a local movement, adopted in the late twentieth-century to take us once and for all beyond man. If that were so then becoming-woman would be a majoritarian shift: something 'we' need to do *once and for all* to overcome the figure of man. Rather, becoming-woman is a minoritarian shift, occurring in multiple, frequent, diverging and always shifting incursions. Becoming-woman would be a perpetual act of war, waged against both the upright morality of man *and* the redemptive otherness of woman. Further, this might relate to the broader project of a counter-organicism: destroying the parochialism in which the thinking body folds the world around its own practical needs, imagining itself as a thing among things. There is another capacity for thinking, which would take thought beyond its own bounded self, and would do so via perception. Becoming-woman might possess some privilege or legitimacy, not just because it was *not* the perception of man, and not because it would be perception from an*other* point of view, but because it would shift the problem of point of view. Becoming-woman would *not be* perceiving *as a* woman, but perceiving in such a way that perception would be a form of becoming.

'It is fatal for anyone who writes to think of their sex." This way of approaching becoming-woman would relate directly to Virginia Woolf's refusal to think of sex alongside her use of point of view, where sentences move ever closer to intuiting the world of the beings that the narrative voice perceives: the worlds perceived by waves, particles, moths, light and air. To accept a transcendental stupidity is to elevate thinking above the upright image of pure thought and to encounter a swarm of becomings. Becoming-woman would be a strategy that refused both the Lacanian notion that 'woman does not exist' (or that woman has served as a lure to cover the fact that we are necessarily subjected to a symbolic order that produces the effect of a lost and mourned originary plenitude) *and* an easy posthuman exit that would escape man and woman altogether in a moment of post-feminist, post-cognitive and post-Cartesian unity. *Becoming*-woman would be an affirmative rejection of reactive negations—would abandon the idea of stepping outside man once and for all—but it would also be a refusal of active submission, a refusal of the idea that we always already think within a system that we repeat parodically or ironically.

Becoming-woman, read as a twin refusal (of both purity and subjection), may well not be a flippant or dated (merely timely) remark in the works of Deleuze and Guattari. Becoming-woman might indicate a different mode of the politics of philosophy: the stupidities that populate the philosophical corpus—including the concept of 'woman'—would be indicative of tendencies that always have two sides. The concept of becoming-woman would be beyond good and evil: neither a sign that we might finally move beyond man to some redemptive outside, nor a mark or stain in Deleuze and Guattari's work that signals a moment of weak (1960s and hippy) and unthinking feminist sympathizing. Rather, the concept itself—considered as a *concept* created to do work in reconfiguring the philosophical plane—serves both to reorient the speeds and styles of thinking, and to confront philosophy's plane of concepts with its own stupidity (Weinstein 2010). To this extent the creation of the concept of becoming-woman might also be aligned with a certain style of modernism: at once recognizing that the canvas is always populated with clichés and that we speak in a waste land of dead phrases (Deleuze 2005, 8, 61), while at the same time insisting that the refusal of cliché and dead letters does not give us some grand present of rebirth, but instead a more profound death. (Later in this chapter I will turn to Woolf's story on the perception of the death of a moth. It is the witnessing and writing of death, the perception of the waning of the spark of life, that takes writing beyond the expressing subject to the life that gives itself in *both* annihilation and survival.)

In the remainder of this chapter I will argue that a certain valorization of becoming-woman is already at play in dominant modes of literary aesthetics and politics, and that it is a refusal of this assumed or *moralizing becoming-woman* that is enabled by a reconsideration of Deleuze and Guattari's mobilization of Woolf's modernism. In brief:

1. If we read modernism as an anti-humanism of impersonality, in which the artist is nothing other than the voices he adopts (distanced as he is from the panorama of futility that he surveys), then we arrive at a modernism of ironic elevation and negation. This would be a modernism of heightened or hyper-subjectivism that in many ways paves the way for today's posthumanisms in which man finds himself at one again with a creative life of which he is but one self-aware fragment.[3]

2. Such a modernism would, therefore, be in line with a long tradition of celebrating literary 'becoming' in which writing is pure act, without determining essence, and in which the pure existence of the creative word destroys man as a being within the world, and allows something like a pure subject to emerge. This subject would be godlike in his distance from any of the determinations through which he expresses an infinite productivity: 'For this is quite the final goal of art: to recover this world by giving it to be seen as it is, but as if it had its source in human freedom' (Sartre 1988, 63).

3. A *post*-modernism that followed such an anti-human and negative modernism would lead to at least one of the modes of posthumanism that is being affirmed today: a posthumanism in which there is, and never has been, anything like 'man,' for man is nothing other than all the events, acts and perceptions that bring him into being (Hayles 1999, 3). Man would always be other than any determined 'man.' Man would always be pure 'becoming,' and whatever was, or has been, determined by the notion of 'woman' would always provide man with a playground for his own self-becoming.

4. Against this, we might consider the Deleuze-Guattari-Woolf concept of becoming-woman in which writing occurs not as a

self-unfolding but as an encounter with another becoming—two quantities entering into a differential relation. Becoming-*woman* would therefore not be a pure becoming in which 'woman' would stand for playful self-invention but would be a becoming in which positive traits or tendencies would orient the event of writing (Lawlor 2008). Becoming-woman would necessarily be only one moment in other becomings, and would then open a necessarily sexual (but not gendered) writing: writing would be sexual because it would always be in relation to other relations, and sexuality would always be a form of writing (but not signification) because encounters would produce distinct maps and orientations.

5. Whereas 'the signifier' indicates the dominant system through which the world would be mediated, and would be central to theories of gender that define 'sex' as that which seemingly precedes and is presupposed by gender norms (Butler 1990), sexuality is tied to a mode of writing in which differences are inscribed in multiple strata. Sexuality would no longer be what takes place among signified genders, for genders would emerge from sexual processes (processes of inscription, tracing, marking, miming, coupling, distancing, perceiving): 'Sexual difference is the principle of radical difference, the failure of identity, destination, or finality. It is the eruption of the new, the condition of emergence, evolution or overcoming' (Grosz 2011, 103).

II.

Before we decide to consign becoming-woman to the dustbin of high theory (and its crazier, French and affirmatively pseudo-feminist moments), it might be best to consider just once more whether the concept (if it is a concept) has any purchase today. Here are the possibilities:

1. **Becoming-woman as transition that is now no longer required:** however we might have articulated and defined feminist projects to date (equality, difference, androgyny, anti-essentialism, strategic essentialism…) we are now in a post-feminist

era. We have achieved whatever could be achieved via gender politics and we now need to move on to more complex terrain, acknowledging complexities of class, sexuality, ethnicity and culture. Becoming-woman would be a post-feminist concept, a way of thinking the transition from molar women's movements to a micro-politics in which both man *and* woman would be abandoned as basic political units.

2. **Becoming-woman still required because of the centrality of 'man'**: 'Becoming-woman' was indeed, as Deleuze and Guattari argued, the 'key to all becomings.' If something like the figure of man has been crucial to the ways in which politics has proceeded—assuming a basic social unit of a reasoning individual who acts in order to extend and maximize his interests—then this is both because a certain notion of becoming has been normative, and because the Oedipal figuration of the man of reason is thoroughly tied to this *pure* becoming.

The liberal subject, as self-defining, is nothing other than his own becoming. One might define this valorization of the self *as pure act* as Oedipal (as Deleuze and Guattari do). According to this structure: the world as it is in itself lies beyond the capacities of finite human reason, and man can only know the world through the systems and order that he himself has constituted: 'The question remains, though, whether the 'social' sphere designated by 'the Name of the Father,' a symbolic place for the father, which, if lost (the place and not the father), leads to psychosis. What presocial constraint is thereby imposed upon the intelligibility of any social order?' (Butler 2004B, 253). Man is submitted and subjected to a system of his own making, beyond which he can neither think nor live. Without that imposed system of differences 'he' would have no being. The Oedipalism of this mode of pure becoming lies in its formalism and proceduralism: man is subject to a general system, and must always speak of the world only in terms that are shared and communicable; beyond that system of communication and ongoing legitimation there is only the chaos or fantasy of some lost origin. The notion of the 'beyond' of communicative reason, and politics generally, would be fantasmatic and other, figured Oedipally as that imagined plenitude that is constitutively lost when man accedes to the order of society.

Man *is* becoming; he is nothing more than his own self-deciding and legislating actions. It follows, for Deleuze and Guattari, that there is no becoming-man; one cannot take on traits or styles or rhythms *of man*, because the very notion of 'man' is that of a being whose existence is nothing other than that of free self-variation (without determining essence or positive predicates). Becoming-woman challenges this normalizing Oedipalism in a number of ways. First, if there *is* such a thing as becoming-woman, or entering into variation by taking up those traits and predicates that lie beyond man, then this is because what is other than man is not some dark night of undifferentiated chaos. There are other durations and pulsations of life.

For Virginia Woolf the task of writing was not—as one dominant definition of modernism would have it—to present the signifier *as signifier* and to de-naturalize a life that has (ideologically) presented itself as natural when it is indeed thoroughly human and historical (MacCabe 1979). Such a constructivist or mediated notion of reality would not only be Oedipal in Deleuze and Guattari's terms (presenting reality always as given only through organizing systems), but would be (in Woolf's terms) fatally destructive because of its location in 'a' sex: it would give the world to us only as it is *for man*. The alternative is not then to write from a specifically woman's world—for that too would be the world at one remove. 'Becoming-animal,' also, would not be an imperative to write the world of the animal, as if life were nothing more than multiple mediated and meaningful worlds (although some claims for animal 'lifeworlds' today seem to be insisting on just this point [Wheeler 1995]). Beyond the world as it is given there would be the durations and pulsations—the moments—from which worlds emerge: the task would be to write the waves and particles that might yield a pure perception. 'Man' would always be the being who—via language, meaning or his own sense of life—gives himself the world. Becoming-woman would be a mode of writing in which the waves and particles that compose the gender of woman might be released.

Second, 'man' as the basic political unit relies on a racial and historical (and, again, Oedipalized) narrative: in the beginning is the individual who enters into social relations for the sake of collective efficiency; from the nuclear family of father-mother-child, sympathies are extended to broader social groupings, with women also—eventually—being granted the right to enter the public sphere. But for Deleuze and Guattari the reverse is the case: in the beginning is the territory, in which human bodies assemble according to various rhythms, durations and sympathies with the earth. From that original grouping, or organization of the 'intense germinal influx,' a certain deterritorialization can occur whereby a single body stands above the group, figured as its point of law. That elevated 'despot' is able to terrorize the network of bodies, at least in part, through an excess of desire—consuming the surplus of production, and taking over women's bodies. (There would be some convergence here between Deleuze and Guattari's account of social machines being constituted through sexual consumption and Gayle Rubin's [1975] insistence that the token of 'woman' is constituted through systems of exchange, with woman established as object of consumption. The difference would lie in Deleuze and Guattari's insistence that before there is exchange of woman, or before woman is constituted as that which is exchanged, there is theft: not theft in the face of scarcity, but a theft that produces a power of excess—the despot who, in seizing the surplus of all forms of production, including sexual production, becomes a distinct and organizing point of power).

When 'man'—in the liberal era—regards himself as the basic social unit, who gives himself law and mediation in order to avoid the chaos and psychosis of bare life, he must do so by repressing the racial and collective history that has passed from the intensive differences of life to the generalizing figure of man. For Deleuze and Guattari it is not the case that life begins with a figure of man who must come to terms with his world (who must become social and extend from the biological family to the social collective); rather it is after a long, complex and inhuman history—in which racial, sexual and organic complex is increasingly reduced to general figures—that the supposedly underlying generality of the human emerges. Becoming-woman would be a way of releasing man from the notion that beyond the sexual binary there is only the primitivism of chaos; by looking at the coming into being of the genders of humanity one would open up a geology. This geology would then open out onto all the racial and historical differentials that have been frozen into the unit of man, and beyond that into all the differentials of life that have been reified into figures of bounded organisms opposed to unorganized matter.

Finally, becoming-woman would challenge both the linguistic figure of modern man, as well as a series of declared post-linguistic (supposedly posthuman) turns. The notion that we become subjects by submitting ourselves to the system of signifiers, and that we then live this subjection as a law that prohibits some maternal beyond, is thoroughly Oedipal. The concept of 'the' signifier is despotic, and both ties modern Oedipalism back to a history in which the complex territories of life have been subjected to a body (including language of culture) that has leapt outside the assemblages of relations, and also looks forward to a 'postmodern' world in which there is supposedly no reality or world other than that given through signifying systems, or in which the pre-linguistic is always given *ex post facto* after the event of sex. If, by contrast, language were considered to be one of many systems—including systems of non-linguistic signs, such as all the gestures we read in a lover's face, or the signs of art in which formed matters can be presented as signs of color or light as such—then it might become possible to liberate writing from 'the subject.' Becoming-woman would signal that there are positive modes of difference and articulation. It is not language that differentiates; the differences of language over-code far more complex systems. Becoming-woman opens up a positivity that not only destroys the notion that language differentiates (because there are traits that one can follow, develop, vary and extemporize beyond the man of linguistic communication), the concept of becoming-woman also challenges various supposedly posthuman or post-linguistic motifs. It would do so by destroying both the natural kinds of bounded sexes (male or female) and the notion of constructed genders; in its place there would be neither a gender politics nor a sexual politics (in which the polity would be a site for the contesting of variously sexualized interests), but there would be a sexuality of becoming. Every becoming would be sexual because no becoming is a power unto itself: there is no self-present, self-sufficient, self-organizing power. There is no life; there is only 'a' life, distinct powers from which an open whole is composed. When we perceive something like an essence (such as what color *would be* in all of its potential manifestations for any time whatever), we perceive the force of its expression, a power's capacity to differ in all its events of encounter and actualization.

III.

There should be something disturbing, destructive and untimely about the concept of becoming-woman. If we were to define becoming-woman as a temporary strategy of the women's movement then we would be assuming an orthography of thought: it would be as though we might use certain concepts provisionally, achieve the aims of the women's movement, cleanse thought of its opacities and stupidities, and then move on. But what if man were a persistent transcendence: a tendency of thought or life to be captivated and rendered docile by images of good sense? If man were a tendency of organicism, a tendency to fold the world around the organized body's view of the world, then becoming-woman would be an ongoing and tireless destruction, a key to becomings.

One of the notions that lies behind various 'turns'—the affective turn, the vital turn, the performative turn, the non-human turn—is that the figure of man, and the notion of linguistic construction, was an error or false turn that can be overcome by turning to the true life and vitality that is man's real milieu. It is as though we might recognize, by an act of reason, that there is no such thing as man and that we are in fact really emotional, embodied, affective and active beings who—following that recognition—can now live interactively, ecologically and dynamically. The Cartesian subject would be an accident or error that we could will away by an act of decision, allowing us to become posthuman and at one with a single world of interconnected life. I would suggest that we think otherwise: Cartesianism is neither an unfortunate and external lapse, but a result of a tendency for thought to be captured by its own images (Toscano 2010). That tendency—like all tendencies—has two sides, and it is the task of becoming-woman to *deterritorialize* those traits from which the 'man' of modernity has been composed. According to Deleuze and Guattari's theory of becoming-woman it is not by annihilating one's being and then taking up a relation of proper knowing towards one's milieu that one overcomes the miserable normality of 'man.' Rather, becoming is always a relation *to* some other becoming: there would be no posthuman world or single ecology that we could arrive at after man. Becoming-woman would be *one* line of exit, one way of thinking some mode of duration and rhythm that would yield a particular refrain. From there one might discover other differential pulsions. There would not be a single ground of life that could be retrieved or found after man; but there would be multiple ways in which one might encounter 'a' life. Each predicate, trait or singularity would open to the infinite in its own way.

By beginning with woman—and not some general notion of becoming—one would be adopting the truth of the relative (which is quite different from the truth of relativism). And it is here again that we might turn to Woolf and writing: the imperative to write is counter-democratic if by democracy one were to refer to consensus or majority opinion (and it is no surprise that in this respect modernism in general has been accused of having a certain contempt for the masses [Carey 1993]). But there might be a destructive, rather than deliberative, democracy in writing and becoming-woman whereby everything that has stood for good sense and propriety is annihilated by a constant and exacting perception. Rather than begin with a relativism, in which there is no view of the world outside that given by various voices, becoming-woman aims to write from a positive perception of traits, with each intuition opening towards a power's capacity. There is a truth of the world, but it is given infinitely, from all the powers to perceive that compose the world in their own way. This might help us to think the specifics of Woolf's style, and the ways in which she writes neither in a strict free-indirect style (in which sentences occupy a certain mode or way of speaking) nor in stream of consciousness.

One of the key features of Woolf's mode of writing might be given in the contrast between a deliberative democracy and something like a democracy of powers, or what Deleuze refers to as the 'swarm' of the world. Jacques Derrida, for example, has argued that literature is tied to democracy in its capacity to 'say anything.' Because the literary text detaches what is said from any ownership of the voice, language circulates freely, *as language* (Attridge 2004). We see text as text in its own right, producing its relations and differences, performing a relation between inside and outside in its 'scene of writing.' Woolf by contrast speaks of her own writing as oriented towards the expression, perception, articulation and life of other powers: waves, moments, particles, predicates, or qualities. If a certain privileging of writing manages to relativize the world, presenting the world as always a world from this or that point of view, then Woolf's privileging of perception and intuition would always tie writing to the forces that prompt its movement. Becoming-woman is not a writing of, or about, sex—but the writing of becoming-woman is sexual in being drawn towards powers not its own. Such writing would not be a form of relativism, but it would open the truth of the relative, that each perception opens *in its own way* onto an infinite and dynamic whole (Deleuze 2006, 21).

There is a truth of the relative that would open towards an ethics of *amor fati,* or an embrace of the encounters that do violence to thinking (without the prima facie assumption that we know what thinking is). Liberalism is, by contrast, a powerful ethics of relativism: I cannot know the law, cannot know the other's good, cannot make an exception of my own desires or opinions on the basis of possessing better or higher knowledge; from there it follows that I can only act and speak through deliberation and an ideal of consensus, aware all the while that every achieved consensus must be open to further deliberation. Relativism would not be an acceptance that 'anything goes,' for it would require me to decide upon those systems that enabled the maximum plurality of opinions; a liberal might have to intervene in cases where unjustified exceptions were imposed. But relativism would be in line with what Deleuze refers to critically as 'equivocity': there is the world as it is on the one hand, and the world as it is known on the other (Deleuze 1994, 410). Deleuze and Guattari's univocity posits one substance expressing itself in infinite difference, in which all voices sing the truth of being in their own way: 'Arrive at the magic formula we all seek—PLURALISM = MONISM—via all the dualisms that are the enemy, an entirely necessary enemy, the furniture we are forever rearranging' (Deleuze and Guattari 1987, 23). The truth of the relative, in contrast with liberal formalism, would pose a quite different imperative. There would be no possibility of a 'veil of ignorance' that would allow one to act *as if* one might speak from an ideal position of 'nowhere.' But if liberalism insists that one can only speak *as if* one might be any subject whatever, Deleuze and Guattari offer a counter imperative to speak for 'any moment whatever': such an imperative intuits what a force or power would be in all its expressions and actualizations. There would not be 'a' world that might be suspended in order to think in a manner that was purely formal or procedural. There would be multiple worlds, each opened from the force of a single becoming. It would be the challenge of perception and thinking to encounter the difference of those worlds, not find some abstract point or field of conciliation.

IV.

If the forgoing is true it follows that becoming-woman is only one possible trait or singularity among others, and that its power lies in moving beyond the historical formation of 'man.' If so, with the end of man and the end of liberalism we might also have reached, happily and finally, the end of woman. As already stated, there can be no becoming-man, no orienting oneself towards the styles and motifs of 'man,' because man *has always been pure becoming.* He is nothing other than that which exceeds and precedes any of his given acts; his essence is to have no essence other than that which he gives himself though existing. Once becoming-woman opens 'us' (we humans) to the notion that becoming is always singular, always the becoming of this or that singularity and always in responsive relation, then writing would be presented with the tireless and ongoing destruction of genders and proliferation of sexes; it is not that there are beings—women—who become. Rather, what something *is* is its rhythm of becoming: 'Children's, women's, ethnic, and territorial refrains, refrains of love and desruction: the birth of rhythm' (Deleuze and Guattari 1987, 330). The refrain that beats time to this rhythm is always in relation to other refrains. Becoming-woman would be an orientation to those traits that had been posed as man's other, but once this orientation opened up positive and divergent becomings we would need to move beyond genders and dehumanize the predicates through which genders and sexual difference had been contained.

Such a jettisoning of becoming-woman would seem to be particularly urgent today, precisely because there is no longer any reason to adopt strategies against liberalism and humanism in a twenty-first century when the problems of climate change, terrorism, systemic economic collapse and mass disenfranchisement are no longer suitably countered by tactics of anti-humanism. It would seem that both sides—both rapacious global capital and post-left, post-feminist thinking—accept that there is no such thing as the man of reason. It is no longer the case that the ruthless market forces of capitalism present themselves as outcomes of free and open individual decision making. In the US, where 'liberal' has become a pejorative (referring to the destruction of family values and leftist interventionism in free markets) the notion of the freely deciding individual seems to have less political force than the sanctity of the markets and efficiency. This is so much the case that when the 2010 US Supreme court decided that corporations were individuals, it was the left that was forced to defend the human individual, against the notion of free buying power that could operate beyond a bounded human person (Cohen, Colebrook and Miller 2012). Bourgeois liberal humanism is not the ideological enemy it once was. It would seem to make sense to exit this terrain altogether. In the era of global finance—where there is no longer any capital to buoy up capitalism, and where systems operate by hedging, default swaps, futures and derivatives—it makes no sense either to return to the individual against corporations, or to celebrate some posthuman end of man in one great ecology of becoming.

'Theory,' too, seems to have long abandoned man, the subject, the system of signifiers and (even strategic) essentialism. After language there was the turn to the body, in which sex could only be known as that which had been belied and reified by gender. If we go beyond the frame of the subject who must recognize herself through the gender system, then we are left with a vital, affective, emotive and nonhuman order that may be *sexual* (in its proliferating relations, attachments and mutations) but certainly not gendered. If we get over all our feminist and leftist gripes, recognizing that workers and women can no longer offer us some outside lever against a patriarchy that no longer has any men left to hold the fort, then it seems the appropriate direction to move towards what would be beyond human figures *tout court*.

To pause and offer a possible conclusion: 'becoming-woman' may have had its time, may have once indicated that without *some* attention to sexual difference there could be no real escape from the rigid logic of man, but after more sustained work on sexual difference beyond gender binaries, we should accept that becoming-woman is, as Deleuze and Guattari suggest, the 'key' to all becomings, and that we have moved beyond the 'key' moment to more nuanced posthuman (perhaps even post-sexual) becomings.

Here is the problem, or series of problems, with such a consignment of this 'key' of becoming-woman to the past: first, do we accept that humans have the capacity to assess their figural and semantic history, locate gender motifs in a blind past, and then move on to the posthuman? Do we grant the human species a capacity to see life as it properly is without the intrusion of rigid stupidities, and would life be the type of 'thing' we might view once we liberated ourselves from humanist framings? (Here, I would suggest that we read Deleuze and Guattari alongside Paul de Man's concept of the sublime, where the exit from anthropocentric projection would not be an intuition of nature or the lived world but a brute sense of materiality.[4]) Second problem: do we accept that within a corpus, such as Deleuze and Guattari's, where the historical event of capitalism and the discovery of the differential calculus disclose some universal truth of life as such, that sexual difference is an unfortunate dated motif that can be grouped with Deleuze and Guattari's almost embarrassing references to drugs (as though they were a little too 60s-ish at certain moments)? Here we would assume some practice of critical hygiene, where the real philosophy and theory might be detached from the unthinking regression of dated stupidities. Doing so would rely upon a distinction between free unimpeded thinking on the one hand, and an external milieu of inherited notions. And it is just that notion of thought as pure self-becoming that Deleuze and Guattari sought to question. Third problem: what do we do with what remains of the archive: do we stop reading all the works of fiction and cinema that are structured around gender binaries, do we (we theorists or literary critics) place ourselves in a world other than that of a still present and insistent gender binary? Do we avoid the evidence that it is easier to imagine the end of the world and the end of capitalism than it is to imagine the end of gender? Perhaps the problem with Deleuze and Guattari's affirmation of becoming-woman as the 'key to all becomings' was not its dated 70s radical-feminist hint of sexual politics, but its suggestion that one might and should move from becoming-woman to becoming-imperceptible. It seems that in our posthuman, eco-aware, post-liberal, post-capitalist and even post-racial world we still remain firmly gendered. This is not because gender is not just one mode of establishing distinct kinds, a mode that could be abandoned once we take on a 'process' notion of being or a vitalist and dynamic conception of creatively evolving life; for gender is *the* difference that has been deployed to figure difference in general.

It would follow, then, that if we do *not* pass through becoming-woman, and if we go straight to becoming-imperceptible without engaging with the logic of man, then all our posthumanisms will remain as ultra-humanisms. And, to return to Woolf, it would not be the case that Woolf *added* the problem of woman to modernist projects, but rather that whatever modernism would be (whether an apocalyptic vitalism or affirmative refusal of the trajectory of the West), writing would be destroyed by thinking of one's sex. Writing would need to take place beyond man, which in turn would require a destruction of 'woman.' The structure of *To the Lighthouse* expresses this at the level of content: the first section of familial gender, where Mrs Ramsay appears as the figure of maternal care and other directedness (opposed to the subject/object philosophy of Mr Ramsay) is severed by the middle section of 'Time Passes.' The final section—following Mrs Ramsay's death and the falling of an immense darkness—describes the young artist Lily Briscoe being taken over by the matters that are presented to her. Her 'vision' follows what Deleuze and Guattari describe as haptic, as though the eye can *feel* the paint and canvas, and draw out its tendencies. The canvas presents itself not as a milieu for creation ex nihilo, but as a resistance or force that elicits a certain mode of becoming. The canvas itself bears a perceptive power or 'cold stare':

> She saw her canvas as if it had floated up and placed itself white and uncompromising directly before her. It seemed to rebuke her with its cold stare for all this hurry and agitation; this folly and waste of emotion; it drastically recalled her and spread through her mind first a peace, as her disorderly sensations (he had gone and she had been so sorry for him and she had said nothing) trooped off the field; and then, emptiness. She looked blankly at the canvas, with its uncompromising white stare; from the canvas to the garden. There was something

(she stood screwing up her little Chinese eyes in her small puckered face), something she remembered in the relations of those lines cutting across, slicing down, and in the mass of the hedge with its green cave of blues and browns, which had stayed in her mind; which had tied a knot in her mind so that at odds and ends of time, involuntarily, as she walked along the Brompton Road, as she brushed her hair, she found herself painting that picture, passing her eye over it, and untying the knot in imagination. But there was all the difference in the world between this planning airily away from the canvas and actually taking her brush and making the first mark.

Lily's becoming is not one of self-unfolding, but an encounter between a physical sensation of surging forth that achieves 'an exacting form of intercourse.' If there is a posthuman element to this becoming it does not lie in a return to life so much as a separation or detachment from the lived:

With a curious physical sensation, as if she were urged forward and at the same time must hold herself back, she made her first quick decisive stroke. The brush descended. It flickered brown over the white canvas; it left a running mark. A second time she did it—a third time. And so pausing and so flickering, she attained a dancing rhythmical movement, as if the pauses were one part of the rhythm and the strokes another, and all were related; and so, lightly and swiftly pausing, striking, she scored her canvas with brown running nervous lines which had no sooner settled there than they enclosed (she felt it looming out at her) a space. Down in the hollow of one wave she saw the next wave towering higher and higher above her. For what could be more formidable than that space? Here she was again, she thought, stepping back to look at it, drawn out of gossip, out of living, out of community with people into the presence of this formidable ancient enemy of hers—this other thing, this truth, this reality, which suddenly laid hands on her, emerged stark at the back of appearances and commanded reluctant. Why always be drawn out and haled away? [...] It was an exacting form of intercourse anyhow[...].

What emerges is not a figure or scene that expresses the world as it is, but something like difference as such, a line that makes no claim to a physical eternity—for the canvas may lie unviewed in an attic until its destruction—even though it expresses the power of color and difference for all time:

> Quickly, as if she were recalled by something over there, she turned to her canvas. There it was—her picture. Yes, with all its greens and blues, its lines running up and across, its attempt at something. It would be hung in the attics, she thought; it would be destroyed. But what did that matter? she asked herself, taking up her brush again. She looked at the steps; they were empty; she looked at her canvas; it was blurred. With a sudden intensity, as if she saw it clear for a second, she drew a line there, in the centre. It was done; it was finished. Yes, she thought, laying down her brush in extreme fatigue, I have had my vision.

But it is not only the young female artist whose perception opens onto a world of other durations. Woolf's short story, 'The Death of the Moth,' begins in standard third-person description, assuming a common shared point of view: 'Moths that fly by day are not properly to be called moths; they do not excite that pleasant sense of dark autumn nights and ivy-blossom which the commonest yellow-underwing asleep in the shadow of the curtain never fails to rouse in us.' This 'us' of common accepted perception is disturbed by the passage of perception, which eventually discerns something akin to 'an energy':

> The rooks too were keeping one of their annual festivities; soaring round the tree tops until it looked as if a vast net with thousands of black knots in it had been cast up into the air; which, after a few moments sank slowly down upon the trees until every twig seemed to have a knot at the end of it. Then, suddenly, the net would be thrown into the air again in a wider circle this time, with the utmost clamor and vociferation, as though to be thrown into the air and settle slowly down upon the tree tops were a tremendously exciting experience.

The same energy which inspired the rooks, the ploughmen, the horses, and even, it seemed, the lean bare-backed downs, sent the moth fluttering from side to side of his square of the windowpane. One could not help watching him.

[...]

Watching him, it seemed as if a fiber, very thin but pure, of the enormous energy of the world had been thrust into his frail and diminutive body. As often as he crossed the pane, I could fancy that a thread of vital light became visible. He was little or nothing but life.

Yet, because he was so small, and so simple a form of the energy that was rolling in at the open window and driving its way through so many narrow and intricate corridors in my own brain and in those of other human beings, there was something marvelous as well as pathetic about him. It was as if someone had taken a tiny bead of pure life and decking it as lightly as possible with down and feathers, had set it dancing and zigzagging to show us the true nature of life. Thus displayed one could not get over the strangeness of it.

[...]

The insignificant little creature now knew death. As I looked at the dead moth, this minute wayside triumph of so great a force over so mean an antagonist filled me with wonder. Just as life had been strange a few minutes before, so death was now as strange.

The 'death' here is not a death drive in which life is a quantity of energy aiming to return to quiescence; it is a positive and multiple death in which the sparks of life become discernible in their distinction and singularity as they approach some degree zero. Deleuze and Guattari's notion of becoming-woman, like becoming-animal, is not one of copying or miming, but operates by the perception of traits: and this positive and relational notion of becoming would help to explain why there could be no becoming-man (Deleuze and Guattari 1987, 320). It would also require a subtle distinction between becoming-woman and various notions of performativity. It is not the case that one becomes who one is by repeating an already given norm or imperative, and then concluding that there must have been a subject who was the agent of the action. On the contrary, what is repeated when one becomes-woman is not the resulting effect—such as female qualities—but the differential power from which such qualities emerge. In this sense becoming-woman is the reversal of a performative pragmatics or strategic essentialism; one does not adopt a style or norm and then destabilize the figure of woman from within, nor adopt the role of 'woman' ironically (Cornell 1991). Rather, one repeats the tendencies, traits or rhythms from which the figure of woman emerged.

The difference, if you like, is that between Madonna (or Lady Ga Ga) and a Marilyn Monroe impersonator. The latter focuses on the end result and may come to that actuality by any possible ends (cosmetic surgery, practice of speech inflections, mirroring of Marilyn's walk, the creation of certain specific dresses); the former repeat tendencies, seizing the event of performance, style, display and movement, becoming a hyper-feminine and yet singular icon. If woman—as an actual social figure—appears as a general composition of certain styles of dressing, moving, desiring, dissimulating, looking, displaying, speaking and feeling, then becoming-woman begins with exploring different modes of dress, appearance, affect and movement. If Marilyn Monroe was a singular expression of a tendency of body-voice-face-screen stylization then repeating that differential power (rather than copying the result) would approach something like becoming-Marilyn. One of the key features of the notion of the trait is tied to a broader notion of singularities or pure predicates: each actual individual occurs as the differentiation of a potentiality. Each human body comes into being by drawing on a range of virtual potentialities, and continues to do so for her entire life: not only does my ongoing biological and neurological identity occur in my relation to other powers (such as my brain becoming a reading brain after encountering script, my eye becoming more and more readily distracted with the purchase of various portable screen devices, my bones becoming stronger after years of running, or my blood pressure rising after decades of a Western diet), it is also the case that my given capacity to become in these ways has a long racial, cultural, sexual and political history. This is the partial truth of evolutionary psychology and cognitive archaeology, which have sought to trace our current responses and capacities back to a hunter-gatherer and warring tribal past, along with the early human gendered division of labor. But the problem with cognitive archaeology is not its seeming sexism, or its assumption that 'men are from Mars and women are from Venus.' The problem is that these 'just so' stories are *not sexist enough*, or that they do not discriminate sufficiently or with any attention to the sexuality of discrimination. Man—the hunter-gatherer and hyper-attentive tribal prototype of our past—is already the result of a desiring history: formed by assembling in territories, organizing the body to react first collectively, and then privately, to visual stimuli. As the history of man and social machines continues what counts as 'man' in general is the result of a history of reduced racial intensities towards an increasingly general whiteness, and the formation of the notion that there is a man in general, eventually emerging as the reading-thinking-reasoning individual of modernity.

To begin to think about the 'traits' that would compose an event of becoming-woman would require both an attention to manifestly stylistic features from which any woman (or man) is composed—so that acts of drag would emphasize the performance of gender in terms of dress, body grooming, and modes of comportment—but also to broader traits, the geologies of which are traced by Deleuze and Guattari in their universal history of capitalism. The reading eye that judges in accord with the measuring hand, and that in turn feels itself to be a subject of speech submitted to 'the' law: this composition of the human animal is, Deleuze and Guattari argue, racial and sexual. The notion that there is some universal underlying humanity, presented in general as 'man' (and about whom various neo-Darwinists might theorize) occurs *after* certain traits have been rendered hegemonic, and after a certain understanding of sexuality as private and familial has reorganized (or reterritorialized) collective qualities onto the individual. It is only if I assume that one becomes human by abandoning one's pathological and exceptional (racial, sexual, ethnic) particularities, and does so in order to enter into the great enlightened conversation of consensus, that sexuality is deemed to be private, personal and individual. For Deleuze and Guattari politics and history are sexual: social machines are formations of desire—both the despot becoming powerful by hoarding, consuming, and visibly enjoying the violence of public torture, and the later formations of fascism where a series of traits mobilize a body politic (swastikas, jackboots, tanks, anthems, the straight lines of modernist design and so on).

V.

The concept of becoming-woman—and I would suggest that we think of it as a concept, created to reconfigure a plane of related notions—is tied to a broader history of capitalism. Capitalism, Deleuze and Guattari argue, has always been 'warded' off by various social machines that seek to limit and over-code flows and exchanges: this ranges from obvious examples, such as early modes of despotism and feudalism in which there is no open market along with a hoarding of goods by a central power, to early modern laws against usury, sumptuary laws, royal displays of excess, and protective subsidies, as well as broader and more subtle ways of quantifying bodies as units of exchange (such as capitalist democracies where laboring bodies and commodities become the two flows of capitalism). Becoming-woman is not a solely feminist gesture, or if it is, it is only because feminism (for Deleuze and Guattari at least) is a path to a broader critique. Capitalism is the abstract essence of social machines: desiring life is composed of quantities entering into relation, and it is from those dynamic relations that relatively stable points of bodies are composed. Bodies—human bodies, political bodies, economic bodies, corporate bodies—are mixtures of powers. Quantities, entering into relation, become qualities and those qualities in turn become relatively stable bodies. Capitalism tends to liberate quantities from bodies, releasing labor power and commodities into a general system without fixed center or transcendent body, but capitalism also limits the free flow of quantities through an axiomatic. Nowhere is this axiom more evident than in liberalism, both in its economic form of laissez faire exchange (which is always an exchange via the market), and in liberal political theory in which I am nothing other than a capacity to deliberate and communicate, always capable of imagining what it would be to think of justice, in general, regardless of my position in the polity.

By contrast, becoming-woman would not abstract from concrete individuals to individuals in general—would not operate *ironically* by imagining that justice or humanity would occur as regulative ideas towards which a process of consensus would tend, but never achieve. Nor would becoming-woman be posthuman if posthumanism were taken to be a return of man to a world of living systems of which he would be but one of many instances. Rather, becoming-woman is the beginning of a humor of depths, moving towards the traits, singularities or predicates that have been actualized by differentiation—and then moving towards the intuition of a virtual potentiality that has a full reality beyond the world as it is given. Becoming-woman would be quite distinct from a performative theory of gender, whereby I become who I am by recognizing, and seeking recognition. Rather, becoming-woman enables a creatively destructive theory of sexuality in which genders are decomposed into traits, and then further decomposed into tendencies, moving towards the infinitely small, or 'a thousand tiny sexes.'

When Deleuze and Guattari write about capitalism they do not adopt the still current criticism that capital reduces the qualitative complexity and richness of the world to system and quantities, with the implication that if we overthrow capitalism's reduction of qualities to quantities, we will return to the full dynamic flux of the world (to the praxis from which technological systems emerged). Deleuze and Guattari are not what Protevi and Bonta refer to as 'flow enthusiasts' (Protevi and Bonta 2004, 37):

> there is no enabling without constraint. (In Foucualt's terms, power is not negative but productive.) Constraint here is a reduction in the dimensionality of the connection space of components while emergent effects mean the substance has increased the dimensions of its connection space (it can do more things, relate to more bodies—or at least more powerful bodies—than a heap of lower-level substances can). (Protevi and Bonta 2004, 37)

The problem, for Deleuze and Guattari, is that capitalism is not systemic enough, not quantifying enough, not sufficiently technical. We allow certain blunt figures—such as the image of the working, desiring man of reason to operate as a limit and lure. It is as though exchange must always serve individual's interests, and yet we do not ask how it is that something like human interests are constituted historically. How has the commodity-acquiring, property-owning, familial, heterosexual, laboring, reading, judging, and political man of modernity been formed? And has not the figure of gender been crucial here: man is deemed to be defined against a femininity that is caring, nurturing, other-directed, domestically attuned, emotional, empathetic and oriented towards a male who (at least according to evolutionary psychology) is chosen because he will provide suitable genetic material? The current vogue for evolutionary psychology or cognitive archaeology is evidence of a tendency to explain quantities and tendencies from already qualified forces: we argue that the gender system emerges from (say) male interests in spreading as much genetic material as possible, and female interests in investing in quality partners. What we fail to look at are how those bounded forms emerged from intensities: how the human body becomes a gendered, familial and identified laboring individual.

Life arrives, historically, at capitalism because of a certain potentiality that has been 'captured' by capitalist political systems, by relatively open markets. Relations amongst intensive quantities, such as the various forces of a body entering an encounter with—say—the intensive potentialities of another body are organized in capitalism as a relation between labor and capital. The standard political response has been to try to find some point outside of exchange; but Deleuze and Guattari aim to take capitalism beyond itself. What is required is not a step outside exchange and quantities, but more exchange, more quantification, a multiplication of powers and encounters. Capitalism is neither quantifying nor systematizing enough; what is required are far more nuanced, discriminating, systemic (rather than imaginary) systems.

Here, then, one might begin to see the force of becoming-woman: what if the figure of 'man,' the supposed basic social unity of life—a unit that today has become entirely rigid in the proliferating pseudo-Darwinian narratives about the emergence of morality, language, art and all other human practices—were to encounter other traits? As already noted, the concept of becoming-woman is not at all similar to strategic essentialism; it is not the tactical adoption of the voice of woman in order to create a political force. On the contrary, becoming-woman acknowledges the reality of traits, intensities and quantities that need to be released from the dull and insufficiently nuanced systems of gender. It is not the case that—as a certain mode of deconstruction would have it—the concept of woman is some imposed abstraction that has no reality, and so one might only speak as a woman parodically or ironically. Nor is it the case that 'woman' is some signifier that we are subjected to, which then creates the illusion of the reality of sex. Rather, what has fallen under the concept of woman has *more reality* than the insufficiently technical and systemic concept of 'woman' in its current form allows: what if, historically, what we know as woman were composed from series of complex tendencies? *Becoming-woman* appears, after all, as a concept in Deleuze and Guattari's *A Thousand Plateaus* where the modern figure of political man covers over a complex, multiple and intensive history of racial and sexual investments. Practices of marriage, kinship, reproduction, pornography, art, fiction, courting rituals, fashion systems, cosmetic surgery, sports, affective rituals, body styles (and so much more): all these are techniques operating in highly complex ways that neither the notions of gender—as two stable kinds—nor sexual difference (as reproductive chromosomal identity) can intuit. It is fatal, when writing, to think of one's sex.

Notes

1. I quote Ronald Reagan from his first inaugural speech as governor of California, January 5, 1967, for whom freedom was 'never more than one generation from extinction.' This Reagan quotation was repeated recently by Julianne Moore (playing Sarah Palin) in the 2012 HBO film *Game Change*. Such a reminder of generation-paced extinction was timely in 2012 when the constant threat of civil rights reversals seemed to actualize into a fully fledged war, both with a supposed 'war on women' and with a resurgence of claims of racial lynching. (Democrats accused Republicans of opening a war on women when certain States legislated for compulsory vaginal probe ultrasounds prior to pregnancy terminations, while Rebublicans countered with an attack advertisement against 'Obama's War on Women' because the Obama campaign accepted donations from a supposedly misogynist

comedian Bill Maher. [http://www.weeklystandard.com/blogs/obamas-war-women_634041.html]) The March 2012 killing of Trayvon Martin was not only compared to a lynching, so were the following calls for his alleged killer's arrest. An article on 'The Lynching of George Zimmerman' (Martin's alleged killer) was posted on Occidentaldissent.com immediately following large rallies calling for Zimmerman's arrest following what Democracynow.org declared to be a 'modern day lynching.' (http://www.democracynow.org/2012/3/20/a_modern_day_lynching_outrage_grows) Wars and lynching: none of these seems at all 'post' anything, and so we might wonder why we would want to complicate matters at all by turning to 'becoming-woman' when the basic 'molar' issues of race and gender seem so intractable. On the other hand, maybe the fact that we seem to be *still* involved in wars and lynching that we might think of other strategies.

2. The idea that the end of the world is easier to imagine than the end of capitalism is widely quoted (though the source is vague). See Jameson 2005, 199 and Žižek 2011.

3. Rosi Braidotti (2012), aware of the various modes, perils, lures and forces of posthumanism usefully distinguishes between anti-humanisms that are set against 'man,' anti-humanisms that retain the revolutionary fervor of secular humanism and her (quite distinct) line of affirmative posthumanism, that creates but does not assume a life and perception beyond man and his others.

4. Paul de Man, *Aesthetic Ideology* 'The dynamics of the sublime mark the moment when the infinite is frozen into the materiality of stone, when no pathos, anxiety, or sympathy is conceivable; it is, indeed, the moment of a-pathos, or apathy, as the complete loss of the symbolic.' 126.

Chapter 9

How Queer Can You Go?

[...] no 'gay liberation movement' is possible as long as homosexuality is caught up in a relation of exclusive disjunction with heterosexuality, a relation that ascribes to them both to a common Oedipal and castrating stock, charged with ensuring only their differentiation in two noncommunicating series, instead of bringing to light their reciprocal inclusion and their transverse communication in the decoded flows of desire (included disjunctions, local connections, nomadic conjunction). [Deleuze and Guattari 1983, 350]

Consider a number of possibilities for what might count as a queer theory: the use of theory (any theory) to expose bias; the criticism of theories themselves for implicit biases; or, a re-description of theory that identifies its orientation as essentially queer. It is this last mode that I wish to pursue in this chapter, and will do so by looking at the ways in which the long-standing model of *theoria* as a distanced look or regard taken upon an object is intrinsically normalizing.

Such a model of theory as the imposition of order and judgement on chaos via a transcendent norm of logic has been identified by a number of thinkers as having its origin in Platonism. John Protevi has identified this model as 'hylomorphic': the ordering of chaotic matter by an external and stable system of reason (Protevi 2001). Luce Irigaray has, following Heidegger, not only criticized the notion of underlying matter (as *hypokeimenon*) that is then rendered intelligent through representation as subjective (for then matter becomes what it ought to be through the perceiving subject's act of knowledge); she has also identified such a notion of theory as phallogocentric. That which is other than the self is the medium through which the self comes to know and affect itself (Irigaray 1985). Perhaps the clearest critique of this notion of *theoria* comes from Martin Heidegger, who argues that the original experience of the world as unfolding and disclosing itself through a time of bringing-to-presence becomes covered over with the idea of 'a' logic that it is, eventually, the task of man to take up as that which renders thought correct and human (Heidegger 1998, 240). Rather than pursuing Heidegger's own way beyond this forgetting of the unfolding of Being, I wish to pursue Gilles Deleuze's reversal of Platonism. This is not because Deleuze manages to move further beyond Plato than Heidegger—rejecting Heidegger's calls to dwelling, caring and attending to the four-fold—but because Deleuze returns to a higher Platonism (Deleuze 1994, 265).

The reversal of Platonism, for Deleuze, is not the overcoming of a transcendent logic in favor of the primacy of lived experience, but an overturning of experience and the lived in favor of radically inhuman Ideas beyond judgment. This reversed or radical Platonism, I will argue, generates not only a new mode of theory, and a new relation between theory and sexuality, but also a new and positive notion of queerness: not as destabilization or solicitation of norms, but as a creation of differences that are no longer grounded in either the subject or generating life. To anticipate my conclusion: this would yield different ways of thinking about practices, and different ways of thinking about sexual identities. In the case of practices, rather than examining the actions of subjects against existing regulations—such as enquiring whether same-sex civil partnerships are a reconfiguration of norms or a submission to normality—we would look at the ways in which bodies enter into relations to produce events, events that transcend those bodies. To use Deleuze and Guattari's phrase from *Anti-Oedipus*, 'ask not what it means but how it works': when faced with a practice try to determine its range of potentiality in the future, not its relation to the present system (Deleuze and Guattari 1983, 206). In the case of sexual identities, rather than thinking of masculinity and femininity as constitutive norms to which bodies submit, we can see the ways in which bodies play with the 'pure predicates' of sexuality (Deleuze 1990, 186): in the case of trans-gender and trans-sexual bodies, such bodies may at one and the same time experience their bodies as female, dress as male, and have sexual relations with partners who are similarly 'counter-actualizing,' or enjoying sexuality in its ideal and inhuman form (Deleuze 1990, 238).

If we think of *normal* theory as the establishment of a paradigm or norm for thinking which criticizes the unthinking absurdities, illusions and stupidities of everyday thinking, then Deleuze's theory is, or aims to be, queer in its liberation from a normative 'image of thought,' while not being simply anti-normative (Deleuze 1994, 131). The task is not to disturb thought's images of itself, but to think imaging as such, via a mode of theory that would detach itself from the lived. It does not follow, then, that such a queer theory would be a form of relativism, or the use of 'a' theory (Deleuze) by a group that takes itself to be the exemplification of liberating sexual practice. On the contrary, as a radical Platonism and a commitment to taking thought beyond itself to Ideas, Deleuze presents thought with the challenge of a radical transcendentalism. Before pursuing that option I want to explore the ways in which thought approaches the queer: how can thinking, from its base of norms and recognition (or what it takes itself to be), approach the queer?

One could use theory to isolate and criticize biases and prejudices within putatively neutral positions and paradigms. Not only would there be nothing queer about *theory*, there would be no relation between theoretical paradigms and one's political objectives. One could criticize heterosexual or normalizing assumptions from a liberal, deconstructive, communitarian or even psychoanalytic point of view. Liberalism, for example, defining itself ideally as a pure formalism devoid of any conception of the good life, would necessarily be opposed to any political or social system that discriminated against persons on the basis of some unacknowledged presupposition regarding personhood.[1] Deconstruction could, in turn, criticize such a liberalist ideal of pure formalism by arguing that there would always be an exemplary or privileged supplement in any system that could not be rendered transparent by the system.[2] It is possible to imagine this deconstructive orientation to metaphysics' unthought or radically stylistic figurations as being of service to a politics that wished to expose normative and normalizing conceptions of the self at the heart of figures of supposedly 'pure thought.' While psychoanalysis from its inception bears an originally normalizing bias, either by positing the Oedipus complex as the transcendental frame for the constitution of subjectivity, or the phallus as the signifier of presence, it can nevertheless be used against its own assumptions. Again, this would be possible only through a critical maneuver, where instead of placing a different notion of the body or subject at the heart of psychoanalysis, the queer theorist would open the genealogy of the psychic subject to permutations not recognized by the original heterosexual frame.

The second possibility for queer theorizing would deploy the notion of queerness in a stronger sense, not only arguing that certain positions are narrowed by an overly normalizing conception of the subject or life, but would go on to point out the ways in which the very structure of a certain notion of theory was normalizing. One might contrast here, for example, the difference between Judith Butler's early criticism of psychoanalytic Oedipalism with Deleuze and Guattari's criticism of the Freudian subject. Butler accepts the structural premises of psychoanalysis—the constitution of the subject in relation to others, the fantasy frame of the self and the other's body, the vicissitudes of the libido in relation to the structures of desire through which the self is constituted as human, and (most importantly) the originally *subjected* nature of the subject[3]: one becomes a self only through abandonment of potentialities not allowed by the heterosexual matrix. The subject necessarily exists in a relation of mourning, melancholia and negativity (even if that which the self mourns is constituted after the event and fantasmatically). For Butler, then, there is nothing intrinsically normalizing about psychoanalysis *per se*, and so a queer theorist can at one and the same time criticize and deploy Freud's corpus. For Deleuze and Guattari, by contrast, it is that negative notion of desire and anxiety—the very structure of psychoanalysis *as a theory*—which remains tied to normalizing notions of 'man' (1983, 348). For Freud it is anxiety that effects repression: the subject, faced with a world of intensity and affect, must delimit and organize the libido into a state of equilibrium or constancy. We can see that notion of the very economy of desire in Butler's work and its influence on queer theory; it is assumed that the becoming-human of the self occurs through a process of recognition that must necessarily abandon and repress desire's more fluid potentialities.

For Deleuze, the notion of theory that begins from the conditions for the possibility of a constituted and normative subject, is not only intrinsically bourgeois in its ideology of placing thought within a position of compromise and contradiction. It is also committed to a normalizing metaphysics (Deleuze 1994, 283–84). The psychoanalytic model of a pool of energy, which is then structured by attachments to desired objects—as opposed to an intensive life that harbors tendencies towards expansive and creative desires—can only produce the man of common sense and good sense. If subjects are understood as having been effected from a general and undifferentiated 'life,' understood along the lines of nineteenth-century thermodynamics, then the relation between the queer and the normal would be entirely conventional. Were we to pursue a queer theory along these lines we would have to argue that queerness would operate as a criticism of presupposed but un-avowed norms. It is because there is a heterosexual matrix that constitutes and delimits subjective possibilities that we could pay attention to those modes of performance and enactment that disturbed normative structures. Our *theory* would not be queer, for we might well be in agreement with the general structure of subjects being constituted through social norms and structures; the queerness would lie in the attention we paid to those supposedly failed or extrinsic modes of subjectivity, to which we may accord a privileged transgressive value. Our approach would be queer only in its difference and distinction from effected models of the subject. Such a theory might also *appear* to be 'posthuman,' for rather than beginning from the man of reason or the subject of phenomenology who synthesizes given experiences into some coherent whole, we would begin from a general pool of force, life or energy that—through action or performance—constitutes subjects. Those subjects may, through misrecognition and metalepsis take themselves to be originators of the act. Theory would set itself the task of demystifying such illusions of agency, demonstrating the ways in which everything begins with performance, act and relationality—the substance or true 'sex' of the subject being constituted *ex post facto*. (I will argue, in the sections that follow that this *seemingly* posthuman theoretical approach remains entirely subjective, and still implicated in a highly normalizing ethics).

In principle, then, it would be a mistake to use the term 'queer theory' to refer to the projects as I have outlined them so far, for what we would really be doing would be queer *studies*. Queer studies would be related to gay or lesbian studies, in its criticism of the assumed normality of heterosexuality, but would go beyond such identified groups to consider the fragility of identity and its excessive character in relation to what Deleuze and Guattari refer to as 'molar politics.' Queer studies might appear to be concerned with molecular or minor forms of politics: not the contestation of paradigms from the point of view of recognizable (even if marginalized) groupings, but the interrogation of constituted subjects from the point of view of a life or desire not yet identifiable *as* this or that specifiable form, a 'people to come' (Deleuze and Guattari 1987, 106). Queer studies would be different, methodologically, from American Studies, Asian Studies, Women's Studies and so on insofar as 'queer' would not refer to a kind but might use various methods to inquire into the stability and instability of kinds. Rey Chow has already challenged notions of area studies according to the degree to which it makes such assumptions about various worlds or areas being available for purview, so it is quite possible that queerness or identity-instability goes beyond queer studies to 'studies' as such (Chow 2006). I would argue, though, that the true challenge of Deleuze and Guattari's thought lies in its difference from *critical* models, and in its transformation of the ways in which we understand theoretical relations, and relationality in general.

The third possibility would be not simply to challenge the norms that dominate a theory—for example interrogating psychoanalysis from within by isolating its unquestioned assumption of male-female relations—but would contest just what it means to theorize. Only then would our *theory* be queer; it would not be the use of theory for queer politics, nor would it be an interrogation of our theoretical premises or figures regarding implicit normative and normalizing assumptions. Instead we would shift the 'image of thought'—mind constituted as an effected point within life—to thought without an image: would it be possible to think of the emergence of qualities, potentialities or Ideas that create an aleatory point? This would not be a position of judgment or critique, but a virtual line of sense. Mind would neither be the site from which synthesis emerges, nor the subject that would be created via the imposition of some subjecting system. Theory would not be the capacity of mind to step back from and reflect upon itself, but a capacity to map all the distinctions, separations and created strata of life, including the creation of various lines and powers of thought. If life can be thought of not as substance from which predicates are then differentiated, performed or effected, but as a plane of force that allows for the creation of relatively stable points, we can think of theory as the creation of a potential which is no longer the power of this or that aspect of life (this or that body) so much as the thought of the transcendental potentiality of life as such, life liberated from any normative image. This is why sexuality would come to the fore in the task of new modes of thinking and theorizing. One might say that the potentiality for queer theory has always haunted theory. Or, one might say that theory has always tended to be queer but has been impeded by a counter-theoretical normalizing tendency. Theory, defined with *theoria* in mind would pertain to looking, perceiving, and possibly imaging. Undertaken in a normalizing manner theory would reflect upon how it is that 'we' see; but if we subtract this 'we,' or if theory is considered *without* the ground of 'the people' then there would be an imaging, perceiving or relation, from which theory would emerge. Theory would arise from relations among powers, and would therefore always be hybrid. This hybridity demands that we reverse the understood relation between theory and metaphysics. If it is the case that our metaphysics—our image of what it is to think—is currently effected from the bodies around us, or the ways in which we 'fold' images around our own ego-centered orientation, then a radical metaphysic of transcendental empiricism would free sexuality from organized bodies. It would no longer be the figure of mind or the good thinking subject that established the relation to theory. The sexual body would not be 'a' body constituted in a social field, but a 'body without organs'; the sexual (rather than gendered body) would be a multiplicity of all those predicates, partial objects, affects and perceptions from which we are composed.

To understand how theory as such might be 'queered' we can distinguish between two senses of the word 'queer': the first would be primarily critical and would concern a difference or distinction *from* a constituted norm or center. The second sense, which I wish to conclude by pursuing here, entails a positive disengagement of substance and subjectivism (so that substance is not that which underlies or precedes; substance does not give us some ultimate subject). This second sense, in refusing substance as some preceding ground, also requires a rejection of what I referred to as the thermodynamic model of desire that underpins psychoanalysis and bourgeois ideology. On the thermodynamic model there is a ground—some form of life, subject or substance—that then requires differentiation; and it would then follow that every actual being would be an instance of more or less. There would be certain figures or norms, such as 'man,' 'woman,' 'family,' 'duty,' 'justice,' or 'democracy,' and every attempt to realize such norms or figures would never quite be the norm itself. Every instance would never quite attain the norm or ideal itself, and this would leave us with a logic of bad consciousness: on the one hand all we have is this world here and now, given some form through systems, and yet (on the other hand) no instance would be adequate to some idea of 'justice' itself. All performances would be in part repetitions of a figure but also disturbances of a figure. There would be no life outside norms, but no pure instance of a norm.

On a positive model, life would not be differentiated through norms, but would be more complex than the norms that have emerged. A *theory* would be queer if it challenged the supposed neutrality or undifferentiated nature of life. Queerness would not concern deviation *from* constituted limits, nor even the acknowledgment—following deconstruction—that the condition for any constituted and repeatable identity is a structure of iteration that bears the necessary possibility of disruption. The possibility of a genuinely queer theory begins, I would argue, only when we challenge the normative image of life that underpins the dominant understanding of Western *theoria*. Perhaps, unexpectedly, it is Platonism in its most radical sense that would allow us to rethink theory beyond its vitalist normativity. In order to make sense of this claim I want first to look at the ways in which the thermodynamic model of life is normalizing and grounded upon an image of thought as good sense and common sense.

According to Gilles Deleuze in *Difference and Repetition* there is an originally violent, disruptive and impersonal potential in Plato that is immediately covered over by normative images of the thinking and theorizing subject (Deleuze 1994, 244). What does it mean to theorize? If everyday thinking is directed towards constancy, recognition and efficiency, it achieves this structure through a certain synthesis of time. Experience is lived as continuous: a self is constituted as the ground for the living and open-ended continuity of life considered as organic or as 'lived.' The recognition and order that make experience coherent was deemed to be possible, according to Plato, only because there existed Ideas that were beyond the lived experience of the self. Such Ideas could not be considered as concepts or categories imposed by subjects onto experience for the sake of creating coherence. These Ideas were radically impersonal *and* radically alien to any sense of time as a coherent and lived sequence. Ideas do not exist at the level of *Chronos* (sequential or chronological time) but *Aion*, or the eternal power to give difference (over and over again, the repetition of difference). Within Plato's own thought this radical nature of the Ideas is, however, immediately domesticated; for instead of considering a memory in which an Idea could be given to thought that was not thought's own, and that was at odds with the lived order of the world, Plato introduced a moral distinction between those experiences that truly reflected the Ideas that they actualized, and the simulated and dangerous doubles that bore a fragile and unreliable relation to the Ideas that were their pure potentiality. Deleuze's overturning of Platonism is a retrieval of the Idea. Deleuze's reversed Platonism is *not* a liberation of life from all order, distinction, difference and essence. Instead, it is a liberation of essence and distinction from the lived world.[4] All our actual experiences that are lived as experiences *of* this or that identifiable and specified form need to be understood not as constructed and arbitrary impositions on an otherwise undifferentiated life, a life that is only known as lived and ordered; rather, actuality needs to be understood as the actualization of Ideas, but the Idea does not—as it would in Plato—issue in a proper form. For the Idea is nothing other than a potentiality for difference, a difference that is given and lived as simulation (or simulacra). An Idea can never be given other than in its variation. It is not that there is an Idea that is then varied; the Idea is variation. It is the *distinctness* of the Idea, its absolutely differential nature—or its capacity to make differences—that entails that it can only be experienced as obscure. Once something is clear—recognizable *as* this or that delimited and perceived object—it loses its distinction. Theory, then, is not the adjudication of this lived world according to the extent to which it properly incarnates an Idea; theory is the intuition of our lived and actual reality *as simulacrum,* as a becoming-clear or identifiable of an Idea (an Idea that exceeds the lived, but exists in nothing other than the lived). In turn, once we see the given as the actualization of an Idea that loses its distinction by becoming-actual, we can then take the next step of theorization, which would be 'becoming-imperceptible': can we try to think of those movements, distinctions and potentialities that allow our sensibly given world to be sensed but which themselves—as Ideas—are only given as simulations?

How then do we move from this level of abstraction to queer theory? We can begin by going back to the thermodynamic model, which Deleuze aligns with bourgeois ideology, good sense and common sense. If we follow the modern paradigm and argue that subjectivity is not some natural and transcendent norm but is constituted through the synthesis of relations, then we *seem* to have demystified all notions of a grounding normality. But, following Deleuze, I would argue that the thermodynamic model (in which an undifferentiated life is given structure through contingently imposed systems) is the highest mode of normalization, for nothing is outside the one grand order of more or less, and every decision is always a compromise that could really just as easily have gone the other way. The subject is not the foundation of experience but is effected through experience:

> Good sense is the ideology of the middle classes who recognize themselves in equality as an abstract product. It dreams less of acting than of constituting a natural milieu, the element of an action which passes from more to less differentiated: for example, the good sense of eighteenth-century political economy which saw in the commercial classes the natural compensation for the extremes, and in the prosperity of commerce the mechanical process of the equalization of portions. It therefore dreams less of acting than of foreseeing, and of allowing free rein to action which goes from the unpredictable to the predictable (from the production of differences to their reduction). Neither contemplative nor active, it is prescient. In short, it goes from the side of things to the side of fire: from differences produced to differences reduced. It is thermodynamic. In this sense it attaches the feeling of the absolute to the partial truth. It is neither optimistic nor pessimistic, but assumes a pessimistic or optimistic tone depending upon whether the side of fire, which consumes everything

and renders all portions uniform, bears the sign of an inevitable death and nothingness (we are all equal before death) or, on the contrary, bears the happy plenitude of existence (we all have an equal chance in life). (Deleuze 1994, 283)

Equality, or the idea that individuals exist in relation to each other via some general standard of the human, partakes of a specifically bourgeois inflection: there is some undifferentiated vague generalization of 'man' that will always approximate some never fully articulated standard. Any concept or decision is as relatively good and compromised as any other. Indeed, each concept would be—as constituted in relation to an otherwise undifferentiated 'life'—an inessential compromise and limitation. The subject of such an anti-metaphysical or post-foundational understanding would bear a number of features. It would, Deleuze insists, be thoroughly at home with contradiction: any constituted concept could never master or express the general life that it represents. As a consequence one would always have to deal with the essentially limited and compromising nature of the terms and figures of our theory (Deleuze 1994, 337). Further, such a subject would be oriented towards judgment, rather than action: aware of the provisional nature of our grasp of our selves and our world, we would always be compelled to consider the limitations and locatedness of our point of view, never capable of appealing to life 'in itself.' Such a position would also be characterized by an 'on the one hand' and 'on the other hand' logic. Deprived of all foundations, norms and essences we would need to acknowledge that any decision would always preclude and belie equally justifiable possibilities.

Consider in terms of queer theory how this logic would work. On the one hand we need to be critical of constituted identities, which might come to function as restrictive norms. On the other hand, without the tactical or strategic adoption of such an identity we risk political invisibility and ineffectiveness. The same logic applies to all issues within queer theory: on the one hand arguments for civil partnerships seem to buy into the normative structures of middle-class lifestyles and capitalist property relations; on the other hand, without such rights and entitlements we risk complete marginalization and disempowerment.

Deleuze argues that such a logic takes a partial apprehension for the absolute. Always thinking within constituted, delimited and actualized terms, politics becomes a negotiation of the system, with perhaps some attempt to transgress or destabilize the system—always aware that no break from normativity in general is possible.

At first, such a logic of more or less, and of the minimal requirements of some normativity, would appear to accord with Deleuze and Guattari's own more explicitly political statements. In *A Thousand Plateaus* they argue against an absolute deterritorialization (while elsewhere arguing for a 'higher' deterritorialization), and they also argue for the necessity of a molar politics alongside the molecular processes of 'becoming-woman' (Deleuze and Guattari 1987, 460). However, by looking at the radically Platonic model Deleuze opposes to thermodynamic and bourgeois ideology in *Difference and Repetition* we can give a more nuanced understanding of the relation between territorialization and deterritorialization in *A Thousand Plateaus*. The latter should *not* be understood as a relation between effected identities and their deviation or becoming different through time. Here, we might contrast Deleuze's own transcendental empiricism with deconstruction. According to Jacques Derrida, the condition for the possibility of any experience of a being or life *as* this or that ongoing and maintained being is that it be marked and lived *through time* as the same. This means, then, that there must be some iterable trace that marks each lived moment as a moment *of* this supposedly constant presence; but if this is the case then something can 'be' or 'live on' only if it has already submitted to some structure of tracing or iterability. And, as all the queer mobilizations of deconstruction have speedily noted: if an identity is effected only by way of a repetition through time of the same, then the condition for identity is also a condition for difference and deviation. The self is nothing other than its repeated performances, and is at once always already different from itself.

From this deconstructive point of view there is an 'essential' queerness to all identity in so far as identity is effected through structures that at one and the same time make ongoing sameness possible while introducing a destabilizing repetition into the marking out of that sameness. I would argue that even this most radical of models could, at a push, be understood as indebted to the late nineteenth-century understanding of life as force or energy from which identifiable terms are effected. Although Derrida (1978) has undertaken a critique of the Freudian theoretical model and the relation between the quantity of force and constituted qualities, the dissemination of deconstruction, especially for queer theory, has resulted in the maintenance of the idea of theory as reflective and destabilizing judgment in relation to differentiating systems.

Against that thermodynamic model of thinking, which Deleuze regards as an overly quiescent adoption by philosophy of scientific models, Deleuze argues for an overturning of Platonism that would pay attention to the distinct Ideas that are actualized in the seemingly clear systems within which we think and move. Life is not, Deleuze insists, a general quantity of force of energy that is then differentiated through the establishment of relations. Nor, Deleuze insists, should we take the other Bergsonian path and think of life as irreducible and unquantifiable quality that would then be subjected to quantifying systems. Instead, Deleuze suggests that we consider 'intensive quantities.' Here, intensities are not qualities that unfold in time and that are belied by quantity. For intensities are potentialities for differential relations which, when encountering other intensities, produce quantities *of* this or that quality. Each experienced, perceived or experienced intensity is necessarily given as a quantity of such and such a quality; what is, necessarily, covered over by this lived experience is the pure intensity from which relations are effected (Deleuze 1994, 210). It is this radically (or passively) vitalist Deleuzian theory of life that, perhaps surprisingly, charts its way between the linguistic mediation or linguistic paradigm *and* the literalism of theories of emergence. The vitalism is passive because it is not the case that there is something like life that surges forth from itself in order to arrive at itself; instead there are quantities of force entering into undecided relations *from which* beings emerge that would then provide some basis for active decisions.

One way of thinking about modern theory, or metaphysics after Kant, is that we can have no knowledge of things in themselves: things are known only as they are given through the categories of experience. The structuralist or linguistic turn, after Kant, places those categories, not in the transcendental subject but in social or linguistic systems. Even though poststructuralism, especially in its Derridean form, criticized the acceptance of structure without the consideration of a structure's genesis, it was the tension between genesis and structure that dominated theory: 'And even when one comes to think that the opening of the structure is 'structural', that is, essential, one already has progressed to an order heterogeneous to the first one: the *difference* between the (necessarily closed) minor structure and the structurality of an opening—such, perhaps, is the unlocatable site in which philosophy takes root' (Derrida 1978, 155).

One can only think of genesis, origins or life as they are given through structure; but any structure must have had its genesis and it is the process of the ongoing maintenance of structure which precludes any stable system. This leaves us with an 'on the one hand' and 'on the other hand' logic, and also with a judging position of the subject in relation to distanced life.

In Judith Butler, for example, we are all necessarily subjected to the heterosexual matrix or the social system of recognition. On the other hand, the condition for the maintenance of any system (repetition and performance) also destabilizes and transforms that system. In terms of specific political terms and issues, we must on the one hand take part in the terrain of politics—accepting its lexicon—while at the same time acknowledging the limits of the given. There could, though, be no appeal to that which exceeds the given. Queerness would then be understood as the destabilization or solicitation of the normative. Theory would be queer only in so far as it attended to the conditions for normality and normativity, exposing a perturbation at the heart of any possible structure.

For Deleuze, by contrast, there is no contradiction or law of exclusion between structure and genesis, and this is because of his reversed Platonism. There are Ideas, absolutely distinct potentialities from which the differentiated world is actualized. Instead of opposing structure and genesis—or the system through which the world is given, and the emergence of that system—Deleuze argues for a 'static genesis' (Deleuze 1990, 124). So we might say this is a case of Deleuze rejecting what he and Guattari refer to as 'exclusive disjunction,' whereby one must decide *either* that one submits to a structure *or* that one falls into non-identity. Instead, they argue for inclusive disjunction: yes, the world is composed of structuring relations, in various strata (including language) but there are *also* potentialities for relations or structures that are not yet actualized. Our given world of relations, qualities, quantities, terms and predicates is dynamic, in flux and organized into relatively coherent series.

Our response to such an actualized differentiated world should not be to think within a given structure while mourning our non-attainability of some ineffable 'outside.' Instead, Deleuze's concept of static genesis prompts us to think of distinct potentialities that exceed thought, but which are only given *as thought*. Structure is not imposed upon an undifferentiated life; rather, life as it is differentiated is the result of powers to make differences that exist *eternally in a plane beyond constituted subjects*. Static genesis allows us to think of a past that is impersonal and radically eternal (not already bound up with this historically constituted world): a potentiality for the creation of intensities, which are given to thought only in extended terms. We should see the languages, relations and structures of this world, then, not as organizations or negations/limitations of an otherwise neutral reality—where queerness would lie in the instability or perturbations of the organizing system—but as actualizations of potentialities or Ideas that will be eternally repeated. Thus, for Deleuze, there is an Idea of revolution, such that we can at one and the same time think empirically of all those revolutions that have occurred within history; *and* the Idea of revolution, which all those instances of revolution intimate but do not exhaust. The memory or reminiscence of that Idea of revolution would take thought beyond human recognition and constituted terms to that strange virtual potentiality, which at once gives itself to be thought while always violating and exceeding thought.

How might we deploy or respond to this abstract attempt to move beyond structurations of some ineffable reality to the positivity and affirmation of structure? What happens if we see the terms within which we think as actualizations of eternal Ideas? The first maneuver would be critical, for we can—as Deleuze did in *Difference and Repetition*—look at the ways in which our image of thought belies and diminishes the force of Ideas. If we think of judgment as negotiation of an arbitrary or imposed system in relation to a life that is lost, diminished or mourned then politics can only be a queering or solicitation of a terrain that will always be other than (retroactively posited) life. If, however, we think of theory as an attempt to reinvigorate the political terrain by reference to a positive plane or 'depth' of problems, we open thought to a positive outside. In terms of 'becoming-woman,' we could then think of new modes of relationality: not a world that is synthesized by man as a thinking subject, who then turns back upon his own organizing systems, but a world of divergent lines of relationality, where forces intersect to produce qualities and quantities without the ground of good sense and common sense. Theory is queer, not in the sense of constant destabilization or contradiction, but in opening itself up to problems. For Deleuze, life is neither oriented to self-maintenance and constancy, nor devoid of positivity and distinction. Instead, life takes the form of a problem. A force that encounters another force is the posing of a problem. We can think of this physically in terms of evolutionary theory, so that bodies are not passive sites for inscription but organized capacities that meet a similarly complex environment and produce relatively stable sets of terms. But this physical understanding does not, for Deleuze, provide a ground for theory. Instead, the task of theory is to take this form or Idea of difference—that we begin not with substances or subjects but potentialities for problematic relations—and create a new mode of thinking, thought liberated from the image.

I want to consider the ways in which two theorists have undertaken this challenge. Elizabeth Grosz has, in her work on time and evolution, argued that we can think of a 'pure difference' that would not be the differentiation *of* some prior, presupposed or posited life (Grosz 2004, 46). Such 'pure difference' as articulated in Grosz's later work can allow us to go back to her earlier positive work on embodiment, and contrast its positive and queer tendency with Judith Butler's approach in *Bodies that Matter*. The key difference lies in the problematization of the linguistic paradigm. Butler acknowledges that we cannot think of language or sociality as imposed upon life, for 'life' exists only as always already split from itself. Here she follows a post-structuralist notion of the signifier: not as a sign that orders reality, but as that aspect of matter which (in presenting itself as partial) creates a gap, absence, or prior real which is always given after the fact. In terms of politics, then, we are always already within subjection and mourning: at once human or recognizable only through given systems, while never fully coinciding with such systems.

> The body posited as prior to the sign, is always *posited* or *signified* as *prior*. This signification produces as an *effect* of its own procedure the very body that it nevertheless and simultaneously claims to discover as that which precedes its own

action. If the body signified as prior to signification is an effect of signification, then the mimetic or representational status of language, which claims that signs follow bodies as their necessary mirrors, is not mimetic at all. On the contrary, it is productive, constitutive, one might even argue *performative*, inasmuch as this signifying act delimits and contours the body that it then claims to find prior to any and all signification. (Butler 1993, 30)

Queerness in Butler's terms, as I have already suggested, can only be the effect of an explicit theorization of the conditions for recognition: it is because one becomes human or a subject only through processes or iteration that there is also, necessarily, a failure or 'queering' of identity. For Grosz, by contrast, the body was never a site for iteration or inscription but always offered its own volatility (Grosz 1994). If we know and live bodies through practices and culture, culture itself is a 'ramification' of a nature that is nothing other than a power of creativity (Grosz 2005). Theory is not, then, critical—operating to de-stabilize, de-mystify, or de-naturalize—but positive and affirmative: an attention to those untimely forces that will not so much persist (as ongoing performances) but *insist*. This is why, for Grosz, one can both insist upon sexual difference, without thereby submitting to some system of recognition. Sexual difference is not the relation between terms, nor a difference posited ex post facto after the gender system has produced relatively stable identities. We could think of sexual difference as an originating queerness that produces positive and creative difference in relation to natural selection. If natural selection is a theoretical postulate that explains, after the event, how randomly effected differences have survived to produce populations that have responded efficiently to the environment, sexual difference introduces an aleatory principle that disrupts life's tendency to equilibrium, striving and self-maintenance (Grosz 2004, 66). We can see this in animal life with the production of extravagant mating calls and visual display.

But Grosz makes an important point regarding human culture, where those forms of sexuality and coupling that are not oriented towards reproduction have ramifying effects that open up spaces and possibilities not accounted for by models of natural selection (Grosz 2004, 83). Indeed, the question of *fitness* comes to the fore once we introduce sexual selection—that is, selection not oriented towards reproduction or ongoing maintenance of the population as it recognizes itself, but the selection of traits that operate as an excessive lure.

This question of fitness is, I would argue, a politic-metaphysical question of the utmost urgency for our time. What modes of life, what forces or selections can be affirmed? This is not the question of a *decision*—of how we might make or recreate ourselves—but the problem of encounters that are queer (not determined according to recognition and reproduction). Queer encounters, from a Deleuzian perspective, are not affirmations of a group of bodies who recognize themselves as other than normative, but are those in which bodies enter into relations where the mode of relation cannot be determined in advance, and where the body's becoming is also ungrounded. Here, we pass directly from Deleuze's transcendental empiricist motto—relations are external to terms—to micropolitics and 'becoming-woman.' It is not the case that there is a world of uniform matter or force, governed or differentiated by a system of laws (this is neither the case physically, where interactions of matters produce distinct fields and modes of relations, nor socially, for the world we live is made up of quite distinct fields of relation that include philosophy, art and science). Nor is it the case that there are individuals who enter into relations. Rather, Deleuze begins with a differentiating 'spatium' that unfolds into various encounters, producing terms and relations through time (Deleuze 1994, 244). Queer theory then has two features. First, it refuses the man of good sense and common sense who must synthesize, judge and perceive the relations of this world. Not only does such an image of thought reproduce already given terms of gender (mind ordering matter, activity organizing passivity, structure giving being to non-being), it relies on equivocity, or two already decided levels of being: the force or energy of 'life,' on the one hand, and the synthesis and organization of that life by 'man' or systems on the other. Second, having refused the location or organization in the mind of man or language we can start to think of theory in Deleuze's sense of intuition: not as a critical destabilization of constituted terms and systems, but as an enquiry into the emergence of terms and relations. This is why Deleuze and Guattari regarded 'becoming-woman' as the key to all becomings. One must escape from the image of thought of bourgeois thermodynamics:

the mind as a negotiating point in a field of effected differences, outside which is the great undifferentiated (Deleuze 1994, 283-4).

There must be at least one other possibility for thinking beyond the man of reason. Sexual difference, or relations that are not oriented to judgment and reproduction, would be the beginning (but not the end) of theory.

I want to conclude by thinking the practical consequences of such a notion for queer theory, now understood not as a theory that sets itself against normativity through either a recognition of another group of bodies or through a destabilization and negation of norms. Rather theory would set as its task the notion of the Idea as a problem: how have relations and terms emerged, what—given effected relations—might have occurred otherwise; what are the forces of potentiality hidden in our experienced encounters? The concept of relations being external to terms, or of forces *for structuration* that exceed human thinking, has been aptly theorized by Levi Bryant. Part of a broader movement of new modes of realism (in which reality is not reality *for* a subject) Bryant insists on the capacity for forces beyond relations as already actualized:

> While I readily concede that objects *can* enter into relations—how else would open systems be possible?—it does not follow from this that objects *are* their relations. In short, if it is to be possible to form closed systems in which constant conjunctions of events occasionally obtain as they sometimes do in experimental settings, then it follows that relations cannot ontologically be *internal* to their terms or the objects that they relate. In other words, objects are not *constituted* by their relations to the rest of the world. While relations to other objects often play a key role in the precipitation of events or qualities in objects, we must here recall that objects are not identical to their qualities but are rather the ground of qualities. Accordingly we must distinguish between objects and their relations, or rather the structure of objects and the relations into which objects enter. I call the former 'endo-relations' (or, following Graham Harman, 'domestic relations'), and the latter 'exo-relations' (or, as Harman calls them, 'foreign relations' ...). Endo-relations constitute the internal structure of objects

independent of all other objects, while exo-relations are relations that objects enter into with other objects. Were objects constituted by their exo-relations or relations to other objects, the being would be frozen and nothing would be capable of movement or change. It is only where relations are external to objects that such change can be thought. (Bryant 2011, 68)

I will now turn to an iconic moment from the literary canon, Herman Melville's *Billy Budd*, and do so through Rosi Braidotti's concept of an 'ethics of affirmation,' which she summarizes as 'giving what you do not have' (Braidotti 2006, 208, 259). Such an ethic might at first appear to be at once thoroughly capitalist—speculate and project profits in virtual markets of the future—and thoroughly Kantian—we may not know our subjectivity but we can acts *as if* we were free. Where the ethics of affirmation becomes ecological, queer and counter-modern is in the liberation of the Idea from the lived: can we offer Ideas to thought that are not our own?

In the following scene from Melville's *Billy Budd*, Claggart perceives Billy at once as an all too desirable object *and* as a force that threatens his personal moral life:

If askance he eyed the good looks, cheery health, and frank enjoyment of young life in Billy Budd, it was because these went along with a nature that, as Claggart magnetically felt, had in its simplicity never willed malice or experienced the reactionary bite of that serpent. To him, the spirit lodged within Billy, and looking out from his welkin eyes as from windows, that ineffability it was which made the dimple in his dyed cheek, suppled his joints, and dancing in his yellow curls made him pre-eminently the Handsome Sailor. One person excepted, the master-at-arms was perhaps the only man in the ship intellectually capable of adequately apprehending the moral phenomenon presented in Billy Budd. And the insight but intensified his passion, which assuming various secret forms within him, at times assumed that of cynic disdain, disdain of innocence—to be nothing more than innocent! Yet in an aesthetic way he saw the charm of it, the courageous free-and-easy temper of it, and fain would have shared it, but he despaired of it. With no power to annul the elemental evil in him, though readily enough he could hide it; apprehending the good, but powerless to be it; a nature like Claggart's, surcharged with energy as such natures almost invariably are, what recourse is left to it but to recoil upon itself and, like the scorpion for which the Creator alone is responsible, act out to the end the part allotted it. [Melville 1986, 356]

One way to read such a scene would be as a representation of subjects constituted within heterosexual normativity: in this all-male environment Claggart as a figure of authority is at once attracted to Billy's beauty (where the beauty already tends towards spectacular effeminacy with its 'dyed cheek' and 'yellow curls'). That very attraction is at the same time repulsive, so that Claggart must destroy what he beholds. The isolation of such scenes in the literary canon would follow from our attention to the ways in which desire at once presents itself within the normative matrix, while also expressing moments of disruption, or what Alan Sinfield (1992) has referred to as 'faultlines.' Another mode of reading would be not simply to read this scene—where we as readers view represented subjects and sexualities—so much as force an encounter with the Idea of reading. If we can read qualities as signs *of* some desire—see Billy as an ideal figure of male youthful beauty—we can then see the world as composed of such signs, the 'secret forms' from which we are composed. In *A Thousand Plateaus* Deleuze and Guattari refer to a positive, productive and *feminine* notion of the secret: not the secret as that 'gray eminence' or hidden absolute which would be figured by the great feminine 'beyond' (Deleuze and Guattari 1987, 280) but the secret as *immanence*, or the metamorphosing and transposing world whose qualities we are. We are given in this scene, a scene of sense, a reading of reading, or what Deleuze also referred to as 'time in its pure state' (Deleuze 2000, 98). We see or read Claggart seeing and reading Billy: we perceive perception, not as representation, but perception as desire. Here art (as one mode of thought among others) strives to encounter the very emergence of relations and qualities. Billy is, as actualized, a body desired as male by another male, destroyed for that socially prohibited line of desire. But the condition for such a series of relations—the eye of Claggart that contemplates an object that threatens his social being—is intimated when one passes beyond the moral to the aesthetic: 'Yet in an aesthetic way he saw the charm of it.' This would approach becoming-woman, or the 'feminine line': qualities or predicates that are actualized but not exhausted by bodies. There is a certain desirability or potential for desire that exceeds the interests and intentions of the subjects it composes. The task of a theory that traced such a desire would be directly political. Can we go beyond the man of good sense, common sense, negotiation and norms and intuit the qualities and the forces of qualities that diminish and compose life? Life itself would neither be that which requires the imposition of norms, nor a domain from which normativity would follow, but would be that creative, queering, divergent, and transposing power that would open up relations beyond those of the thinking or acting subject.

Notes

1. It was in this regard that feminists criticized the supposed pure formalism of John Rawls, who argued that subjects should imagine their ideal polity from a veil of ignorance. Such a notion of a pure subject liberated from partial attachments precludes the consideration of traditionally feminist political problems, such as childcare and childbirth: one can either, as 'corporeal feminists' have done, criticize the theory itself for harboring an implicit gender bias (Diprose 1994), or one can make adjustments to the theory according to its own ideals of pure formalism (Okin 1994).

2. Figures of auto-affection, self-fathering, or mind that gives form and order to matter, have been identified by Jacques Derrida, and others, as 'remainders' within Western metaphysics that enable the figuration of a pure and ideal point of view. Thus 'man' would not be one term among others in the system but an irreducible norm from which systematicity is figured (Derrida 1981). In a more explicit use of deconstruction for queer theory Lee Edelman considered 'homographesis' as the general scene through which homosexuality presents itself as a series of differences to be read, but which at the same time thereby opens up sexuality in general to the problem of *differance* (Edelman 1994).

3. In *Giving an Account of Oneself*, Butler does, however, distance herself from her earlier insistence on the exclusivity of subjection, and suggests other modes of relation that are not purely negative. Even so, her central criticism of Rosi Braidotti's feminism—which is the mode of theory I will be pursuing here—is the status of the negative. I would therefore disagree with Butler's

own mapping of the relation among her own work, the work of Deleuze, psychoanalysis and Braidotti's feminism: 'Every time I try to write about the body, the writing ends up being about language. This is not because I think that the body is reducible to language; it is not. Language emerges from the body, constituting an emission of sorts. The body is that upon which language falters, and the body carries its own signs, its own signifiers, in ways that remain largely unconscious. Although Deleuze opposed psychoanalysis, Braidotti does not' (Butler 2004, 198). I will contest this supposed opposition of Deleuze to psychoanalysis; Deleuze opposed the personalization of the unconscious, favoring a more radical unconscious or 'unthought' that was radically inhuman and positive: the Ideas or problems through which we think, which give themselves to be thought, even if they cannot be thought: 'schizoanalysis attains a nonfigurative and nonsymbolic unconscious, a pure abstract figural dimension' (Deleuze and Guattari 1983, 351). As Butler continues, 'Psychoanalysis seems centered on the problem of lack for Deleuze, but I tend to center on the problem of negativity. One reason I have opposed Deleuze is that I find no registration of the negative in his work, and I feared he was proposing a manic defense against negativity' (Butler 2004, 198). Even if there are modes of subjective relation that are—contra Nietzsche— not those of force and violence, there can be (for Butler) no mode of self or theory which is not constituted in relation to norms. It is precisely, though, in Butler's (2005) critical reading of Nietzsche's force as violence—in the sense of violence done by selves to others—that the limits of her theory lie. Another reading of Nietzsche (one pursued by Gilles Deleuze [1983] and Elizabeth Grosz [2004]) posits a positive and generating force, not as force among bodies or as force of one body over another. To say that 'life' begins with force is to reject the original position of bodies and terms (or even the system through which terms are distributed)—force as relations between or among bodies—and instead see force as the differential production of bodies and relations. Force in that differential and originally unequal sense is queer: not the force *of* a body, quality or quantity. We could see such a reading of force as a radicalization of Spinoza's 'field' metaphysic (Bennett 1984): there is not a space that is filled with bodies, nor a general pool of energy which is then organized into distinct terms; instead, everything begins with a dynamic potentiality for relations, which are then actualized to produce a space or field of quantities and qualities.

4. In a remarkably lucid article, Elisa Glick (2000) has criticized Judith Butler's 'linguistic idealism' and privileging of representational politics in favor of a more Marxist interrogation of the lived practices and historical and economic contexts from which practices such as 'drag' emerge. Glick draws on David Harvey's work to argue that Butler reinforces a postmodern capitalist lifestyle commodity culture in her emphasis on performativity (precisely *because* performance effects, rather than follows, subjectivity). Here I would like to pursue an opposite critique: Butler's performativity is not too detached

from lived experience, but too reliant on an image of life as coming into being and recognition through effected, critical and destabilizing subjects. If we think of life *beyond* constituted bodies, as Elizabeth Grosz does in her re-reading of Darwin, Freud and Nietzsche (2004), or as Rosi Braidotti does in her notion of metamorphoses and transpositions that can be considered *ecologically* beyond the human (2002; 2006), then we have a new model of queer politics. We abandon the exemplary queer subject of drag and parody, to examine the abstract potentialities from which subjects are composed. Concretely, this would mean that subjects are not produced as masculine *or* feminine through some decisive cultural matrix ('exclusive disjunction' in Deleuze's sense), but that masculinity and femininity are potentialities that can be mobilized inclusively: one can be male *and* female (what Deleuze refers to as inclusive disjunction: both a and not-a). This would go beyond being a socialized man dressing *as* a woman: for such parody would be equivocal, or a playing of natural being *against* representation. Instead, we would begin by acknowledging something like 'becoming-woman' that would be a potentiality for life *as such,* beyond women as socialized groups. Significantly both Grosz and Braidotti maintain a positive idea of sexual difference from an Irigarayan perspective, which they (correctly) see as compatible with a Deleuzian impersonal vitalism. If life is not a general undifferentiated force that is then represented by 'man,' sexual difference (becoming-woman, or understanding life beyond the image of man) opens up a new mode of relationality.

Chapter 10

Postmodernism Is a Humanism: Deleuze and Equivocity

The Politics of Postmodernism

There was an intense and long-running debate in the feminist theory of the 1980s regarding the politics of postmodernism. Was the attention to representation, signification and cultural difference a liberation from an essentialism that had mired women in their biology? Or was the focus on representation yet one more way in which the feminine can be appropriated and homogenized within one all-determining system? One way to solve this problem was to shift from feminism, which begins its critique from one side of a sexual binary, to gender, thereby problematizing the nature or construction of that binary. The very concept of gender provided a way out of the impasse of negotiating whether women ought to seek equality or difference, for the problem of gender lay not in whether women were really different but just how that difference had been produced through the representational system.

I want to argue that the very structure of the concept of gender is a symptom, a symptom that pastes over a certain failure to think. It is quite possible, even expected, today to use gender as a self-evidently critical term without asking about the nature of those kinds or 'genres' to which gender refers. Gender difference is either one form of constructed cultural difference among others, just one more way in which man as a representational animal produces his differentiated world. Or, gender difference is a privileged figure or phantasmatic frame through which we construct the symbolic order. Either way, we are always at one remove from difference, already within the frame of gender. Against this tendency towards gender, the problem of the status of sexual difference has re-emerged recently in a certain attack on postmodernism undertaken in the name of Lacanian sexual difference: one cannot reduce the world to a system of circulating differences or constructed genders, for one can only live such a constructed or symbolic frame through the fantasy of a 'real' excluded from that frame, and this 'real' that resists symbolization absolutely is figured through 'woman' (Lacan 1982:144). This is why, for Lacan, there can be no sexual relation, no happy postmodern cohabitation in a world of constructed differences with each term being differentiated from every other. For one term of that relation—woman—is not an object within the system but a fantasized 'one' outside or beyond the system (Copjec 1994:235; Žižek 2003:12). For all their virulence, these attacks on what Slavoj Žižek and Joan Copjec among others take to be postmodernism do not go far enough, for they remain within the problem of gender, the problem of the construction of kinds through signification. Whereas the postmodernism under attack supposedly presents the world as a system of unfounded difference, of hybridity, multiplicity and simulation, the Lacanian anti-postmodern riposte merely points out the conditions that must prevail in such a constructed or signified world: one must always presuppose a subject for whom these signifiers signify, a sense barred by the signifier and therefore a 'beyond' of the signifier or 'not-all' that we phantasmatically live as woman. What I will argue is that even if we accept the Lacanian fantasy that underpins the postmodern condition of signification we should go further and ask just whose fantasy this is and whether one might not be liberated from it.

The very concept of gender—the notion of constituted, represented or signified kinds—is tied up with a certain understanding of sexual difference. Sexual difference becomes 'gender' in postmodernism precisely because postmodernism remains a humanism, with the subject as the point of construction or representation through which the world is constituted. The very idea of genders, as signified kinds or binaries, relies upon an equivocal distinction between that which signifies and that which is signified. Man in his modern and postmodern incarnations is not a rational animal so much as a being who, by virtue of the fact that he speaks or signifies, can never be included in the real to which he refers.[1]

There is an idea of postmodermism at the center of Alain Badiou's, Žižek's and Copjec's defence of sexual difference: postmodernism supposedly imagines a world of circulating differences without foundation, ground, subject or center. According to the post-Lacanian critique of this postmodern celebration of difference and hybridity, sexual difference is what must be presupposed, even if disavowed, in such affirmatory logics. In Copjec's case, without the idea of sexual difference—or the idea of woman as the Thing that subtends signification—one could not have a system. In order to signify, the system must be the signification *of* some being, some non-included object, and this being that is extracted from the domain of signifiable, differentiated things is woman, who strictly speaking does not exist. That is, in order to imagine the 'all' of being one has to complete the set of signified objects with that one lost object (Copjec 2003:35-6). The entry into the system of signifiers, which is lived as prohibition or renunciation, produces woman as that which must be renounced. Everything begins with prohibition or the injunction that not all desires are permissible (Žižek 2003:103-4), and from that 'not' one fantasizes the desired thing beyond the law. For Copjec, the way out of this fantasy is to face the non-all of being, that there is no lost object, that woman does not exist. If women, unlike men, are not constituted through the fantasy of this lost object they offer a new model of ethical agency, the possibility of acting without the mourning or nostalgia for a precluded plenitude. One does not happily inhabit a post-gendered world; one lives through the trauma of sexual difference, the necessary gap or hole in being that has always been phantasmatically imagined as woman.

Badiou takes this attack on postmodernism further, insisting that historicism, sexuality, multiculturalism, the reduction of the work of art to culture, as well as a general laziness and quiescence of thinking, abandon the event, an event that tears the actual world of things from itself but that is also belied once we take this disruption as a truth within the world. For Badiou the event is the rupture of the domain of already constituted things, and it is the exposure of the event that produces the subject of truth, a subject at odds with, or irreducible to, one's world. It is in the Lacanian relation of love, and not in the world of sexuality, that this event opens being (Badiou 1999:83).[2] So for Badiou what is wrong with postmodernism is its celebration of differences and the absence of a subject at odds with this actual multiplicity. I want to sustain the force of this critique of postmodernism—that it is a failure or banality of thinking, a reduction of thought to quotation, repetition and signification—and argue that Badiou, Žižek and Copjec do not go far enough. Rather than assert the subject, the sexual relation or the event as a gap or not-all of being, one needs to traverse the fantasy of 'man' as submitted to a signification that is radically other. We can do this by taking the psychoanalytic genesis of sense one step further. If the emergence of the world, as a domain of representable objects, can occur only through signification, and if we live this signification phantasmatically—as imposed by an other who has subjected my desire to the system of things, thereby denying me 'the Thing'—then we can go one step further. Fantasy and signification, including the subject of speech, are only possible through sense. Rather than remaining within the Oedipal fantasy frame of sense, we might set ourselves the challenge of intuiting the emergence of sense.

We might consider this liberation in Deleuzian-Spinozist terms: from a finite point of consciousness within the world, we see ourselves as subjected to relations (Deleuze 1992); but if one thinks further, if one strives to think from the point of view of the emergence of relations, one will no longer enslave oneself to constituted terms, such as the gender system, the heterosexual matrix or the framing fantasy. One will ask what life must be such that fantasy is possible: what must the body be such that its relations to other bodies would take the form of a sexual narrative? In general, rather than seeing signifiers as imposed on life, we should ask what life is such that it yields signification. This will take us to sexual difference in the non-Lacanian sense: bodies are such that their interactions, desires and affects yield a surface of sense. Sense is not an imposed or alien system that negates, diminishes or orders life; sense is the infinitive (Hughes 2008; Williams 2008).

In addition to his extended argument in *The Logic of Sense*, Deleuze describes the emergence of sense in his first book on cinema. Following C. S. Peirce, we can think of firstness or powers and forces of life; then we have secondness or actions, the ways in which powers act upon each other. Thirdness, or relations properly speaking, take the form of sense: one power does not just encounter another but adds to the encounter the sense or perception of the perception. (The eye does not just encounter light but sees something *as something*, something that could be seen again, and is seen as having the power to be perceived.) Sense, then, is the emergence of the relation, not just between two terms, but a relation to an exchange, a giving or interpretation (Deleuze 1986:197). One can only have signifiers—a system of ordered relations—if there is already a potential in life for the perceived to refer beyond itself. The perceived is not just perceived as having a certain sense—we do not just see the world *as* this or that—for seeing something *as* something requires that the perceived bears a potential to repeat itself, or to be sensed: redness is perceived as redness because of a singularity, a 'to red' that allows for the emergence of sense. This is not an essence in the sense of a predicate—redness in general—but an infinitive, a power to be repeated, varied, extended, actualized, 'to red …' (Deleuze 1990:221). So sense emerges from bodies but is not reducible to bodies, and sense also emerges through the desire of bodies. The psychoanalytic insistence on corporeal genesis takes us to the proper problem of sense (Deleuze 1990:197). At the level of bodies there is a corporeal perception, such as the eye encountering light, but at the level of sense there is an incorporeal event. If the eye exceeds the located present and sees a color as a power or potential to be perceived beyond the present, a 'to red …,' an infinitive emerges that takes the encounter beyond the present and recognizes its force for all time: the eternal truth of the singular (Deleuze 1990:99). Sense is not an order imposed on an undifferentiated world; rather sense is orientation or relations effected from singularities. This means that there is a not a subject or system that signifies; rather, signification and subject are the effects of the sense (or effected relations) of singularities:

> Only a theory of singular points is capable of transcending the synthesis of the person and the analysis of the individual as these are (or are made) in consciousness. We can not accept the alternative which thoroughly compromises psychology, cosmology, and theology: either singularities already comprised in individuals and persons, or the undifferentiated abyss. Only when the world, teaming with anonymous and nomadic, impersonal and pre-individual singularities, opens up, do we tread at last on the field of the transcendental. (Deleuze 1990:103)

Thinking sense in this way requires the challenge of univocity: not remaining within the myth of the construction of life through signification, separating life on the one hand from representational mediation on the other. Rather than regarding desire as that which extends the bodily drive beyond life to an other who does not exist (Žižek 2003:95), univocity sees sense as the surface that regards bodies as located within time, but perceives in them a potential for all time.

So, if there is a criticism of postmodernism that it has failed to take into account the structure of the subject—that to have a lived world of signifiers one cannot avoid positing the subject for whom those objects are presented, and a thing or being that those presentations are presentations of—this does not mean that one should not take this possibility beyond the Oedipal structure it causes. That is, one should go beyond the fantasy and structure of signification to its possibility. This involves three problems that I will address here. First, how has this fantasy—of signifying man relating to an absent object of desire—been constituted (what are its specific historical and political conditions)?

Second, how is fantasy as such, or sense, possible? How is the world always more than itself, not lacking an object that would complete sense, but productive of sense as an incorporeality or extra-being? Finally, if there is an event or possibility of sense that exceeds a system of signifiers how might this lead us to read, and how might we deal with a postmodernism that has so readily reduced what is other than the signifer to an effect of signification? These problems need to be approached through the concept of equivocity, for it is just the postmodern refusal to consider being or ontology beyond signification that is itself ontological and equivocal. How is it that the world is lived as somehow signified through a system that is not of being itself?

The Ontology of Postmodernism: Equivocity

How then is the idea of the postmodern entwined with an equivocal ontology? To begin with, we can follow Gilles Deleuze and Felix Guattari (who, in turn, follow Lacan) and argue that the very concept of the signifier relies on the logic of the subject.[3] In both *Anti-Oedipus* and *A Thousand Plateaus* Deleuze and Guattari trace the historical genesis of the subject through the logic of signification. Once we see life as necessarily mediated through a single point of law and system, and once this system is identified with language as such, then the subject is formed as nothing more than an effect of this one system that 'overcodes' all other systems.

Both Copjec and Žižek, following Lacan, also insist on the subject as the subject of signification. In so far as I speak and am submitted to a law that allows me to articulate my demands in relation to an other—an other who is always given to me through the system of signs—I necessarily imagine a remainder of desire, the real subject, that is other than any of its signified acts (Žižek 1999:159).

Postmodernism, if it is understood as a system of signification that is radically detached from the real or that produces and constitutes the real, is equivocal. As opposed to Deleuze's ontology of univocity in which there is just one plane of expression, equivocity posits two radically incommensurable levels. This is made clear in the Lacanian insistence on the logic of the 'not-all': the linguistic system must, if it is language, posit that to which it refers, and in so doing the subject must also be posited as the desire to signify that underpins the linguistic system as such. The logic of sexual difference here is both subjective and equivocal: subjective because it is only through the desire to speak to or be recognized by an other that the subject who precedes and exceeds the sign is generated: 'sexual difference can articulate itself only in the guise of the series of (failed) attempts to transpose it into symbolic oppositions' (Žižek 2002:12). And this logic is equivocal precisely because that which is other than system and signification is not one more thing or being, but that which can only be imagined as other than any signified being, and yet generated from the very logic of the signifier as that which determines and represents beings. The not-all or the failure of being to be given in the form of a totality entails both some fantasized point beyond the system of signified objects, and the recognition that this beyond is produced by the system's own failure:

> At the core of this matter of the unforgettable but forever lost Thing, we find not just an impossibility of thought, but a void of Being. The problem is not simply that I cannot think the primordial mother, but that her loss opens up a hole in being. Or, it is not that the mother escapes representation or thought,

but that the *jouissance* that attached me to her has been lost and this depletes the whole of my being. (Copjec 2003:35-6)

As Copjec goes on to explain, what is important is not some unrepresentable beyond, but the formation of a drive that directs itself to some representation of this beyond, some part object or thing that we desire that is a fragment or sign of the Thing beyond relations (Copjec 2003:37). What makes this logic truly equivocal is the extreme rigor of Copjec's position: the Thing, or noumenal beyond, is given as other than representation only through a peculiar structure of representation. The drive is just the formation of a representation of a thing that is desired because it is not the Thing: one desires the breast, not for its fulfillment of the needs of life but because it is a fragment of, but not identical to, that which is other than all life, the mother or Thing: 'It is not a means to something other than itself, but is itself other than itself. The bi-partition takes place within the object, not between the object and the satisfaction that lies beyond it' (Copjec 2003:38).

Copjec herself suggests a utopian beyond to this equivocity in the title of her book (itself a quotation from Lacan). To 'imagine there's no woman' is to refuse the masculine fantasy of the Thing or *jouissance* beyond the law. The position of woman—for whom there is no beyond precisely because she is not submitted to the law of castration—might therefore offer the model of an ethical act; unlike man who looks back to a lost totality, it is woman who acts without the support of truth or a barred thing in itself (Copjec 2003:7). Like Alain Badiou, who is highly critical of Deleuze's univocity, Copjec insists on the ethical act as a break, rupture or tear in the fabric of being. Not surprisingly, while Copjec cites the tragic Antigone as exemplary of such an act, Badiou and Žižek appeal to the Christian and Pauline images of a disruption of truth from beyond being (Badiou 2003; Žižek 2001). It is just this religious, transcendent or ir-real affirmation that is most problematic in their critique of postmodernism.

We may want to be critical of the world as a closed system of signifiers that can only be troubled from within, but does this mean we need to leap out of the system by an appeal to a beyond of being? The strength of the contemporary Lacanian position is its appeal to truth as other than received systems, but such a truth can be better and more responsibly secured by Deleuze's insistence on univocity, and this for affirmatively ethical reasons. The problem with equivocity is just its terrifying religious heritage, that it affirms that which is other than communication, representation, experience, justification and language.

Indeed, this must be so if we understand language as signification, as an imposed and arbitrary system, as radically other than its putative referent. So I would argue that both the simple image of the postmodern—as a world of simulation, signification, representation or social construction—*and* the criticism of this notion are equivocal without justification. The idea of language imposed on the world begins from a binary between a world in itself and the mediating or differentiating system. By the same token, the criticism of postmodernism that insists on the necessary fantasy or event of the 'in itself' also accepts truth as other than the lived real. But this equivocal understanding of the signifier should be challenged by the thought of univocity, in which truth may be intuited as that which expresses itself, not as that which is 'in itself' only to be belied by relations, but as that which gives birth to—while remaining irreducible to—relations.

Expressionism, which follows from the commitment to univocity, is not the affirmation of a human subject and his relation to the world; expressionism accounts for relations as emerging from one substance, but a substance that is given not as a single whole but as a play of forces and differences from which points of relative stability emerge. Expressionism aims to intuit the real possibility of relations: to perceive is to establish a relation, to connect or mix corporeal bodies; any such mixture results in an event—say, a perceived quality within time—and this event then opens another time, a time of singularities or eternal truth whereby the *what* that is perceived can be thought independently of the *that* through which it is perceived. The subject who perceives and speaks is made possible through sense. And sense is not the effect of a system of signifiers, for there can be signification only if the signifier refers beyond itself to a signified. Each actual body that we perceive within time has emerged from a potentiality that exceeds its concrete material appearance. It is possible for language to refer, concretely, to 'women,' because that specific and extensive grouping is an actualization of a broader and excessive potentiality. It is this beyond of the signifier—that to which it refers—that Lacan describes in Oedipal terms: to be submitted to language is to seek the sense of what we say, some beyond of the signifier, a beyond imagined as prohibited by the one who holds the phallus, with the phallus as a paradoxical element, for it offers itself as signifier of signifiers—*that there is sense*—while strictly bearing no sense. For Deleuze, who follows Lacan up to this point (Deleuze 1990:228), one needs to go one step further. That there can be sense, that a body part can detach itself and present itself as the sense or law of bodies is possible only through the event of sense in general: the capacity for bodies—through their mixtures, causes or relations within time—to release the thought of that which is for all time.

This event or infinitive is sense: it inheres in language but cannot be reduced to language. Regardless of whether I affirm, remember, imagine, deny or desire what is expressed, the expressed itself remains the same; the expressed is therefore not the thing itself (what is denoted). The expressed is perceived as that in the thing that marks it out as being the thing that it is. So when I say 'morning star' or 'president of the United States of America' I refer beyond the corporeal object (the physical body of the planet Venus, or the individual Barack Obama) to that body's particular way of being referred to, and if I tried to explain this sense—by saying the morning star is the evening star, or saying that the president of the United States is the husband of Michelle Obama—I would then have to give you another sense; we can never say sense itself or that which sense expresses. Nor is the expressed the mental or psychological idea of the I who speaks (manifestation), for the sense of, say, 'the author of *Hamlet*' is more than the corporeal body of William Shakespeare (for there would still be an 'author of *Hamlet*' if we were to find that the physical individual named as William Shakespeare did not actually write the plays we had taken him to write. Sense is also more than any individual's articulation of sense, for we can identify the same sense in different articulations. Sense is the result of bodies and their encounters, the expression of relations, but it also takes on a being of its own that should not be regarded as other than being, as imposed on being, but as 'extra-being.'

Univocity enables responsible and responsive thinking: not accepting the world as signified, as mediated through signs, but interrogating the emergence of signs. Equivocity, by contrast, is banality, not thinking through the events within which we are immersed, but accepting already given distinctions between two substances; equivocity reads art as representation, selves as constructs, and genders as mediated kinds. Equivocity accepts two levels—signifier *and* signified, sign *and* world, representation *and* the real—without asking the genesis of this difference.

Deleuze explains equivocity in his book on Spinoza by referring to two ways of apprehending signs. If Adam sees the prohibition placed over the tree of knowledge as a command or imposed order, then the sign or command is seen as other than the world, tyrannically imposed. It is as though there is the world on the one hand, and then the laws and commands of its governing creator on the other. If, however, Adam sees the prohibition as an expression of the world's relations, as a sign of the harm that will follow from eating the forbidden fruit, then God is nothing more than the full knowledge of the world's powers (Deleuze 1992:247). To see signs *as signifiers*, as differences arbitrarily imposed on an otherwise lawless and undifferentiated world, is to imagine the system of speech and the speaking subject as radically other than the world itself. There is posited being on the one hand and the subject who posits on the other; this results in the radical split of the subject and the symbolic, for any thought of being as a whole must always have a remainder, blind spot or not-all that conditions the system but is never able to be articulated within the system. The subject is produced in and through subjection (Butler 1997).

There are both ontological and practical or pragmatic reasons to reject equivocity. Ontologically, equivocity might be defined as the privileging of ontology, or as the decision to grant some being a foundational status (whether that foundation is the subject, life, actuality, culture, signification, God, humans, matter and so on). It follows that equivocity would also entail a certain mode of pragmatism, whereby we accept what is true in terms of what is true *for us,* or what works *for us*—which is of course no truth at all. By contrast, univocity does not concern itself with what *really is* and so there could (and should) be arguments about whether one can include numbers, fictional characters, relations or values in one's ontology; there would be no privileged being that would provide the yardstick for all other beings. It follows that if there is a pragmatism it would be without ground: no longer a decision of truth according to what works for us, but truth as that which works as such, as that which takes hold or possesses force. (And if one were to answer that this seems like totalitarianism—for doesn't Nazism 'have force'—one would reply that, Nazism doesn't possess force because it has to operate by vanquishing and denying force. (In fact totalitarianisms are necessarily equivocal, grounding the truth of the world on some higher logic of what really and truly is.) Univocity affirms one expressive plane of life in which languages and signs express or flow from the real, and yet do so in ways that are contingent (or that could have issued in different systems). By contrast, in equivocal ontologies signifiers imprison and order a life that in itself remains radically other or phantasmatic. Our submission to a system of signs gestures to an outside that is signified, but out of reach. According to equivocal logics, the signifier is a law or command, an order or norm to which thought ought to submit. And it is in this process or act of submission that the subject is split from being; a gap or 'not-all' opens a symbolic order that both produces and precludes its mourned outside.

It is just this equivocity that engenders postmodernism and its discontents, for it establishes the signifier, system and subject on the one hand, and the real or the retroactively constituted world on the other. For Jean Baudrillard, the simulacrum is defined through a loss or absence of the real and is therefore both other than the real as well as being the only real, or hyperreal, to which we have access (Baudrillard 1994). There have also been positive affirmations of this post-metaphysical condition, a condition abandoning the real and recognizing our linguistic condition. For Richard Rorty, postmodern liberal humanism is just this acceptance of our existence within contexts along with the abandonment of any grand claims to foundations, justification or life as such (Rorty 1983). Jurgen Habermas, while critical of what he takes to be the postmodern relativism of deconstruction, nevertheless insists that only by working within speech and negotiation can there be any politics; politics abandons any metaphysical outside to focus on procedures of legitimation and communication (Habermas 1992). Judith Butler, who maintains both the idea of a mourning for a lost real, and the recognition that such a real is produced only through mourning, insists that it is just this recognition of subjection that might enable political mobility:

> One can certainly concede that desire is radically conditioned without claiming that it is radically determined, and that

there are structures that make possible desire without claiming that those structures are impervious to a reiterative and transformative articulation. The latter is hardly a return to 'the ego' or classical liberal notions of freedom, but it does insist that the norm has a temporality that opens it to a subversion from within and to a future that cannot be fully anticipated. (Butler 2000:21)

Gender, if one took this dominant equivocal point of view, would be an identity or position adopted in order that we might speak, act and perform as subjects; but this very condition of required submission and normativity would also allow for instability. One must recognize oneself *as* this or that gendered identity in order to take part in what Butler refers to as the heterosexual matrix; but, precisely because this matrix is constituted through speech, acts and performatives, it is also always capable of being rendered otherwise, of producing new relations. Gender is a system of norms and prohibitions; it is only through the prohibition of the object of desire—say, the maternal body—that the subject is produced *as other than* that which he must have desired. One's sex, or that which precedes the gender system, is, for Butler, positioned *as real* only after the event of its loss or abandonment. Sex remains as impossibly other precisely because submission to the system of gender is not something one does or does not do; there is not a self who then adopts the law. Rather, there is law—the norm of speaking as this or that gender—and from there one recognizes oneself as a sexed subject who was destined to take on this or that position. One is produced as a subject through the fantasy of submission. On the one hand, then, Butler appears to be anti-postmodern, for she rejects the idea of a system of signs imposed on an otherwise neutral and inaccessible sex. On the other hand, she represents the epitome of equivocal logics. Our position within a system of norms produces a radical difference between norm and that which the norm supposedly orders, organizes and represents. It is in the repetition of the norms or signifiers of gender that one produces oneself, one's sex or the real as that which was there to be signified:

> This is not to say that, on the one hand, the body is simply linguistic stuff or, on the other hand, that it has no bearing

> on language. It bears on language all the time. The materiality of language, indeed, of the very sign that attempts to denote 'materiality,' suggests that it is not the case that everything, including materiality, is always already language. On the contrary, the materiality of the signifier (a 'materiality' that comprises both signs and their significatory efficacy) implies that there can be no reference to a pure materiality except via materiality. Hence, it is not that one cannot get outside of language in order to grasp materiality in and of itself; rather, every effort to refer to materiality takes place through a signifying process that, in its phenomenality, is always already material. (Butler 1993:68)

What makes this logic equivocal is not that it is binary so much as the character or nature of the binary. In equivocal logics there are no true binaries or differences, only one privileged term—such as the signifier (or mind or representation)—that generates its pale and dependent others. Equivocity or the positing of two substances, going back to Descartes' distinction between mind and matter, precludes real difference. If one begins from numerical difference between, say, two substances such as mind and matter, then one has to establish a relation between these two, and this will always take the form of one substance negotiating its other: mind as cause of matter, mind as reflection of matter, matter as cause of mind. Once one privileged substance, such as mind or the signifier, accounts for relations and differences, differences can always be seen as different instances predicated on some quality that is parceled out among numerically different bodies. Red, say, would be a generality that could appear now here, now there, differentiated as a quality by the real body of which it is predicated. Univocity, by contrast, allows only for real difference. Two instances of red are really and singularly different, each with their own singular power; this real difference is released in sense, in the perception of this singularity as not being a variation of some generality through time, but as a *'potential to...,'* or an infinitive, that has as much being as anything else. If there is only one being, then differences—such as the difference between incorporeal sense and the bodies it expresses, as well as different qualities—are all equally real and equally different. This is revealed most clearly in the singularities of art: what I might perceive or think here, on this canvas, is not redness in general, redness as the variant of some generality, but a 'to red ...' that bears a repeatability for all time. Univocity or one being enables real difference, for difference is no longer differentiation of some being that is other than the differentiated.

In postmodern equivocal logics, however, difference is determined in advance on the basis of a difference between one type of being or substance and another. One term—the signifier—produces, constitutes and orders its other. For Butler, the real or matter is just that which divides itself into inside and outside, before and after; and the signifier is precisely that portion of matter that divides life from itself (Butler 1993:68). The norms of gender are read as signs of some real and underlying self. So the difference between form and matter, subject and world, sex and gender, signifier and signified, are produced by one substance—the signifier, language or the speech-act—generating its radically incommensurable other. As signifiers, gender norms produce a sexual subject who supposedly precedes the act. For Butler, then, there is no being, substance or life that is the one ground subtending all acts; rather there are acts of a certain form or type—performatives or significations—that then produce their real or cause. So what *seems* like a difference or a binary, the difference between sex and gender, real and signifier, presence and representation, is actually the effect of one term (the signifier) producing a phantom, a lost and imagined other. And this is only possible because there is a distinction made between what really is or has being—the signifier—and its generated and lesser other (the illusory subject or sex). Postmodernism is equivocal precisely because one event or relation of life—the signifier—explains and typifies all relations. Signification is the explanation, cause and logic from which all other relations take their being.

Not only is postmodernism equivocal—depending on the signifier and an absent or constituted real—it is also the culmination of subjectivism. (And in this respect we would have to note the profound value of Butler's work in bringing intelligence, rigor and force to the tradition of ontology that has for the most part *not* faced up to the logic of the signifier that Butler so astutely unpacks.) According to Martin Heidegger, western thought as a whole is subjectivist. Some point or underlying ground—*hypokeimenon*—precedes and orders all other relations; differences are the effect of, or flow from, some point or logic outside life.[4]

But this substance that grounds and orders life is also, for most of western thought, imagined equivocally as other than perceived and lived life. For Heidegger, and Deleuze after him, overturning Platonism does not entail the reversal of the hierarchy of being over becoming, but the recognition that both sides of this binary have their ground in a single life, a life expressed through, but never exhausted by, language. Language is not the sign or order of some world; the world gives itself through language (Heidegger 1998:200) and through multiple series of signs beyond human language (Deleuze and Guattari 1987:117). Western thought becomes enslaved to equivocity, for Heidegger, precisely when the truth of the world, the logic of being, is located in some source point beyond the world itself, when Plato's Ideas, for example, become correct ideas or forms through which the world might be viewed. For Deleuze, this subjection to equivocity has a political origin. Whereas primitive societies regarded their inscriptive systems as expressive and productive—with rituals of tattooing, scarring and symbolization producing the connection among human bodies and the world with which they work (Deleuze and Guattari 1987:176)—modern man regards inscription as signification, as one system of signs that is relatively translatable and that has as its single condition and point of origin 'the' speaking subject (Deleuze and Guattari 1987:159-60).

For both Heidegger and Deleuze, western thought, particularly in its humanist mode, is both equivocal and subjectivist, precisely because the subject—'*das Man*' for Heidegger, the signifying subject for Deleuze—is that point through which all the differences of the world are generated, a single point of generation or synthesis that is the ground of all relative differences. Humanism is equivocal, not just because there are two substances—mind and matter—but because one substance is the ground of the other: the subject is the point from which the logic and relations of the world are recognized and given actuality. Without the synthesizing power of mind the order of the world would not be brought into being.

In postmodernity it is the system of signification, the law of speaking, communicating man, that constitutes a political ground: 'The State gives thought a form of interiority, and thought gives that interiority a form of universality' (Deleuze and Guattari 1987:375). In *Anti-Oedipus*, Deleuze and Guattari explain the ways in which the logic of capitalism is built on a fantasy of man and an equivocal ontology. The idea that we are all submitted to a system of signs, and that outside the system of communication and recognition there is only the chaos of the undifferentiated, and that there must have been an object that was abandoned for the sake of order: all these fantasies of submission center on the affective image of signifying man (Deleuze and Guattari 1987:182). Two key aesthetic political points need to be made here. The first is critical. The idea that 'we' are submitted to a system or law that produces us as subjects set over against a necessarily prohibited object is a sexual fantasy. Psychoanalysis tells me not to kill my father and desire my mother and I realize that that's what I wanted. We should, however, not see ourselves as submitted to a system of speech beyond which lies the undifferentiated night of chaos and incest. On the contrary, for Deleuze and Guattari, systems of signs are expressive; they flow from life, and a life that is *more* differentiated than any formalized system of signs. Signs are not arbitrarily imposed. They do not differentiate and order the real. They are themselves real, have their ground in the real and flow from the real. Signs become signifiers—an imposed system generated from the point of law and the subject—only with the aesthetic investment in the affective perception of man as a speaking animal, or what Deleuze and Guattari refer to as 'faciality' or the regime of the 'despotic signifier' (Deleuze and Guattari 1987:117).[5] Contrary to the view that we can include Deleuze and Guattari within a postmodernism that has freed itself from the real or substance, they insist that the structures, forms and systems within which we operate are substantial. Their theory of language insists that there is a form both to the signs emitted—a form of expression—and a form to what those signs express—a form of content—and these forms, stratifications or expressions take place through substance. 'The signifier' for example expresses the subject, the body of man organized through the face. This affective investment in the signifying body—'the interpretosis of the priest'—can be historically delimited:

> the form of the signifier has a substance, or the signifier has a body, namely, the Face [...]. Not only is this semiotic system not the first, but we see no reason to accord it any particular privilege from the standpoint of an abstract evolutionism. We would like to indicate very briefly certain characteristics of

> the other two semiotic systems. First, the so-called primitive, presignifying semiotic, which is much closer to 'natural' codings operating without signs. There is no reduction to faciality as the sole substance of expression: there is no elimination of forms of content through abstraction of the signified. To the extent that there is still abstraction of content from a strictly semiotic point of view, it fosters a pluralism or polyvocality of forms of expression that prevents any power takeover by the signifier and preserves expressive forms particular to content, thus forms of corporeality, gesturality, rhythm, dance and rite coexist heterogeneously with the vocal form. A variety of forms and substances of expression intersect and form relays. It is a segmentary but plurilinear, multidimensional semiotic that wards off any signifying circularity (Deleuze and Guattari 1987:117)

Deleuze and Guattari write here of 'warding off' circularity, which is precisely how one might describe postmodern equivocal logics: a signifier is not a signifier unless it is the signifier *of* something signified, and yet the signified is given *as signified* only by way of the signifier. So, from the critical point, where we reject the idea of signs imposed on life, we can move to the constructive point of asking whose life is expressed in this Oedipal fantasy of man submitted to language for the sake of being saved from the dark night of maternal incest? (And how did what is other than the signifier—the form of content—get reduced to a pre-linguistic, undifferentiated and unthinkable abstraction?) When confronted by a language—such as the language of postmodernism, the language of signifying man—we can ask about the genesis of linguistic system, and about the desires it expresses.

Now, according to the early Deleuze, there is a sexual genesis to sense, and he follows psychoanalysis strictly on this point. The self-preservative and destructive drives produce a series of partial objects, which are then related to the phallus as a paradoxical object: for the phallus is that body part that signifies but does not yield the sense of what it signifies. There are two series: the concrete body parts that make up our actual body, and then the *organism* that experiences itself as a unified identity only through reference to some organizing point. In the case of the Oedipus complex, the self is unified by imagining that its bodily integrity or the image of the body as a coherent whole might be fragmented if another body—the father who possesses the law—were to impose castration. Oedipalism creates a specific causal series: it refers the series of multiple parts to an imaginary whole—the self or subject who speaks and answers to the law—and then (*ex post facto*) regards fragmentation as that which would follow if the self were to transgress the prohibition on desire. The body's actual parts are organized via a virtual scene. And this enigmatic resonance between two series—the series of bodily objects and the series of the object elevated above the body—yields sense only with the Oedipus complex, which refers the series beyond itself to the event (Deleuze 1990:220). For Deleuze, here, the event emerges from sexuality but then liberates itself from a personal sexuality. So, for example, the mouth that connects to the breast through the drives of life, articulates a demand that is addressed to an other who is beyond life (for the breast is also a promise of love, and an indication of an other whose desires can be imagined but never known). It is with speech, emerging from sexual relations, that a sense irreducible to speech is liberated; any act of speech expresses a sense that is at once within a context (referring to this sense here and now) but also beyond a context, for the same act of speech could be repeated in other contexts. Sense is sexual in a ramified sense. Sense is a pure attribute, an infinitive or power that detaches itself from bodies.

Concretely, one can say that bodies allow for perceptions or qualities. One can perceive a certain quality, and this perception might then be expressed in a proposition. It is in and through this expressed proposition that sense is liberated: a perception *of x* is perceived as a power *to x*, a redness, for example, that is capable of being repeated and varied in any time whatever. Sense may emerge dynamically from Oedipal relations among bodies, but can never be reduced to bodies. You and I can converse and understand each other only because our language transcends us both, and exceeds any single body. Indeed, if we are to *think*, one needs to move beyond constituted sexualities to the sense that appears as their 'quasi-cause': it seems that we speak only because we are subjected to a single system that grants us our distinct identity, but this supposedly foundational or causal law is possible only because of relations among bodies.

This allows us to move to the positive argument of univocity. There is an affective component of any system of signs, any assemblage; there is a form of expression (or a particular character to the regime of signs) as well as a form of content (or a particular distribution of what is expressed). In capitalism we imagine the form of expression to be the signifier, an imposed and purely differential system, and we imagine the form of content, or what is signified, to be the undifferentiated, negative or retroactively posited real. But if all regimes are expressions of life, and if we question the universality of the signifying model, we can ask what mode of life the despotism of the signifier expresses. How did we come to think of ourselves as subjected to systems? How did we come to think of life as that which can only be thought (phantasmatically) as other than the law? What investments, desires, connections must be presupposed for me to think of myself as a speaking subject positioned within a law that is radically other than some supposedly negated pre-Oedipal real? If we see signs not as radically other than life but as expressions of life we can undertake two tasks.

First, we can ask what the image of signifying man expresses. What configuration of desire has produced a submission to law that remains forever in a state of negation, loss and mourning of the real? Deleuze and Guattari give a direct answer in *Anti-Oedipus*. Lacan is quite right to note that we are all Oedipal, but this Oedipal subject is historically, politically and sexually specific. It is the man of the bourgeois family who sees himself as dominated by an internalized father. And this internalized, punishing and castrating father—this man of law within us all—has a political and historical origin. Whereas law and force once emanated from the despot, the king or the tribal ruler, we now see law as 'human,' as generated from the simple fact that we are speaking beings. A certain body—that of white, laboring, familial man, the man of propositions and judgments—provides the affective image that underpins the Oedipal fantasy. (And underpinning that Oedipal fantasy is the 'image of thought' in general, or the equivocal notion *par excellence*: that there is some thinking being, subject or performativity that precedes and conditions the world.) The fantasy of signification is therefore expressive of a reactive desire, a desire that posits man as a speaking animal, submitted to the logic of the signifier, set over against a desiring life that can now only be imagined as retroactively constituted through the very fantasy of prohibition. And as long as we do not question this fantasy we remain within what Deleuze refers to as the 'neurotic novel'; we repeat the symptom as our own (Deleuze 1990, 276). Žižek has recently defended this persistence of desiring negativity on two grounds: first, without the gap of desire or the illusion that there is a distance between the emptiness of the subject and the world, the desires we would be left with nothing, but subjectivity lies in this 'less than nothing,' in acknowledging that the subject *is* an illusion but one that nevertheless persists through the desire of the drive. Second, this allows for creativity: no object answers to my desire, and 'my' subjectivity is nothing other than this gap or distance between desire and what I can grasp, know or have:

> Far from being the same as the nirvana principle (the striving towards the dissolution of all tension, the longing for a return to original nothingness), the death drive is the tension which persists and insists beyond and against the nirvana principle. In other words, far from being opposed to the pleasure principle, the nirvana principle is its highest and most radical expression. In this precise sense, the death drive stands for its exact opposite, for the dimension of the 'undead,' of a spectral life which insists beyond (biological) death. [...]. What Lacan calls 'symbolic castration' is a deprivation, a gesture of taking away (the loss of the ultimate and absolute—'incestuous' —object of desire) which is *in itself giving*, productive, generative, opening up and sustaining the space of desire and meaning. The frustrating nature of our human existence, the very fact that our lives are forever out of joint, marked by a traumatic imbalance, is what propels us towards permanent creativity. (Žižek 2012)

This dimension of Žižek's thought comes close to the Deleuzian insistence that one also recognize the subject as a production: the key difference lies in the nature of production, whether it can be located in a death drive of the psyche or whether there is a broader extra-human field of force of which the human death drive would be but one actualization. I would suggest that the difference lies in the commitment to univocity:

should we affirm the subject as *the* gap or 'less than nothing' that introduces an 'undead' haunting or absent element allowing for creativity, *or* should we distribute distance across an entire field, beyond organisms, subjects and what is taken to be life? Univocity would not deny the force of subjects and desires, but would locate such forces or drives in a larger plane—with no mode of drive being any more significant than any other. This would also mean that one would challenge certain accounts of 'the political,' such as Judith Butler's account of subjects and bodies as being given through political systems:

> If one can speak about the 'being' of the body, it is a 'being' that is always given over to others, to norms, to social and political organizations that have developed historically and that allocate precariousness differentially. It is not possible first to define the ontology of the body and then to refer to the social significations the body assumes, or the social networks that form its conditions for subsistence. Rather, to be a body is to be exposed to social crafting and form; it is to be this very exposure. That is what makes the ontology of the body a *social* ontology. In other words, the body is exposed to socially and politically articulated forces as well as to claims of sociality—including language, work, and desire—that make possible the body's persisting and flourishing. (Butler 2011, 382)

If we think beyond the polity then we move from equivocity—the polity and the bodies its creates by way of subjection—to univocity, where there is no polity so much as a field of forces that are micro-political, creating thousands of tiny interactions, relations and resistances.

The challenge of both thought and art is to construct a symptomatology: to read the symptom as a response to a problem, to read the work of art not as an arbitrary or contextually bound signification but as an event of sense. For Žižek the imperative is to 'enjoy your symptom,' because without the subject's attachment to some contingent object that promises (but also stands in the way of) full enjoyment there would be no life, force or resistance. For Žižek the gap or distance of the symptom is tied to the distinct difference of language:

Everybody now knows that 'we can do things with words': [...]. And indeed, is not the very kernel of psychoanalysis embedded in the dimension of language embedded in the dimension of language as speech *act*? Is it not confined to this dimension by the very fact that it is a *talking cure,* an attempt to reach and transform the real of the symptom solely by means of words, i.e., without having recourse to an immediate operation on the body [...]. The point is not to arrive at the factual truth of some long-forgotten event—what is effectively at stake here is, quite literally, the recollection of the past, i.e., the way this remembrance of the past bears on the subject's *present* position of enunciation, how it transforms the very place from which the subject speaks (is spoken). (Žižek 2001, 32)

For Deleuze, by contrast, symptoms trace back to a field well beyond subjects, to a plane of forces from which relatively stable points emerge. Expressionism works against the craven *ressentiment* that would proclaim: 'I am constituted through the system of signifiers therefore I can only think what is beyond signification as some absent cause.' Expressionism prompts us to look beyond the fantasy of signifying man to the very possibility of signs. Expression—seeing signs as events that flow from the real—is tied to univocity: not world and signification, not real and system, but one flowing life. And yet this flow of life gives itself in articulation, in ever and ever finer distinctions, cuts, bifurcations, disturbances; the cuts are not differentiations *of* the real, for 'the real' *is* the force of distinction and difference. Both expression and univocity in turn are dependent on the recognition of affect, and yet affect is *not* emotion. If affects are considered to be what we feel when our bodies respond to certain forces or perturbation, then affect is once again the sign *of* some outside. Part of the force of Deleuze and Guattari's philosophy is to detach affect from the lived and from feelings and emotions; one might say that there are affects or the powers and forces that occur in the relations among quantities, some of which are felt. Forces of light meet with the resistance of my skin; I feel warmth. I probably do not feel the other quantities produced (vitamin D, melanoma, ageing and so on.). What if a painter could paint this light? Not light as felt or absorbed, but light in its capacity *to warm*? Then an affect would be seized upon that might stand alone. Further, we might say that persons and other organisms are possible because there are affects: powers of encounter from which we are assembled.

It is the critical concept of affect that allows us to ask just what the equivocity of postmodern man expresses. It is through affect and its extension that we can explain the emergence of the image and fantasy of man. In his book on David Hume, Deleuze explains how all life is affect or sympathy (Deleuze 1991:34); a body lives and desires in its partial connections and attachments to other bodies. From the connection of one body part to another the self forms regular sympathies with present bodies, say in the formation of a family or tribe (territorialization). But one can extend these sympathies to bodies that are not present. A body can become exemplary, and represent the law or identity of the whole (deterritorialization). For Hume, the family produces the father as the exemplary body, and we can imagine communities as extended families, such that social virtues are fictions that enable us to think of imaginary wholes that express and extend sympathies (Deleuze 1991:35). This fictive extension can produce the image of man or humanity: a community of those who are not present or can be thought of only potentially (Deleuze 1991:41). Two points need to be made and the first is directly aesthetic-political: the extension of sympathy or affect begins from expressivity and image. One body stands in for the whole, allowing us to think the community of bodies or the family of man. And this allows us to understand why our supposedly universal concepts of humanity, or man in general, are always different and micro-political. The supposedly generic 'man of reason,' is more often than not the white, bourgeois man of modern capitalism. (In the beginning is not the polity, but the affect or attachment from which a figure of 'the body' is assembled.) The sense of 'man' or the subject is always the affective extension or deterritorialization of this or that body. Despite all our proclamations of humanity, human rights and universal sympathy recent events ought to lead us to question why, when we know this distant, different suffering other has as much right as my similar neighbor, we nevertheless feel more sympathy for those who are like 'us.' The western trauma of September 11 is a salutary reminder of just how affective our image of humanity is, for was not this incident traumatic precisely because it was an attack on the West, on us, on 'man'? Only an affective and expressive approach to sense—not a logic of the signifier—can deal with a politics that is pre-discursive. Far from insisting on the logic of sexual difference, *as differentiation,* which would have to do with the formal structure of signification, thinking of sex expressively allows us to intuit the articulations of the body that is imagined and presupposed in our fantasy of the speaking subject.

The subject of rights and language, who is supposedly any speaker whatever, is a body who precedes exchange, who communicates, calculates, labors and submits to inter-subjective norms; this affective body of the 'speaking subject' is produced from the body of white western man, a body governed by the signifying face and expressive eyes:

> The face is not universal. It is not even that of the white man; it is White Man himself, with his broad white cheeks and the black holes of his eyes. The face is Christ. The face is the typical European, what Ezra Pound called the average sensual man, in short, the ordinary everyday Erotomaniac [...]. (Deleuze and Guattari 1987:176)

Deleuze and Guattari also argue that the image of speaking, judging and signifying man—the subject produced through the system that differentiates life and negates the real—is equivocal. Its desire for that which is necessarily or constitutively prohibited, the definition of man through Oedipal or negated desire, sets the signifying subject radically apart from 'his' world. On the one hand there is the order of speech, signification, difference and relations; on the other hand there is a real that remains forever out of reach, retroactively produced or imagined only from within the limit of the system: man and his other(s). Nowhere is this more apparent than in fetishized ethical models of the face, where the radical distance and absence of *the* other closes the world upon the subject and what cannot be apprehended. For Deleuze, reading through Proust, the face, like all fragments, does not present itself as a radical alterity set apart from the world, but it does open out onto proliferating worlds:

> By setting fragments into fragments, Proust finds the means of making us contemplate them all, but without reference to a unity from which they might derive or which itself would derive from them. [...]

Even the final revelation of time regained will not unify them nor make them converge, but will multiply the 'transversals' that themselves are not interconnected[...]. Similarly, the faces of the other have at least two dissymmetric sides, like 'two opposing routes that will never meet' : thus for Rachel, the way of generality and that of singularity, or else that of the shapeless nebula seen from too close and that of an exquisite organization seen from a right distance. Or else for Albertine, the face that corresponds to trust and the face that reacts to jealous suspicion[...], and again the two routes or the two ways are only statistical directions. We can form a complex group, but we never form it *without its splitting in its turn, this time as though into a thousand sealed vessels:* thus Albertine's face, when we imagine we are gathering it up in itself for a kiss, leaps from one plane to another as our lips cross its cheek, 'ten Albertines' in sealed vessels, until the final moment in the exaggerated proximity. And in each vessel is a self that lives, perceives, desires, and remembers, that wakes or sleeps, that dies, commits suicide, and revives in abrupt jolts: the 'crumbling,' the 'fragmentation' of Albertine's departure, must be learned by all these distinct selves, each at the bottom of its urn. (Deleuze 2000, 124)

Expressionism

For Deleuze the problem that poses itself if we think of expression, rather than signification, is how we might discern and intuit a life that exceeds and solicits the enclosure of the subject. If postmodern subjectivity depends on the affective image of man—the self positioned within exchange, communication and the negation of life—then the path to expression might be through sexual difference, a difference that would have to be rethought at the level of style. Instead of seeing sexual difference as the logic through which life is signified—with the man of speech and law set over against the feminine 'not-all' or beyond of signified objects—one might imagine sexual difference as the style of life.

If there is not life on the one hand and signification on the other, but one expressive life that gives itself only in its styles, then we can propose a series of connections. Sense is sexual precisely because the corporeal body and its relations create a sexual surface, a series of zones and territories that extend and thereby transform the drives of life. Sense is possible through the Oedipal relation that creates a surface or frontier between the body on the one hand and the incorporeal expressed on the other. Even in *The Logic of Sense,* Deleuze will insist on a further metaphysical surface: the impersonal singularities that are irreducible to the Oedipal relation from which they emerge. But in *Anti-Oedipus,* with Guattari, he is more stringent: the mother-father-child schema is *one* fantasy of sense, one way in which bodies and their connections deterritorialize, or allow a body or body part—the phallus—to provide the sense of all bodies.

The way to think through the Oedipal enclosure of sense is through style, for style creates sense, especially in the form of the paradox. Paradox is only possible through sense but also displays sense as emerging through a language that it also exceeds. 'I do not mean what I say'; 'this has no meaning'; 'this is not what I'm saying'; 'I am lying'; or 'this is not true': such acts are performative contradictions. They are so because the 'I' who speaks is split from the 'I' denoted; paradoxes allow the speaking subject to inhabit the system of sense, while also refusing sense. This is only possible because sense operates in two directions at once, down towards the denoted or what is said, and outwards towards the expressed that is released from the denoted. Sense, therefore, relies on an aleatory or paradoxical element, such as the 'I' that at once grounds the speech in a here and now and releases a sense of the act that exceeds this 'I' (Deleuze 1990, 77). It is this creation of a surface or paradoxical element that occurs through style. Style is sexual if we take sexuality to be the extension of the drive beyond its object. Sense is not tied to sexuality because a sexual scene or fantasy of difference is required in order for the signifier to be split or barred from the subject; sense is sexual because by sexuality Freud referred to the event: the power for an affect, quality or perceived to be thought and imaged beyond the corporeal body.

Styles do not refer to or organize some underlying life; styles are problems, expressions or strivings of a life that gives itself in its variations (Deleuze and Guattari 1987:318). These variations or styles are sexual because they are productive, connective and desiring. 'Becoming-woman' can then be seen to indicate a counter-Oedipal movement of sense: not the 'woman' who does not exist because she is man's projected, fantasized other, but woman as variation. There are becomings, or positive expressions of life, that occur as powers or styles of variation that are different from the centered subject of speech and enunciation. Whereas the image of the subject is that of some site or point that manages, subtends or imposes difference, becoming-woman is always 'becoming-towards.' It is not creation *ex nihilo*. Becoming-woman can be intuited as an expression of that life of which man is only one distinct effect: 'A woman has to become-woman, but in a becoming-woman of all man' (Deleuze and Guattari 1987:292). 'Man' and 'woman' are not binary differentiations or genders; both terms are expressions of a sexuality that goes beyond the human (233), a sexuality that can only be intuited if we go beyond the logic of signifying man and think of a life that articulates itself in distinct powers or potentials to become. There is no single point, term or actuality—no man as subject—that can act as ground and enunciating center for all becoming:

> There is no becoming-man because man is the molar entity par excellence, whereas becomings are molecular. The faciality function showed us the form under which man constitutes the majority, or rather the standard upon which the majority is based: white, male, adult, 'rational,' etc., in short, the average European, the subject of enunciation. (Deleuze and Guattari 1987:92)

Conclusion

In order to give this reference to style more specificity we might consider Virginia Woolf's novel *To the Lighthouse*. First we can consider the novel critically, at the semantic and narrative level, as both an allegory and manifesto of aesthetics. The first section of the novel, 'The Window,' sets up a series of oppositions that take the binary form of equivocity: one term—man—is the ground, origin and center from which the other term 'woman' is effected as different. Mr Ramsay the philosopher who works with defined and closed problems and who is concerned about his place in history (or whether he will be remembered in the great canon of philosophers) is set against Mrs Ramsay who is the classically other-directed, emotive, empathetic, beautiful and uncomprehending 'woman.' Lily Briscoe is trying to paint Mrs Ramsay as an iconic representation of all things human and wholesome, but has to deal with the phrase emanating from Tansley, one of Mr Ramsay's university colleagues, that 'women can't paint, women can't write.' The binaries of this first section are equivocal precisely because they organize sensible, physical and emotional being as the lesser, dependent and distinct other of intellectual being. Lily's painting of Mrs Ramsay will be a representation of meaning, of the female body as the principle of life and nurturance; it will also take its place within history. Just as Mr Ramsay is fearful that his personal contribution to philosophy might pass unnoticed and that his proper name might remain unrecorded, so Lily's painting aims to take its place in the great hall of art. We could see this first part of the novel as critical.

Woolf repeats the standard oppositions of western thought—male/female, reason/body, logic/emotions, philosophy/art and viewer/viewed—in order to expose their rigidity. As Jane Goldman has noted, there is more than one way to read Woolf's declaration that on or about 1910 human nature changed (Goldman 1998). 1910 was the year of the Post-Impressionist exhibition, when forces of light and difference were freed from the organizing point of the human eye. We should therefore consider the style of the novel with regard to the problem it expresses, what the novel as an event of sense is striving to do, and the potentials or infinitives it releases. This is given at two levels in the novel. First, in the concluding section of the novel Lily Briscoe no longer represents Mrs Ramsay, nor is her artwork pure form and imposition; she is invaded by perception. Her work is neither an intended act, nor a performance that produces her as a distinct subject, so much as a perception in which two terms—Lily's desire and the painting—are produced as distinct through their specific relation.

> With a curious physical sensation, as if she were urged forward and at the same time must hold herself back, she made her first quick decisive stroke. The brush descended. It flickered brown over the white canvas; it left a running mark. A second

time she did it—a third time. And so pausing and so flickering, she attained a dancing rhythmical movement, as if the pauses were one part of the rhythm and the strokes another, and all were related; and so, lightly and swiftly pausing, striking, she scored her canvas with brown running nervous lines which had no sooner settled there than they enclosed (she felt it looming out at her) a space. (Woolf 1977:148)

It is the event of sense, or the emergence of a difference, that creates Lily and the surface to which she is directed. (Lily and canvas operate in modes of mutual creation or transversal becoming.) Lily finally draws a dark line on the canvas, thus reversing the idea of a single light that illuminates and gives form: 'with a sudden intensity, as if she saw it clear for a second, she drew a line there, in the centre' (Woolf 1977:192). Here it is dark—the zero degree of light, the positivity of light's absence—that expresses a pure difference, not this or that different thing, but the pure potential *to differ*. If the God of Genesis gives form to being and matter through light, Lily's creation produces form through dark on light, a light that is not differentiating so much as given in difference. This iconic moment in the novel expresses a manifesto or desire for a certain style: style as the response to differing light, and not style as a form-giving or illuminating power set over a dark matter.

With this iconic moment in mind, we can now read the style of Woolf's novel as a whole in terms of its refusal of the position of subject and object and its tracing of singularities. The power of Woolf's sentences, we might say, is that they fail to connect or logically follow. How, we might ask, can a sentence, such as the following, describe *a light that allows something to be heard*, a sound that harbors a memory and longing, and that illuminates lost objects, and then draws a smell, and ultimately produces a tactile sensation of grit. In the following sentence the subject of the sentence is a perception, first of light ('the sun poured'); this light then enables the auditory ('so that every footstep could be plainly heard'); the sound evokes a distant scene or desire ('sobbing for her father'); and then, we might ask, just what is it that 'lit up bats'? For this same subject that illuminates, allows to be heard and recalls is eventually referred to as olfactory—'a smell of salt and weeds'—before concluding with the tactile 'gritty':

while the sun poured into those attics, which a plank alone separated from each other so that every footstep could be plainly heard and the Swiss girl sobbing for her father who was dying of cancer in a valley of the Grisons, and lit up bats, flannels, straw hats, ink-pots, beetles, and the skulls of small birds, while it drew from the long frilled strips of seaweed pinned to the wall a smell of salt and weeds, which was in the towels too, gritty with sand from bathing. (Woolf 1977:13)

No longer adopting the propositional style of a subject who predicates qualities of an outside world, nor of a subject who is nothing more than the mechanical repetition of a disembodied system, Woolf's style moves beyond the free-indirect inhabitation of styles towards monadic points of perception. The sentences confuse perceiver and perceived, at the same time as they express a substance that does not exhaust itself in any of its terms. Essence is power, and power is the capacity to affect and be affected. To intuit the essence of a text, to think beyond its composed terms, is to strive to perceive or be affected by the problem to which it is a response. From the rigid binaries of male and female, light and dark, Woolf's style moves to the singular differences covered over by dependent oppositions; sexual difference supplants gender. There are no longer distinct kinds or generalities, or genders, so much as essences that operate as powers *to differ*, essences that are sexual precisely because they have their sole being in creation.

Notes

1. '[T]he paradox is that the Real as external, excluded from the Symbolic, is in fact a symbolic determination—what eludes symbolization is precisely the Real as the inherent point of failure of symbolization' (Žižek 2000:121).

2. The relation of love, in Badiou's work, is only one way in which we might consider the event, which also manifests itself in the poem, the matheme and the revolutionary situation. I am here deliberately narrowing the terms of debate to the question of sexual difference and gender. The figures whom I am contrasting with Deleuze—Judith Butler, Joan Copjec, Slavoj Žižek, as well as Alain Badiou—do offer highly nuanced reflections on the problem of sexual difference. By drawing a stark contrast between their approaches and that of Deleuze—despite the fact that there are certain sympathies—I hope

to focus on the ways in which the work of thinkers like Butler has (however unwittingly) led to an unthinking celebration of the performance, discourse and constitution of gender at the expense of the positivity of sexual difference.

3. Deleuze and Guattari historicize what Lacan takes to be a transcendental condition. We are, they concede, subjected to the signifier, regarding our desires as mediated through the law of the father; but this is the consequence of capitalism's shift of the law away from an external prohibition towards a general axiom. It is the act of speaking as such, existing in a world with others, that now imposes a command of prohibition. We are now tyrannized by a supposedly general human condition of lack.

4. If Luce Irigaray and Deleuze share the same project of sexual difference, albeit with different outcomes, this is because they both draw on Heidegger's recognition that western thought has been dominated by a Platonism that the works of Plato, if read carefully, would allow us to challenge. That which truly is, substance or *hypokeimenon*, cannot be identified with or exhausted by any of its expressions or representations. The thought of substance is just the opening of thought to that life or being that is beyond thought's own limited images; the thought of substance therefore allows for real difference. However, once substance is seen as numerically distinct from perception as other than or different from the represented world then we fall into equivocity: the perceived world on the one hand, and its different ground on the other. Man or the subject becomes that point in the world from which difference and representation are explained in advance.

5. Deleuze and Guattari therefore spend a great deal of time in *A Thousand Plateaus* describing regimes of signs and various strata. Strata refer to various ways in which the one expressive life produces distinct levels, such as the strata of language in the narrow sense that borders the life it signifies on one side, and the system of speaking subjects on the other. But there are other stratifications, such as the social arrangement of bodies that faces law on the one side, and the desires of bodies on the other. One side of a stratum faces towards territorialization or organization, while the other faces towards deterritorialization or the freer flow of singular, not yet connected, differences. This allows us to think of various regimes of signs, with formal language being one of many. A sign, for Deleuze and Guattari, is not other than life, not an order imposed on life, but a relation within, or of, life. Sexual difference can be considered as a sign, with one body's perception and desire of another body producing a relation that is both sexual—because it is desiring, connective and productive—and a sign , for life is just this relation of singular differences that must somehow read, code or perceive other differences both in terms of its own life and striving, while also being transformed through this perception. So all perception is (a) sexual or desiring, (b) a sign, because the difference encountered must be read, (c) anti-interpretive, because this reading or perceiving does not posit a meaning

behind what it perceives but creates a body and relation, a territory of assemblage, and (d) expressive, because these signs, perceptions and strivings are not signs of a life that lies outside them, for life is just this striving, perceiving whole.

Chapter 11

On the Very Possibility of Queer Theory

Is queer theory a reflection on what it means to be queer, or does the concept of queerness change the ways in which we theorize? On the one hand the concept of theory appears to be inextricably intertwined with the concept of the human: man is that rational animal possessed of a soul capable of intuiting the essential, or what truly is, and thereby liberating himself from determined and merely actual perception (Irwin 1988). On the other hand, the possibility of a true theory—a mode of thinking that operates without a normative image of thought—seems to be opened only after the death of God and the death of 'man' (Deleuze 1994: 109). For Deleuze, true thought and true theory—a real break with the normative image of 'man'—must include *both* the intuition of the ground from which sense, truth and problems emerge, *and* must fulfill the promise of transcendental inquiry, which has all too often fallen back upon a self or subject who subtends theory. Contrary to a popular idea of a simple anti-humanism Deleuze does not reject the intuition of essences, the eternal, genesis and grounds; on the contrary, his work is best understood as an argument in favor of a superior transcendentalism that would think beyond the residual humanism maintained both by forms of Kantian critique and by popular notions of community and interrogation (Deleuze 1994, 197).

While abandoning the idea of a metaphysical outside or 'beyond' which might ground metaphysics, post-Kantian thought has nevertheless maintained the possibility of renovating thought from within (O'Neill 1989). If, in modernity, we have abandoned the idea of *theoria* as an intuition of essences, we can nevertheless sustain some commitment to critique: an interrogation of our situation from within (Habermas 1992). From such a commitment to interrogation from within, or resignation to an ironic attitude, it might seem that the values of queer theory would be the values of the postmodern, posthuman, post-metaphysical attitude in general. If our situatedness is, by definition, that which also counts as normal and normative, then theory *as such* might be intrinsically queer, as an attempt to deviate from, or pervert, that which appears self-evident, unquestionable and foundational. Accepting such a definition of queer theory would render the enterprise both parasitic and relative; queer theory would always be a solicitation of the normal, and if homosexuality and bisexuality were to become legitimate social models, then queerness would not have withered away, but merely shifted terrain: queer theory would be queer politics and would proceed by way of interrogating any supposed normality or normativity, having no intrinsic power. What I would like to consider in this final concluding chapter is a less negative and less relative formulation of queer theory, one concerned more with the intuition of essences than with the critical distance from the natural attitude.

There are two ways to think about the theoretical point of view in modernity. The first is critical. After Kant's 'Copernican turn' we recognize that there can be no 'view from nowhere.' To experience or live a world we must be related *to* that world through knowledge or perception; there cannot, therefore, be any intuition of that which exists outside the relations through which the world is received (Langton 1998). All our concepts are concepts *of* some intuited world, and all our intuitions are formed as conceptually meaningful and ordered. Kant therefore defines theoretical knowledge as given through the forming power of concepts and the receptive power of intuition. There can be no theoretical knowledge of any supposed foundation or law that would lie beyond experience: to know is to relate to, and conceptualize, what is other than oneself. There cannot be a theory of that which underpins experience; theory is, by definition, always situated, relational and grounded. Theory can, however, reflect on the conditions of our situation, and this would yield practical rather than knowable outcomes. If there can be no law intuitable beyond experience, then we are compelled to give a law to ourselves (O'Neill 1989). We cannot appeal to a foundation or ground, for we are always already grounded. Asking the question of grounds requires some grounded position from which questions can be posed. Theory can only tell us that we exist within mediation and experience, but cannot step outside that mediation.

Practically, though, this recognition of our location within experience allows for a radical anti-foundationalism. In the absence of any law or ground we must give a law to ourselves, and because this law is ungrounded—because there is no position beyond experience—no point of view can claim to speak for the law. One must give a law to oneself, always aware of that law's provisional status. As a consequence, liberalism remains a primarily critical and reflective ethic. Even though one is always located, one must strive to imagine a law that could *in principle* be agreed to by any subject whatsoever; one must neither make an exception of oneself—say, by not acting in a manner that would be universalizable on the grounds that one knows better—nor can one attribute one's located preferences to others. One can only will, ethically, that which would be willed as such (Kant 1990). Such a critical recognition of locatedness has served feminism and radical politics well. No one can be excluded from the practice of self-determination; there can be no exclusion from the public sphere of reason on the basis of spurious empirical claims. Thus, Mary Wollstonecraft (1975) argued that there was no way of knowing whether women were less capable than men at the art of reason; there could be no exclusion of women from education and argument, for if there is such a faculty as reason then it behooves us all to extend that faculty to its highest power. It is precisely the absence of foundations and the impossibility of basing theory on anything other than our situatedness that releases the subject from 'imposed tutelage' and issues in the central value of autonomy, of giving a law to oneself (Kant 1990).

In addition to Kantian liberal anti-foundationalism, the other possibility for modern political theory would appear to be some form of communitarianism. On this model, like liberalism, there can be no view from nowhere; however, the liberal appeal to the rational self-constituting individual cannot function as a legitimate point of departure. Selves, including the modern ideal of the autonomous self-critical subject, are constituted through others. One is a self only through relations; to be a self requires that one maintain oneself as recognizable through time, as having this or that character. Such recognition requires others, both so that one might be recognized as who one is now, and also so that there will be a context of norms, traditions, expectations and narratives through which one understands what it is to be human. On this communitarian model, theory does not take the form of abstracting from one's particularity to produce a purely formal procedure. Theory is not the regulation of those who would seek to exempt themselves from the claims of a universal unfounded reason. Theory is reflection on constituted norms, and is often enabled not by limiting contradiction and particularity, but by paying acute attention to those cultural moments when the conflict of founding (but irreconcilable) values are brought to the fore. If autonomy—relying on no law other than the law one can give to oneself—is the key value of liberal anti-foundationalism, recognition is the key value of communitarianism. Both values follow from an acknowledgement of the theoretical predicament: that to live or be a self is to have a law, but no such law can be known or intuited. Autonomy asks how one must regulate oneself in the absence of a founding shared law; recognition looks at the ways in which such shared laws are founded communally, historically and culturally.

Judith Butler's work, from its very beginning, has maintained the force of both these founding values of modern theory. On the one hand, the self is not given as a knowable substance but must be performed or given to itself through action. On the other hand, such self-giving or performing is only possible through others and recognition. It is for this reason that Butler's work is not so much a mobilization of twentieth-century theory for queer politics, but a theory in which the queer body becomes exemplary. For it is the queer body that exposes the essential tension between autonomy and recognition. One must both be recognized as a subject who subtends various performances, but there must also be a self who is not reducible to performances, such that actions can be posited intelligibly as issuing from this or that coherent self-fashioning subject. To be a self requires that one take on a norm; one must be recognizable *as* this or that subject. The condition of being a self—that one remain the same through time—requires a certain iterability: there is no self *who* repeats, for it is through the event of ongoing repetition that a self is constituted. The various performances or actions that the self undergoes must be recognizable *as* repetitions *of* some style or mode of being. Gender is one of the ways in which various differing performances can be recognized as differences *of* this or that sexual subject; if one's actions do not bear this iterability then one cannot be recognized as a subject. At the same time as the self exists only in performing itself as a self to be recognized, one must not be reducible to one's performances alone. If performances are normative, intelligible or readable then one can be recognized as a sexual subject who exists above and beyond any of her recognized actions. The self who asks to be recognized is, in the very claim for recognition, never reducible to the norm or system through which she speaks and performs. Without a difference or deviation in the repetitions of the norm one could not be a subject who subtends or performs that norm. Theory, then, maintains the necessary and essential tension between subjection (to the norm) and activation: the norm has its being only through the various performances but these performances also introduce differences and instabilities.

In many respects we might consider Butler's work to be both exemplary of the precarious model of the self that is presupposed in cultural studies, as well as being critical of the premises of identity politics. Without the mutability of the self the critique of cultural norms makes no sense; but this radical capacity for self-redefinition is also at the heart of contemporary capitalist modes of identity. On the one hand, one can be a self only through some recognizable identity; on the other hand, the performance of that identity is also the condition for the subject's destabilization and possible (but not necessarily enabling) undoing. Such a theory at once provides a way to think through the classic problems of representation in cultural studies. How do we judge images of political identity? On the one hand we might argue that stereotypical representations of certain images in the media reinforce rigid norms, preclude self-constitution and do not allow for subjects outside limited norms to be recognized. On the other hand, there can be no creation of oneself *ex nihilo*. Butler's answer to the politics of representation is not to judge between good and bad representations, dividing the authentic from the imposed. Rather, the conditions of representation themselves will yield a politics in which one can be a self only through the repetition of a norm, at the same time as that very repetition is essentially queer. For the queer is not radically outside or beyond recognition and selfhood; it is that which makes a claim to be heard as human—within the norms of speech, gender, the polity and the symbolic—at the same time as it perverts the normative matrix. Perhaps too much has already been said about Butler's early championing of parody and drag (Bersani 1995), but her work is dominated by the claim that it is the necessary repetition of a norm that both allows a self to be recognized, at the same time as the repetition is the self's undoing. To perform *as queer* is to maintain and demand recognition for that which has, hitherto, exceeded the bounds of cultural recognition. Thus, the queer is that which both partakes in the norm—one can be recognized *as* male or female—and destabilizes that norm, for this male or female will not take on the desires of the heterosexual matrix.

Butler's theory therefore allows for the (albeit problematic) maintenance of identity politics: the assertion of oneself *as* this or that subject demanding recognition is both necessary for the social system at the same time as it introduces a necessary dynamism into the system. At the same time as it maintains specified groupings, identity politics must also be recognized as queer: one is not asserting one's difference *from* some already recognized other. One is asserting difference as such: that one is a self only insofar as one, through repetition, also creates and performs differently. If I were merely the exemplification of a norm, if being straight or gay exhausted my identity, then I would have no identity at all. The condition for identity is difference, but for Butler this is iterative difference. There is not a substance or subject who then goes through time and difference; it is by way of the repetition of this differing act that a subject might be retroactively posited. Theory, in its Butlerian or critical mode, is an analysis of the conditions of performative difference; this mode of critical and destabilizing analysis exposes the fragile and precarious status of the supposedly stable and conditioning norm. The conditioning norm is itself conditioned, possible because of processes of iterative difference.

Against the model of iterative difference, which allows for the critical maintenance of identity politics, Gilles Deleuze offers a theory of positive difference. Crucial to the understanding of the distinction between the post-Hegelian iterative model of difference and Deleuze's understanding of difference is the status of relations. In her early work on Hegel, Butler explains Hegel's critique of internal relations: if relations were internal, then the way in which any being related to the world would be determined in advance. Encounters, journeys and interactions would merely unfold from what that being already is (Butler 1987: 35). Against this, Hegel argues that something *is* only in its relations; it is not that there are beings that then encounter difference. Rather, there is difference or relationality *from which* points of stability and recognition emerge. Absolute consciousness is just this differing—or *not* being the self-same—recognizing itself as its own negating power. Subjectivity is a relation to relationality, a consciousness aware that it is nothing other than its distance and difference from itself:

> The Hegelian subject cannot know itself instantaneously or immediately, but requires mediation to understand its own structure. The permanent irony of the Hegelian subject consists of this: it requires mediation to know itself, and knows itself only as the very structure of mediation; in effect, what is reflexively grasped when the subject finds itself 'outside' itself, reflected there, is this very fact itself, that the subject is a reflexive structure, and that movement out of itself is necessary in order for it to know itself at all. (Butler 2012, 7-8)

We might say, then, that we have abandoned internal relations: the encounters, qualities, events and individuality of a being do not unfold from any single point but occurs in relation to another relation. There is an unfolding of relations that then produces a specific difference between terms; consciousness is just this coming to recognition of oneself as nothing more than relationality. The essence of what something is—that which makes it what it *is*—is its existence, its actualization, or the way in which it has established itself as this or that complex of relations.

Butler remains committed to the idea that relations are produced through a process of difference and repetition. Something *is* identifiable *as* something only if it is repeated through time, but each repetition also introduces a certain difference or *not* being at one; the self in remaining itself is always subjected to, or negated by, that which is not:

> When we ask, what are the conditions of intelligibility by which the human emerges, by which the human is recognized, by which some subject becomes the subject of human love, we are asking about conditions of intelligibility composed of

norms, of practices, that have become presuppositional, without which we cannot think the human at all. So I propose to broach the relationship between variable orders of intelligibility and the genesis of the knowability of the human. And it is not just that there are laws that govern our intelligibility, but ways of knowing, modes of truth, that forcibly define intelligibility.

[...] Subjectively, we ask: Who can I become in such a world where the meanings and limits of the subject are set out in advance for me? By what norms am I constrained as I begin to ask what I may become? And what happens when I begin to become that for which there is no place within the given regime of truth? (Butler 2004A, 57)

Quite recently new developments in theory have subtly shifted the emphasis on relations (Harman 2012). If we insist that something can neither be, nor exist outside of the relations through which it is actualized, then this might lead us—as Butler has done—to insist on a subject as relationality (and perhaps to attribute that subjective relational capacity to linguistic or social beings alone, the latter including animals). But there is another inflection of the insistence on relations, which is to say that a thing comes into being through relations but has a force to produce other relations, and that for every actual relation there are a 'thousand tiny' virtual relations not given (but that 'swarm' in the background, accessible only in part and fleetingly). In most modes of theory relations are external to terms; very few writers today would insist on substances being nothing more than that are what they are, with relations being determined in advance by a being's intrinsic properties. In Deleuzian theory relations not only yield the dispersed world of actual beings but also remain as real virtual potentialities beyond the world as we know it, and beyond the world as it is at present.

That is, whatever systems or relations happen to have been formed, the forces that produced those relations could always have produced other relations. Relations do not follow from self-sufficient terms, but they do emerge from tendencies. Deleuze posits a positive virtual plane, or 'pure past,' that is actualized in each encounter to produce both the term that is repeated, and the difference established in each term. Tendencies are never known or given as such, only in their inflections. Deleuze seeks to find syntheses of difference and repetition that are asymmetrical, positive and pre-individual. In *Difference and Repetition,* Deleuze makes two key points with regard to the establishment of an active synthesizing subject. First, the self *who repeats* and from whom relations to the world are established depends upon passive, pre-individual syntheses: the individual who acts is composed of a thousand tiny egos, each effected from an encounter. Thus, it is not the self who must receive sensation and organize a world, for sensations are already the effect of intensive encounters or syntheses, and emerge from potentialities *to be sensed*. Synthesis does not occur as the repetition of the same through time; synthesis is not the maintenance of sameness. Rather, there can only be a relative stability through time of a quality if two forces of difference have entered into relation. Synthesis occurs first as difference *before* identity. Color, for example, occurs as relation between waves of light and an organism's eye, but the eye, in turn occurs as the relation between organic living matter, milieus of light, and evolutionary tendencies towards formation. An intensity's synthesis (or the coming into being of a quality) is not the repetition through time of the equal but is an asymmetrical synthesis; a quality, such as color, occurs as the relation between quantities. There can be more or less light, more or less of a quality, because of a relation of quantities, or forces entering into encounters. Before there is the 'I' of the self who repeats itself actively, there is the 'eye,' which is already the establishment of a qualitative relation or the unfolding of an intensity. The 'eye' is the result of a passive synthesis that has organized the problem of light, and light—as intensity—is that which might also have unfolded or been explicated in other relations or other qualities: so that each of our organs, according to Deleuze, is a contemplative soul, not receiving so much determining data, but giving a quality to the intensities of all it encounters:

> The passive self is not defined simply by receptivity—that is, by means of the capacity to experience sensations—but by virtue of the contractile contemplation which constitutes the organism itself before it constitutes the sensations. [...] There is a self wherever a furtive contemplation has been

established, wherever a contracting machine capable of drawing a difference from repetition functions somewhere. The self does not undergo modifications, it is itself a modification—this term designating precisely the difference drawn. Finally, one is only what one *has:* here, being is formed or the passive self *is,* by having. Every contraction is a presumption, a claim—that is to say, it gives right to an expectation or a right in regard to that which it contracts, and comes undone once its object escapes. (Deleuze 1994, 100)

Second, while the self is nothing other than repeated modifications, what is repeated is not the actual, existing, material or bare present. Nor does repetition happen *to* an individual: what is repeated is the pure past. Each event is the actualization of a pure potentiality, a power *to be* which each present repeats. All revolutions are the repetition of the power or potentiality of revolution; all selves are repetitions of a potentiality for modification. All the objects that constitute an individual's reality are haunted by another series of virtual objects that are never fully present; these are not psychic, wished for or imagined, but exist as pre-individual potentialities. A virtual object opens any material objective individual series to a contemplation beyond the self, a pure intensity that is beyond the habitual time of the body, and the remembered time of the psyche. The beyond of pleasure—or the outside of any individual's definition through a series of desired objects—is not an indeterminate negativity or undifferentiated 'beyond.' Deleuze objects to psychoanalysis' grounding of the 'beyond' of pleasure on an opposition between death and life, between the self and its return to a state of inanimate matter. Instead, Deleuze insists on the pure past as a virtual, eternal, intense, pre-individual and positive series that each actualized present repeats. If the individual appears in the form of organized, actual and life-serving objectifications—the desired objects towards which the subject is directed—this is because the individual is grounded upon a series of virtual objects. These virtual objects are pure fragments, or shreds of the past: a past that was never present and does not exist, but is always absent from itself and *insists* (Deleuze 1994, 124–5).

To give this concrete form, we can note that any actualized, existing, acting, repeating subject—a self who defines itself both against others (autonomy) and through others (recognition)—has as its prior condition pre-personal series. The aim of Deleuze's ethics and politics is to analyze, affirm and open these series. Most importantly, in terms of theory and the *life* and humanity of theory, Deleuze insists on the importance of the ground or dark precursor. Any two series of resonating differences—such as the differences of a language and the differences of our bodily identity—resonate with each other and can experience forced movement only through a 'dark precursor' or ground. So, in order for the self who says 'I' and speaks the language of man to be coordinated with the bodily movements of the self-interested, active and organized human organism there has to be some silent, unstated, undecided, passive ground (or *sense*) that itself cannot be simply stated. Much of *Difference and Repetition* is concerned with trying to intuit those silent presuppositions of representation and identity that tie the series of philosophical concepts—of the self, the 'I,' truth, identity and recognition—with the body of man oriented toward maintaining a state of equilibrium.

For Deleuze, thinking *beyond* the human requires some forced movement; this force can be thought of as the pure past, as desire, as the dark precursor, as the body without organs, and as the virtual—all of which open the constituted field of relations to that which is given through relations, but is not exhausted by any actualized relation. In *Difference and Repetition*, Deleuze writes of the 'beyond' of a life and pleasure of self-maintenance: this beyond would be 'death,' but not a death opposed to life and Eros. *Thanatos*, he argues, is Eros carried to its 'nth' power: desexualized, or rendered purely virtual and inhuman. Only here would we encounter pure intensity. The self or 'I' who loves another self (erotically) is already the effect of a whole series of virtual and intersubjective objects. Any actual couple draws upon, while repeating and transforming, the history of erotic encounters. To think the power of Eros beyond bounded bodies, would be to imagine syntheses beyond the organism and beyond the maintenance of life—a positive and annihilating 'death.' This conception of a 'beyond' of pleasure does not rely on the notion of returning to a state of nothingness, but it does raise the thought of how we might think intensities tending towards minimal thresholds. If we took desire beyond its human and bounded form, what minor intensities of desire might we discern: the movements of plants towards the light, the movements of particles towards (and away) from each other? Such a conception of desire in terms of small intensities, enables a redefinition of the objects of desire, and a non-Oedipal approach to psychoanalysis. If the self is given positively through the objects it desires, then it makes sense to see certain privileged objects as the outcome of a pre-individual and supra-individual plane of history. The phallus would not be a universal signifier of promised presence, the desire for which orients all subjectivity to an always concealed absence. Any actualized object that a body desires is possible because of a positive history, or a series of events that might have issued in an entirely different present. (The positivity of history is outlined in *Anti-Oedipus* where the phallic totem begins as a collective investment: Deleuze and Guattari insist that once capitalism develops as a concrete form, it is *then* possible to discern that capitalism was always lying in wait as a potentiality.) The phallus, through historical and political syntheses, becomes a virtual object; it organizes desires and bodies prior to their actual and individual encounters. Deleuze refers in *Difference and Repetition,* and in *The Logic of Sense,* to the aleatory object which allows series to resonate. So, before 'I' can love or recognize 'you,' our perceptions have already been synthesized in advance by the *sense* of our encounter: the sense or orientation of what counts as human, what counts as love, what counts as a recognizable body. For Deleuze this virtual plane is precisely not linguistic, for language as such can only organize bodies after those bodies have been intensively and affectively organized or synthesized. The true aim of thinking or theory would be to go back to the singular points from which relations and affects have been determined:

> Underneath the large noisy events lie the small events of silence, just as underneath the natural light there are little glimmers of the Idea. Singularity is beyond particular propositions no less than universality is beyond general propositions. Problematic Ideas are not simple essences, but multiplicities or complexes of relations and corresponding singularities. (Deleuze 1994, 203)

How does each individual or the self who says 'I' repeat and modify a virtual series of affections, encounters and intensities that are not its own and that might also be repeated otherwise? Against iterative difference—which is a repetition *of* a being that has no existence outside its seriality, or that produces that which repeats only through a maintaining of the same through time—Deleuze insists on the positive insistence of the virtual in all its intensity.

If we were to draw an example from genetics we might say that iterative difference gives us the idea of an organism that would undergo change and modification through repeating itself; each generation or copy introducing more and more instability and alterity. Deleuze's positive difference shows how each modification of an individual is preceded by micro-perceptions or encounters: before the self repeats itself there are repetitions of intensities or pure qualities. A virus might be repeated in my body, creating not a different organism but a different potentiality—a new virus or the modification of an organ, which might then effect my body's motility—not the ways in which I act but the ways in which I am acted upon. Difference is not the reiteration of some quality but occurs through the eternal return of the power to create relations, to produce connections. Concretely, this idea of difference does not result in an organism being modified through selection, but an individuation and selection that disregards the organism, creating connections among bodies that are the undoing of any organized body:

> For the I and the Self are perhaps no more than indices of the species: of humanity as a species with divisions. [...] The I is therefore not a species; rather—since it implicitly contains what the species and kinds explicitly develop, in particular the represented becoming of the form—they have a common fate, *Eudoxus* and *Epistemon*. Individuation, by contrast, has nothing to do with even the continued process of determining species but, as we shall see, it precedes and renders the latter possible. It involves fields of fluid intensive factors which no more take the form of an I than of a Self. Individuation as such, as it operates beneath all forms, is inseparable from a pure ground that it brings to the surface and trails with it. (Deleuze 1994, 190)

In political terms we can also distinguish iterative and positive repetition. For Butler, an individual does not exist *ex nihilo* but can be a self only through an other whom the proto-subject repeats and modifies. Claiming to be a queer *subject* might involve laying claim to certain normative practices—such as marriage and gender—which would have the effect both of normalizing the self by subjection to convention and recognition, but also disturbing convention by introducing a new mode or style of claim. To a certain extent all politics is queer politics, or an ongoing negotiation between the degrees of repetition to which the self submits and the amount of deviation or difference from normativity that the self can effect. The queer, on such an understanding, would be negative, defined as the difference *from* those conditions of recognition and normativity that both enable and preclude autonomy. Deleuze offers a quite different ontology and ethics of non-being. We are mistaken if we think of non-existence as the failure, deviation or difference from the present and actual. We need to think of non-being as positive, real and affirmative. Each existing, actualized individual is therefore the actualization of a non-being, which is better defined as '?-being' or as a series of problems. The queer self might be better thought of as a counter-actualization of the material repetitions that make up 'man,' rather than as a deviation from actual norms of man. Similarly, we could think of queer politics, not so much as a de-formation of what is constituted as normal, but as the composition of questions based on what bodies might be able to do. We could see marriage in its current bourgeois normative and heterosexual form as the solution to a certain problem or question: how the self forms its gender, manages its desires and property, and organizes its child-rearing. The queer self would repeat, while also recomposing, the problems that orient the self: counter-actualizing the present by drawing on the pure past of the questions from which we have emerged. How might a self desire, what might count as an object of one's desire, what future relations or events might the couplings of bodies produce and enable?

Whereas Butler's model of theory is to begin with the subject and then interrogate its conditions of possibility in the tension between recognition and autonomy, Deleuze's theory is one of positive intuition. Here, we go beyond composed selves and problems to the affects and intensities from which they are organized. For Butler a queer theory is one in which the conditions of being a subject are essentially queer—one must claim to speak as a self, but can do so only through an other who is *not* oneself. At the same time, the condition for being queer is to become a subject: one must be recognized as having a claim to speak, a claim to be and exist. For Deleuze, the conditions of theory require a going 'beyond' of the self and the organism. As long as we are concerned with identity, with the repetition *of* who we are, we remain within constituted matter and lived time. To think transcendentally we need to think the pure form of time and difference, the pure intensities that each present repeats and actualizes both in the present and for all time. For Deleuze, then, the conditions of the queer and the conditions of the new are the same: to counter-actualize the present, to repeat the intensities and encounters that have composed us, but not as they are *for* us.

In quite specific terms this requires a radical and distinct break from identity politics. As long as ethics is defined as the maintenance of individuals as they are we restrict the potentiality of life to one of its constituted forms. Only by thinking intensities beyond the human can we begin to live ethically. Thus queer politics would involve neither recognition of the self, nor a refusal of normativity, but the affirmation of the pre-personal. Rather than assessing political problems according to their meaning and convention—or the relations that organize certain affects and desires—we need to think desires according to virtual series, all the encounters that are potential or not yet actualized.

Such a queer politics has two direct consequences. First, practically, once we abandon conditions of recognition we can interrogate a practice according to the potentiality of its encounters. Rather than seeing gay marriage, trans-gendering or gay parenting as compromised maneuvers in which the queer self repeats and distorts given norms, we need to look at the positivity of each encounter. How do bodies establish relations in each case, and what powers are opened (or closed) to further encounters and modifications? Second, aesthetically, against an art of parody or drag that would repeat the norm in order to destabilize it from within, positive repetition and difference make a claim for thinking time in its pure state, by attending to those powers to differ that are pure fragments. Art would not be the representation or formation of identities but the attempt to present pure intensities in matter, allowing matter to stand alone or be liberated from its habitual and human series of recognition. The sensations presented in art are not those of the lived subject but are powers to be lived for all time, allowing us to think the power of perception beyond the selves we already are.

This aesthetics would, in turn, give us a new distinct model of reading. On the critical identity-based model of queer theory, where the queer self is the destabilizing repetition of an enabling normativity, we look at the ways in which works of art introduce a difference or dissimulation into the image of the human. A reading of Shakespeare's *A Midsummer Night's Dream*, for example, might focus on the ways in which the final image of normative heterosexual desire has to go through a series detours and deviations in order to arrive at the supposedly normal destined end. Queer reading would attend to all those moments in the text in which the normal has to be achieved, produced, effected and also, therefore, exposed as contingent, constituted and open to change. To a great extent the queer theory industry has been mobilized around a re-reading of the literary canon's images of heterosexual desire to show moments of instability, deviation and mobility. Deleuze, however, offers a quite distinct model of reading, both of the literary work in *Difference and Repetition*, and of art in general in *The Logic of Sensation* and (with Guattari) in *What is Philosophy?* In *The Logic of Sensation* (2003) Deleuze describes all art as the repetition of the history of art, but a repetition that struggles to release sensations from their subjection to figuration and repetition. There is, for Deleuze, no such thing as a bare canvas, for we are always already composed and dominated by clichés. The creative future can arrive, not through the assertion of greater and greater individuality, but only in a destruction of the personal to release the figure. This would not be the figuration *of* some repeatable form, but the delineation or process of differing from which this or that determined figure is drawn. In *Difference and Repetition*, Deleuze draws upon Shakespeare's *Hamlet* and Proust's *Remembrance of Things Past* to describe the profound syntheses of time that go beyond the body that is composed of habits, and the self that is composed of memories. The act in *Hamlet* exists above and beyond Hamlet's individual existence; it is a pure potentiality, something that he may or may not live up to, actualize or bring into the present. The future, or the opening of the new, can come about not through Hamlet drawing upon himself, his desires or his personal past, but by living out or allowing that power to differ which exists above and beyond him:

> As for the third time in which the future appears, this signifies that the event and the act possess a secret coherence which excludes that of the self; that they turn back against the self which has become their equal and smash it to pieces, as though the bearer of the new world were carried away and dispersed by the shock of the multiplicity to which it gives birth: what the self has become unequal to is the unequal in itself. In this manner, the I which is fractured according to the order of time and the Self which is divided according to the temporal series correspond and find a common descendant in the man without qualities, without self or I, the 'plebeian' guardian of a secret, the already-Overman whose scattered members gravitate around the sublime image. (Deleuze 1994, 112)

Here, for Deleuze, the art of theatre is not about the representation of plots, individuals and desires, but somehow giving form to a power of the pure past. Beyond the habitual repetitions that organize a body—'this is what I do'—and beyond the repetitions that constitute a self—'I am who I am by being the same through time'—drama exposes this higher repetition which destroys the self and its world of coordinated actions: 'Drama has but a single form involving all three repetitions' (Deleuze 1994: 115). The task of art is the presentation of this higher power, and reading the work of art is intuiting this power of time. In Proust the art of the novelist lies in presenting a self with its habits and recollections, and then presenting the pure potentiality from which that self was actualized: the past not as it was actually lived and recalled, but as it never was, but only *could be*, 'in a splendour which was never lived, like a pure past which finally reveals its double irreducibility to the two presents which it telescopes together: the present that it was, but also the present which it could be' (Deleuze 1994, 107). Against a critical reading, which would look at the ways in which art or literature queers the pitch of the normal, Deleuze offers a positive reading in which temporality in its pure state can be intuited and given form as queer, as a power to create relations, to make a difference, to repeat a power beyond its actual and already constituted forms.

Works Cited

Adorno, Theodor and Max Horkheimer. 2002. *Dialectic of Enlightenment: Philosophical Fragments*. Ed. Gunzelin Schmid Noerr. Trans. Edmund Jephcott. Stanford: Stanford University Press.

Agamben, Giorgio. 1993. *The Coming Community*. Trans. Michael Hardt. Minneapolis: University of Minnesota Press.

Agamben, Giorgio. 1998. *Homo Sacer: Sovereign Power and Bare Life*. Trans. Daniel Heller-Roazen. Stanford: Stanford University Press.

Agamben, Giorgio. 2004. *The Open: Man and Animal*. Stanford: Stanford University Press.

Agamben, Giorgio. 1999. *Potentialities: Collected Essays in Philosophy*. Trans. Daniel Heller-Roazen. Stanford: Stanford University Press.

Anderson, Nicole. 2010. '(Auto)Immunity: The Deconstruction and Politics of 'Bio-Art' and Criticism,' *Parallax* 16:4 (2010): 101–116.

Attridge, Derek. 2004. *The Singularity of Literature*. Derek Attridge. London; New York: Routledge.

Atwood, Margaret. 2009. *The Year of the Flood: A Novel*. New York: Doubleday.

Austin, J. L. 1962. *How to do Things with Words*. Oxford: Clarendon Press.

Badiou, Alain. 2000. *Deleuze: The Clamor of Being*. Trans. Louise Burchill. Minneapolis: University of Minnesota Press.

Badiou, Alain. 2001. *Ethics: An Essay on the Understanding of Evil*. Trans. Peter Hallward. London: Verso.

Badiou, Alain. 1999. *Manifesto for Philosophy*. Trans. and Ed. Norman Madarasz. Albany: State University of New York Press.

Badiou, Alain. 2003. *Saint Paul: The Foundation of Universalism*. Trans. Ray Brassier. Stanford: Stanford University Press.

Bainbridge, David. 2003. *The X in Sex: How the X Chromosome Controls Our Lives*. Cambridge: Harvard University Press.

Baudrillard, Jean. 1994. *Simulacra and Simulation*. Trans. Sheila Faria Glaser. Ann Arbor: University of Michigan Press.

Bennett, Jonathan. 1984. *A Study of Spinoza's Ethics*. Indianapolis, IN: Hackett Pub.

Bergson, Henri. 1911. *Creative Evolution*. Trans. Arthur Mitchell. London: Henry Holt.

Bergson, Henri. 1912. *Matter and Memory*. Trans. Nancy Margaret Paul and William Scott Palmer. London: G. Allen; New York: Macmillan.

Bergson, Henri. 2004. *Matter and Memory*. Trans. Nancy Margaret Paul and W. Scott Palmer. New York: Dover.

Bergson, Henri. 1913. *Time and Free Will: An Essay on the Immediate Data of Consciousness*. London: G. Allen. Trans. F.L. Pogson.

Bersani, Leo. 1995. *Homos*. Cambridge, MA: Harvard University Press.

Boyd, Brian. 2009. *On the Origin of Stories: Evolution, Cognition, and Fiction*. Cambridge: Belknap Press of Harvard University Press.

Braidotti, Rosi, Ewa Charkiewicz, Sabine Häusler, and Saskia Wieringa. 1994. *Women, the Environment and Sustainable Development: Towards a Theoretical Synthesis*. London: Zed Books.

Braidotti, Rosi. 2002. *Metamorphoses: Towards a Materialist Theory of Becoming*. Cambridge: Polity Press.

Braidotti, Rosi. 2006. *Transpositions: On Nomadic Ethics*. Cambridge: Polity.

Brennan, Teresa. 1993. *History After Lacan*. London: Routledge.

Bryant, Levi. 2011. *The Democracy of Objects*. Ann Arbor: Open Humanities Press.

Butler, Judith. 2000. *Antigone's Claim: Kinship Between Life and Death*. New York: Columbia University Press.

Butler, Judith. 1993. *Bodies that Matter: On the Discursive Limits of 'Sex.'* New York: Routledge.

Butler, Judith. 1990. *Gender Trouble: Feminism and the Subversion of Identity*. New York: Routledge.

Butler, Judith. 2005. *Giving an Account of Oneself*. New York: Fordham University Press.

Butler, Judith. 2004B. *Precarious Life: The Powers of Mourning and Violence*. London: Verso.

Butler, Judith. 1997. *The Psychic Life of Power: Theories in Subjection.* Stanford: Stanford University Press.

Butler, Judith. 2011. 'Queer Bonds.' *GLQ: A Journal of Lesbian and Gay Studies* 17. 2-3: 381-387.

Butler, Judith. 2012. *Subjects of Desire: Hegelian Reflections in Twentieth-Century France.* New York: Columbia University Press.

Butler, Judith. 2004A. *Undoing Gender.* London: Routledge.

Carey, John. 1993. *The Intellectuals and the Masses: Pride and Prejudice Among the Literary Intelligentsia, 1880-1939.* New York: St. Martin's Press.

Carr, Nicholas. 2009. *In the Shallows: What the Internet is Doing to Our Brains.* New York: Norton.

Carroll, Joseph. 1995. *Evolution and Literary Theory.* Columbia: University of Missouri Press.

Chow, Rey. 2006. *The Age of the World Target: Self-Referentiality in War, Theory, and Comparative Work.* Durham: Duke University Press.

Churchland, Patricia. 2011. *Braintrust: What Neuroscience Tells Us About Morality.* Princeton: Princeton University Press.

Clough, Patricia Ticineto with Jean Halley. 2007. *The Affective Turn: Theorizing the Social.* Durham: Duke University Press.

Copjec, Joan. 2003. *Imagine There's No Woman.* Cambridge, MA: MIT Press.

Copjec, Joan. 1994. *Read My Desire: Lacan Against the Historicists.* Cambridge, MA: MIT Press.

Cornell, Drucilla. 1991. *Beyond Accommodation: Ethical Feminism, Deconstruction, and the Law.* New York: Routledge.

Damasio, Antonio. 1994. *Descartes' Error: Emotion, Reason, and the Human Brain.* New York: Putnam.

Damasio, Antonio. 2000. *The Feeling of What Happens: Body and Emotion in the Making of Consciousness.* New York: Harcourt

Damasio, Antonio. 2003. *Looking for Spinoza: Joy, Sorrow, and the Feeling Brain.* Orlando: Harcourt.

Damasio, Antonio. 2010. *Self Comes to Mind: Constructing the Conscious Brain.* New York: Pantheon.

De Botton, Alain. 2000. *The Consolations of Philosophy.* New York : Pantheon Books.

Deleuze, Gilles. 1986. *Cinema 1: The Movement-Image*. Trans. Hugh Tomlinson and Barbara Habberjam. Minneapolis: University of Minnesota Press.

Deleuze, Gilles. 1994. *Difference and Repetition*. Trans. Paul Patton. New York: Columbia University Press.

Deleuze, Gilles. 1991. *Empiricism and Subjectivity*. Trans. Constantin V. Boundas. New York: Columbia University Press.

Deleuze, Gilles. 1993. *The Fold: Leibniz and the Baroque*. Trans. Tom Conley. Minneapolis: University of Minnesota Press.

Deleuze, Gilles. 2003. *Francis Bacon: The Logic of Sensation*. Trans. Daniel Smith. London: Continuum.

Deleuze, Gilles. 1984. *Kant's Critical Philosophy*. Trans. Hugh Tomlinson and Barbara Habberjam. Minneapolis: University of Minnesota Press.

Deleuze, Gilles. 1990. *The Logic of Sense*. Trans. Mark Lester with Charles Stivale. Ed. Constantin. V. Boundas. New York: Columbia University Press.

Deleuze, Gilles. 1983. *Nietzsche and Philosophy*. Trans. Hugh Tomlinson. New York: Columbia University Press.

Deleuze, Gilles. 2000. *Proust and Signs*. Trans. Richard Howard. London: Athlone.

Deleuze, Gilles. 1991B. *Pure Immanence: Essays on A Life*. Trans. Anne Boyman. New York: Zone Books.

Deleuze, Gilles and Félix Guattari. 1983. *Anti-Oedipus: Capitalism and Schizophrenia*. Trans. Robert Hurley, Mark Seem and Helen R. Lane. Minneapolis: University of Minnesota Press.

Deleuze, Gilles and Félix Guattari. 1987. *A Thousand Plateaus: Capitalism and Schizophrenia*. Trans. Brian Massumi. Minneapolis: University of Minnesota Press.

Deleuze, Gilles and Félix Guattari. 2004. *A Thousand Plateaus: Capitalism and Schizophrenia*. Trans. Brian Massumi. London: Continuum.

Deleuze, Gilles and Félix Guattari. 1994. *What is Philosophy?* Trans. Hugh Tomlinson and Graham Burchell. New York: Columbia University Press.

De Man, Paul. 1996. *Aesthetic Ideology*. Minneapolis: University of Minnesota Press.

Dennett, Daniel. 1991. *Consciousness Explained*. Boston: Little, Brown and Co.

Derrida, Jacques. 1969. 'The Ends of Man.' Trans. Edouard Morot-Sir, Wesley C. Puisol, Hubert L. Dreyfus, and Barbara Reid. 1969. *Philosophy and Phenomenological Research* 30.1: 31-57.

Derrida, Jacques. 1981. 'Economimesis.' Trans. Renata Klein. *Diacritics* 11.2: 2–25.

Derrida, Jacques. 1978. 'Freud and the Scene of Writing.' *Writing and Difference.* Trans. A. Bass (London: Routledge).

Derrida, Jacques. 1998. *Of Grammatology.* Trans. Gayatri Chakravorty Spivak. Baltimore: Johns Hopkins University Press.

Desmond, William. 1995. *Being and the Between.* Albany: SUNY Press.

Diprose, Rosalyn. 1994. *The Bodies of Women: Ethics, Embodiment, and Sexual Difference.* London: Routledge.

Due, Reidar. 2007. *Deleuze.* Cambridge: Polity.

Edelman, Lee. 1994. *Homographesis: Essays in Gay Literary and Cultural Theory.* New York: Routledge.

Esposito, Roberto. 2008. *Bios: Biopolitics and Philosophy.* Trans. Timothy Campbell. Minneapolis: University of Minnesota Press.

Felski, Rita. 2013. *Schools of Suspicion: Literary Studies and the Limits of Critique.* Unpublished ms. Forthcoming.

Flanagan, Owen. 2011. *The Bodhisattva's Brain: Buddhism Naturalized.* Cambridge, MA: MIT Press.

Flanagan, Owen. 2003. *The Problem Of The Soul: Two Visions Of Mind And How To Reconcile Them.* New York: Basic Books.

Flanagan, Owen J. 2007. *The Really Hard Problem: Meaning in a Material World.* Cambridge, MA: MIT Press.

Foucault, Michel. 2002. *The Order of Things: An Archaeology of the Human Sciences.* London: Routledge. 2nd ed.

Freud, Sigmund. 1959. 'On Narcissism'. In *Collected Papers:* Vol. 4. Ed. Joan Riviere and James Strachey. New York: Basic Books.

Freud, Sigmund. 2000. *Three Essays on the Theory of Sexuality.* Ed. James Strachey. New York: Basic Books.

Gilson, Etienne. 1994. *The Christian Philosophy of Thomas Aquinas.* Trans. L. K. Shook. Notre Dame: U of Notre Dame P, 1994.

Glick, Elisa. 2000. 'Sex Positive: Feminism, Queer Theory, and the Politics of Transgression.' *Feminist Review* 64: 19–45.

Goldman, Jane. 1998. *The Feminist Aesthetics of Virginia Woolf: Modernism, Post-Impressionism and the Politics of the Visual.* Cambridge: Cambridge University Press.

Grayling, A. C. 2001. *The Meaning of Things: Applying Philosophy to Life.* London: Weidenfeld & Nicolson.

Greenfield, Susan. 2008. *ID: The Quest for Identity in the 21st Century*. London: Sceptre.

Gregg, Melissa and Gregory J. Seigworth, eds. 2010. *The Affect Theory Reader*. Durham: Duke University Press.

Grosz, Elizabeth. 2011. *Becoming Undone: Darwinian Reflections on Life, Politics, and Art*. Durham: Duke University Press.

Grosz, Elizabeth. 2004. *The Nick of Time: Politics, Evolution, and the Untimely*. Durham: Duke University Press.

Grosz, Elizabeth. 2005. *Time Travels: Feminism, Nature, Power*. Durham: Duke University Press.

Grosz, Elizabeth. 1994. *Volatile Bodies: Toward a Corporeal Feminism*. Sydney: Allen & Unwin.

Habermas, Jurgen. 1990. *The Philosophical Discourse of Modernity: Twelve Lectures*. Trans. Frederick G. Lawrence. Cambridge, MA: MIT Press.

Habermas, Jurgen. 1992. *Post Metaphysical Thinking: Philosophical Essays*. Trans. William Mark Hohengarten. Cambridge, MA: MIT Press.

Hansen, Mark B. N. and Clarke, Bruce. 2009. *Emergence and Embodiment: New Essays on Second-Order Systems Theory*. Durham, NC: Duke University Press.

Haraway, Donna. 2008. *When Species Meet*. Minneapolis: University of Minnesota Press.

Hardt, Michael and Negri, Antonio. 2000. *Empire*. Cambridge: Harvard University Press.

Haugeland, John. 1998. *Having Thought: Essays in the Metaphysics of Mind*. Cambridge: Harvard University Press.

Hayles, N. Katherine. 2007. 'Hyper and Deep Attention: The Generational Divide in Cognitive Modes.' *Profession* 13: 187–199.

Heidegger, Martin. 1998. *Pathmarks*. Ed. W. McNeill. Cambridge: Cambridge University Press.

Heidegger, Martin. 1967. *What is a Thing?* Trans. W.B. Barton, Jr. and Vera Deutsch. Lanham: University Press of America.

Hitchcock, Peter. 1993. *Dialogics of the Oppressed*. Minneapolis: University of Minnesota Press.

Hughes, Joe. 2008. *Deleuze and the Genesis of Representation*. London: Continuum.

Husserl, Edmund. 1977. *Cartesian Meditations: An Introduction to Phenomenology.* Trans. Dorion Cairns. Dordrecht: Kluwer.

Husserl, Edmund. 1970. *The Crisis of the European Sciences and Transcendental Phenomenology.* Trans David Carr. Evanston: Northwestern University Press.

Husserl, Edmund. 1983. *Ideas: First Book.* Trans F. Kersten. Dordrecht: Kluwer.

Hyland, Terry. 2011. *Mindfulness and Learning: Celebrating the Affective Dimension of Education.* Dordrecht: Springer.

Irigaray, Luce. 1985. *Speculum of the Other Woman.* Trans. Gillian C. Gill. Ithaca, NY: Cornell University Press.

Irwin, Terence. 1988. *Aristotle's First Principles.* Oxford: Oxford UP.

Israel, Jonathan. 2001. *Radical Enlightenment: Philosophy and the Making of Modernity, 1650-1750.* Oxford: Oxford University Press.

Jameson, Fredric. 1991. *Postmodernism, or, The Cultural Logic of Late Capitalism.* Durham: Duke University Press.

Joyce, James. 1922. *Portrait of the Artist as a Young Man.* Cambridge: B. W. Huebsch.

Kant, Immanuel. 1990. *Foundations of the Metaphysics of Morals and, What is Enlightenment.* Trans. Lewis White Beck, 2nd edn, rev. New York: Macmillan.

Korsgaard, Christine. 1996B. *Creating the Kingdom of Ends.* Cambridge: Cambridge University Press.

Korsgaard, Christine. 1996A. *The Sources of Normativity.* Ed. Christine Marion Korsgaard, Onora O'Neill. Cambridge. Cambridge University Press.

Kristeva, Julia. 1981. 'Women's Time.' *Signs* 7.1: 13–35.

Lacan, Jacques. 1982. *Feminine Sexuality: Jacques Lacan and the Ecole Freudienne.* Ed. Juliet Mitchell and Jacqueline Rose. New York: W. W. Norton.

Langton, Rae. 1998. *Kantian Humility: Our Ignorance of Things in Themselves.* Oxford: Clarendon Press.

Laplanche, Jean. 1999. *Essays on Otherness.* London: Routledge.

Laplanche, Jean. 1976. *Life and Death in Psychoanalysis.* Baltimore: Johns Hopkins University Press.

Latour, Bruno. 2010. 'An Attempt at a ".Compositionist Manifesto."' *New Literary History* 41. 3: 471-490.

Latour, Bruno. 1999. *Pandora's Hope: Essays on the Reality of Science Studies.* Harvard University Press.

Latour, Bruno. 2004 A. *Politics of Nature: How to Bring the Sciences into Democracy.* Trans. Catherine Porter. Cambridge, MA.: Harvard University Press.

Latour, Bruno. 2004B. 'Why Has Critique Run out of Steam? From Matters of Fact to Matters of Concern.' *Critical Inquiry* 30: 225-248.

Lauwereyns, Jan, 2010.*The Anatomy of Bias: How Neural Circuits Weigh the Options.* Cambridge, MA: MIT Press.

Lawlor, Len. 2008. 'Following the Rats: Becoming-Animal in Deleuze and Guattari.' *SubStance* 117, 37.3: 169-187.

Lawrence, D.H. 1929. 'Snake.' *Collected Poems*. Vol 2: *Unrhyming Poems*. New York: Jonathan Cape and Harrison Smith. 217-19.

Leclaire, Serge. 1998. *A Child Is Being Killed: On Primary Narcissism and the Death Drive.* Stanford, CA: Stanford University Press.

LeDoux, Joseph E. 1996. *The Emotional Brain: The Mysterious Underpinnings of Emotional Life.* New York: Simon and Schuster.

Lévy, Pierre. 1997. *Collective Intelligence: Mankind's Emerging World in Cyberspace.* Trans. Robert Bononno. New York: Perseus Books.

Lovelock, James. 1988. *The Ages of Gaia: A Biography of Our Living Earth.* New York: Norton.

Lovelock, James. 2009. *The Vanishing Face of Gaia: A Final Warning.* New York: Basic Books.

MacIntyre, Alasdair C. 1984. *After Virtue: A Study in Moral Theory.* Notre Dame: University of Notre Dame Press.

Malabou, Catherine. 2009. *Changer de difference: le féminin et la question philosophique.* Paris: Galilée.

Mark Bonta, John Protevi. 2004. *Deleuze And Geophilosophy: A Guide And Glossary.* Edinburgh University Press.

Massumi, Brian. 1995. 'The Autonomy of Affect,' *Cultural Critique* 31, The Politics of Systems and Environments, Part II.: 83-109.

Maturana, Humberto and Franciso J. Varela. 1980. *Autopoiesis and Cognition: The Realization of the Living.* Dordrecht: Kluwer.

Maturana, Humberto and Francisco J. Varela. 1987. *The Tree of Knowledge: The Biological Roots of Human Understanding.* Boston: New Science Library.

Maturana, Humberto and Varela, Francesco. J. 1992. *The Tree of Knowledge: The Biological Roots of Human Understanding.* Boston: Shambhala.

Melville, Herman. 1986. *Billy Budd and Other Stories.* Penguin Classics. Ed. F. Busch. Harmondsworth: Penguin.

Nehamas, Alexander. 1985. *Nietzsche: Life as Literature.* Cambridge, MA: Harvard University Press.

Nietzsche, Friedrich. 1989. *Beyond Good and Evil: Prelude to a Philosophy of the Future.* Trans. Walter Kaufman. New York: Random House.

Nussbaum, Martha C. 1994. *The Therapy of Desire: Theory and Practice in Hellenistic Ethics.* Princeton, N.J.: Princeton University Press.

Nussbaum, Martha C. 2011. (reported by Julie Hare). 'Democracy at Risk from Emphasis on "Useful Machines."' *The Australian.* August 12, 2011.

O'Neill, Onora. 1989. *Constructions of Reason: Explorations of Kant's Practical Philosophy.* Cambridge: Cambridge University Press.

O'Neill, Onora. 2010. 'Real Life is Too Complex.' http://www.guardian.co.uk/commentisfree/belief/2010/jul/30/assisted-suicide-legislation

Okin, Susan Moller. 1994. 'Political Liberalism, Justice, and Gender.' *Ethics* 105.1: 23–43.

Patton, Paul. 2007. 'Political Normativity and Poststructuralism: The Case of Gilles Deleuze.' http://www.uu.nl/SiteCollectionDocuments/GW/GW_Centre_Humanities/political-normativity-deleuze.pdf

Plant, Judith. 1997. 'Learning to Live with Differences: The Challenge of Ecofeminist Community.' In *Ecofeminism: Women, Culture, Nature.* Karen J. Warren and Nisvan Erkal Eds. Bloomington: Indiana University Press.

Pound, Ezra. 1956. *Cantos.* New York: New Directions.

Pound, Ezra. 2003. *Poems and Translations.* New York: Library of America.

Protevi, John. 2009. *Political Affect: Connecting the Social and the Somatic.* Minneapolis: University of Minnesota Press.

Protevi, John. 2001. *Political Physics: Deleuze, Derrida, and the Body Politic.* London: Continuum.

Ramachandran, V.S. and William Hirstein. 1999. 'The Science of Art A Neurological Theory of Aesthetic Experience.' *Journal of Consciousness Studies* 6.6-7: 15–51.

Rawls, John. 1972. *A Theory of Justice.* Oxford: Clarendon Press.

Rivkin, Jeremy. 2009. *The Empathic Civilization: The Race to Global Consciousness in a World in Crisis.* New York: Penguin Books.

Rogers, John. 1996. *The Matter of Revolution: Science, Poetry, and Politics in the Age of Milton*. Ithaca, N.Y.: Cornell University Press.

Rorty, Richard. 1983. 'Postmodernist Bourgeois Liberalism.' *Journal of Philosophy* 80: 583-89.

Rorty, Richard. 1986. *Consequences of Pragmatism: Essays, 1972-1980*. Minneapolis: University of Minnesota Press.

Rorty, Richard. 2009. *Philosophy and the Mirror of Nature*. Princeton: Princeton University Press.

Rowlands, Mark. 2010. *The New Science of the Mind: From Extended Mind to Embodied Phenomenology*. Cambridge, MA: MIT Press.

Russell, Peter. 2001. *The Global Brain: The Awakening Earth in a New Century*. Edinburgh: Floris.

Ruyer, Raymond. 1952. *Néo-finalisme*. Paris: Presses Universitaires de France.

Ruyer, Raymond. 1958. *La genese des forms vivantes*. Paris: Flammarion.

Ryle, Gilbert. 2000. *The Concept of Mind*. Chicago: University of Chicago Press.

Schwab, Gabriele. 1996. *The Mirror and the Killer-Queen: Otherness in Literary Language*. Bloomington: Indiana University Press.

Schwartz, Regina. 1998. *Remembering and Repeating: Biblical Creation in Paradise Lost*. Cambridge: Cambridge University Press.

Sinfield, Alan. 1992. *Faultlines: Cultural Materialism and the Politics of Dissident Reading*. Berkeley: University of California Press.

Stengers, Isabelle. 2011. *Thinking with Whitehead: A Free and Wild Creation of Concepts*. Trans. Michael Chase. Cambridge, MA.: Harvard University Press.

Stiegler, Bernard. 2010. *For a New Critique of Political Economy*. Trans. Daniel Ross. Cambridge: Polity.

Stiegler, Bernard. 2009. *Technics and Time: Disorientation*. Trans. Stephen Barker. Stanford: Stanford University Press.

Susan Bordo. 2004. *Unbearable Weight: Feminism, Western Culture, and the Body*. Berkeley: University of California Press.

Sykes, Bryan. 2003. *Adam's Curse: A Future without Men*. New York: Bantam Press.

Tallis, Raymond. 2004. *I Am: A Philosophical Inquiry into First-Person Being*. Edinburgh: Edinburgh University Press.

Thompson, Evan. 2007. *Mind in Life: Biology, Phenomenology, and the Sciences of Mind.* Cambridge, MA: Belknap, Harvard University Press.

Warren, Karen. 2000. *Ecofeminist Philosophy: A Western Perspective on What It Is and Why It Matters.* Lanham, MD: Rowman and Littlefield.

Wheeler, Michael. 1995. 'Escaping from the Cartesian Mind-Set: Heidegger and Artificial Life.' In *Advances in Artificial Life: Proceedings of the Third European Conference on Artificial Life.* Ed. F. Moran, A. Moreno, J. J. Merelo, and P. Chacon. Berlin and New York: Springer-Verlag. 65–76.

Williams, James. 2008. *Gilles Deleuze's Logic of Sense: A Critical Introduction and Guide.* Edinburgh: Edinburgh University Press.

Wolfe, Cary. 1995. 'In Search of Posthumanist Theory: The Second-Order Cybernetics of Maturana and Varela.' *Cultural Critique* 30: 33-70.

Wollstonecraft, Mary. 1975. *A Vindication of the Rights of Woman.* Ed. Carol H. Poston. New York: Norton.

Wollstonecraft, Mary. 2008. *A Vindication of the Rights of Woman.* New York: Cosimo.

Woolf, Virginia. 1977. *To the Lighthouse* [1927] London: Panther Books.

Woolf, Virginia. 2006. *To the Lighthouse.* Ed. David Bradshaw. Oxford: Oxford University Press.

Worringer, Wilhelm. 1953. *Abstraction and Empathy.* New York: International Universities Press.

Žižek, Slavoj. 2001A. *Enjoy Your Symptom: Jacques Lacan in Hollywood and Out.* London: Routledge.

Žižek, Slavoj. 2001B. *The Fragile Absolute: Or, Why Is the Christian Legacy Worth Fighting For?* London: Verso.

Žižek, Slavoj. 2012. *Less Than Nothing: Hegel and the Shadow of Dialectical Materialism.* London: Verso.

Žižek, Slavoj. 2003. *Organs without Bodies: Deleuze and Consequences.* London: Routledge.

Žižek, Slavoj. 1999. *The Ticklish Subject: The Absent Centre of Political Ontology.* London: Verso.

Permissions

Earlier versions of some chapters appeared in the following publications.

'Feminist Extinction' in *Undutiful Daughters: New Directions in Feminist Thought and Practice*, ed. Henriette Gunkel, Chrysanthi Nigianni and Fanny Soderback (Palgrave 2012)

'Norm Wars,' in *Revisiting Normativity with Deleuze*, ed. Rosi Braidotti and Patricia Pisters (Continuum 2012)

'Queer Aesthetics,' in *Queer Times, Queer Becomings*, ed. E.L. McCallum and Mikko Tukhanen (SUNY Press, 2011)

'Queer Vitalism,' in *New Formations* 68.5 (2009): 77-92

'Difference, Time and Organic Extinction,' in *Sex, Gender and Time in Fiction and Culture*, ed. Ben Davies and Jana Funke (Palgrave 2011)

'On the Very Possibility of Queer Theory,' in *Deleuze and Queer Theory*, ed. Chrysanthi Niggiani and Mel Storr (Edinburgh 2009).

'How Queer Can You Go?' in *Queering the Non-Human*, ed. Noreen Giffney and Myra Hird (Ashgate 2008).

www.ingramcontent.com/pod-product-compliance
Lightning Source LLC
Chambersburg PA
CBHW022055160426
43198CB00008B/235